MAKE ANOTHER SIGNAL

Heading:	C-O-N-F-I-D-E-N-T-I-A-L

FOLLOWING FROM PRIME MINISTER TO CAPTAIN AND SHIPS COMPANY

USS WASP AND ACCOMPANYING SHIPS :

MANY THANKS TO YOU ALL FOR TIMELY HELP X WHO SAID

A WASP COULDN'T STING TWICE

(SIGNED) WINSTON CHURCHILL

Date		TOR TOD		Opr.		Sys.		Freq. or Method
FROM: ADMIRALTY Ref. No.		**ACTION TO:** USS WASP ;USS LANG USS STERETT; HMS EAGLE HMS ECHO; HMS INTEREPID;HMS SPARTRIDGE; HMS SALISBURY;HMS CHARYBDIS; HMS RENOWN;						**INFORMATION TO:**

Unit Comdr	Unit Gen	Unit Eng	Unit Comm	Unit Disb	Unit Med	Capt	Exec	OOD	Eng	Gun	1stLt	Torp	Comm	Stores	Comsy	Office

U.S.S. *Lang's* copy of a grateful signal for great support.

In April and May 1942 Winston Churchill prevailed on President Roosevelt to allow the U.S.N. Carrier Wasp *to ferry desperately needed Spitfires to Malta. On 20th April forty seven were flown off within range of Malta, but they came under immediate attack from the Luftwaffe, with heavy losses.* Wasp *returned to Scapa Flow, and nothing daunted sailed again in early May wi th another load which reached Malta safely on 10th May. This time the Spitfires held their own against the Luftwaffe, and marked the turning point of the air battles over Malta.*

MAKE
ANOTHER
SIGNAL

CAPTAIN
JACK BROOME

WILLIAM KIMBER · LONDON

First published in 1973 by
WILLIAM KIMBER & CO. LIMITED
Godolphin House, 22a Queen Anne's Gate,
London SW1H 9AE

Copyright © Jack Broome, 1973
ISBN 07183 0193 5

Typeset by
Eyre & Spottiswoode Ltd, Portsmouth
and printed in Great Britain by
Robert MacLehose & Co. Ltd., Glasgow

CONTENTS

ILLUSTRATIONS

All illustrations are by the author except for those listed below.

PREFACE

This is a book about naval signals. A signal is a sign which conveys information. When ships first found themselves beyond shouting range the language of naval signals was born.

In the beginning this language was expressed by the positions, colours and meanings of flags and banners. The more manoeuvrable and co-operative ships became the more the language expanded, until it reached its most colourful peak in the early part of this century. But now it is changing altogether. Soon, the very word signal will be obsolete, for signs are no longer needed to convey information. Today, information is poured, irrespective of distance, from brain to brain. The air is saturated with it. One day it will condense and, paradoxically, form fog.

This book is concerned mainly with the pre-microphone period; with signals that travel alone and, like telegrams, have to be carefully worded to be readily understood. Unlike telegrams, however, they are impersonal and public. They carry the authority of a ship or a squadron. They are paid for with reputations, sometimes even with human lives.

The era of such signals produced craftsmen who could compose on a pad the exact phrase to suit the situation. Their signals had power and penetration; they inspired, provoked, amused or debunked with an aptitude all their own. A signal at sea which commended was round the ship like a flash of light. One which reproved spread gloom just as quickly.

A signal records the immediate reaction of the man-on-the-spot; a recorded sequence of them gives a lively impression of the incident it covers. To illustrate this I have taken several operations and incidents—most of which are already well known—and reconstructed them on the framework of the signals which conducted them.

I have also included some signals which, in themselves, have undoubtedly influenced the course of history; though to what

extent must remain in doubt. But for that primitive signal in 480
B.C., what would have happened to the Greeks in the Battle of
Salamis? How much more effort did Nelson wring from those
under his command by his famous signal at Trafalgar? How many
ships did the Admiralty's signals to Russian Convoy P.Q.17 cost?

Last in the book is a collection of individual signals. Some are
seasoned chestnuts; but a few, I hope, are new. Now, at the close
of that era of individuality, seems the time to harvest them. One
cannot imagine such pithy exchanges as some of those between
Admirals Somerville and Cunningham, being spoken on radio
telephone.

When I began to make this collection, I did not think it would
be very difficult—just a matter of skimming through old signal logs
and drawing off the cream. I went first to the late Mr Ellmers, of
Admiralty Records, and explained my object. Casually, I asked
how many signals had been sent in the Royal Navy during World
War II. His reply: "About two hundred tons."

Mr Ellmers' department was highly efficient. Provided one knew
when, where and by whom a signal was made, his team would
delve into that great signal rick and emerge in a remarkably short
time, dusty but triumphant, with what one was seeking. Unfortunately, in many cases I was not at all sure what I was seeking
until I saw it. The only other source of supply was living memory;
and I would like here to express my sincere gratitude to all
those—from Sea Lord to Signal Bos'n—who have taken the trouble
to search their memories and send me the result.

Since this book is mostly concerned with the text of signals, no
attempt has been made to introduce personalities which are not
already well known. The same applies to technicalities; even
latitudes and longitudes are omitted. To some signals there are
several different versions. If the wrong one appears, I apologise;
living memory is not always strictly accurate. There was, you may
recall, the case of Nelson's great friend, Captain the Hon. Henry
Blackwood, who commanded H.M.S. *Euryalus* at Trafalgar. In a
letter written the day after the battle he quoted Nelson's famous
signal as:

ENGLAND EXPECTS EVERY OFFICER AND MAN WILL
DO THEIR UTMOST DUTY.

And even Admiral Collingwood, Nelson's second-in-command, had a ring inscribed with the words:

ENGLAND EXPECTS EVERYTHING: MEN DO YOUR DUTY.

It is some twenty years since I wrote the above Preface to the original volume of *Make a Signal*, which has been out of print for over ten years.

The last part of paragraph 2 was a timely prediction for, in its old naval sense, the word SIGNAL *has* become obsolete. In the heat of the communication explosion which started shortly after that Preface was written, the words SIGNAL and COMMUNI-CATION fused together. Fog is still forming.

Once again, my thanks to all those who have contributed some more of those good old types of naval signals and also to Captain David Tibbits, D.S.C., R.N., Deputy Master of Trinity House, Captain Barrie Kent, R.N., when commanding R.N. Signal School, Mr Ray Kirk, O.B.E., Superintendent of London's Air Traffic Control, Commander Dickie Richardson, R.N., Thames Harbour Master, and Rear Admiral Roy Foster Brown, C.B., for helping me with new material.

J.E.B.
Gannock Cottage
Nettlebed.
March 1973.

From Age to Age

Once upon a time, our forefathers decided to ease themselves down from the trees whereup they lived and become human beings. Having made this decision, the operation must have been planned. Some particular forefather must have been in charge. By grunt or by gesture someone must have given the signal.

This means of intercommunication had limitations. Probably, at the conferences which followed, one particular forefather was told to look into the matter and draw up some improvements. The matter has been under review ever since.

Even in those days there was plenty of material to work on. The possibilities of signalling by sound were suggested by the trumpeting of the mighty Mastodon. Our forefathers soon found they could tell whether he was seeking a meal or a mate. The reflection of the sun from wet pebbles was noted. Smoke by day and fires by night were suitable for spreading a warning. In the Old Testament a dove conveyed a timely weather report and later Jeremiah called upon his people to "set up a sign of fire . . . for evil appeareth to the North, and Great Destruction."

Some forefathers felt the call of the sea as soon as they reached

the ground. It drew them out to the coasts with that force which still prevails on Bank Holidays, and there they stayed.

They learnt to swim, but found they could not live in the water. They preferred to keep warm and dry. This gave them a lively interest in anything which floated, especially if it would support them. The first forefather to catch and fry a fish added interest.

Having launched the shipbuilding industry they soon found it necessary to identify their craft. People were suspicious in those days. Everyone was a potential disturber of everyone else's peace until he could prove himself otherwise. Individuals and communities were therefore identified by their standards. A standard in this, its earliest sense, was a tall pole supporting some distinctive object. A shipowner took his standard to sea with him. Designs on pottery made by the pre-dynastic Egyptians as far back as 4000 B.C. show what is believed to be boats, used on the Nile at that time, with the standard mounted on the aftermost cabin.

For the next three and a half thousand years there seem to have been more pressing matters to attend to than the development of signalling. Then, in 480 B.C., came the first record of an operational signal made between ships at sea.

It happened during the battle of Salamis. As this signal was the ancestor of all the others in this book, the story is worth telling, Xerxes, the Persian ruler, had spent four years raising an army to overthrow the Greeks. The force he raised was not a happy army, but it was the biggest the world had yet seen. At the outset of the campaign Xerxes was unopposed. The smaller Greek states showed no national patriotism. Athens became alarmed and sent Themistocles, the best leader they could find. He managed to raise some opposition, and it was largely due to his counsel and energy that the Greeks were not completely overwhelmed.

But Xerxes and his hordes swept on. When he reached the Dardanelles he built a bridge of boats, crossed over, and turned down the coast towards Greece. Offshore a fleet of miscellaneous ships backed him up with supplies.

At the pass of Thermopylae, the gateway to Athens, the Persians found 1,400 Spartans under the leadership of Leonidas blocking their path. After fighting with great heroism every single one of this gallant little army was killed; but they left their mark on the Persians, and it was in a chastened mood that they entered Athens.

At this stage it seemed to Xerxes that he had achieved his object and conquered Greece. But he had not reckoned with the Greek navy.

This small fleet was lying off Salamis. When the grim news came through from Athens, there was disagreement between the Commanders. Some favoured retirement to the Isthmus of Corinth, but Themistocles, who was still very much alive, urged battle with the Persian supply fleet. He let it be known that the Greeks intended to withdraw, which enticed the Persians to give chase. When the two fleets met, the Greeks were outnumbered by four to one. But they soon proved that they were craftier than their pursuers.

Having formed into an orthodox line of battle, the Persians looked as if they were going to have it all their own way. But, suddenly, the scene changed. In the Greek flagship an oar was raised. Attached to the oar was a red cloak. The moment it appeared the Greek ships swung round together and bore down upon their adversaries who were soon in complete confusion.

The Greek victory which followed relieved the threat to European civilisation. The first manoeuvring signal at sea had made its mark.

About that time the Chinese were beginning to make use of an article which, later, in the seventeenth century, came under the generic term of Flag, Flagg, Flagge, or Vlag, depending whether you were Norseman, Swede, German or Dutch.

They used it in the Orient on land to marshal armies, and also to conduct operations, as the Greek admiral had done with his cloak.

Gradually the flag spread to Europe. First it embellished the Roman military standards where it hung from a transverse bar at the head of the staff, decorated with silver charms and battle honours, and even portraits of the reigning emperors. The pride and significance of Regimental Colours seems to emanate from such occasions as when in 103 B.C. Caius Marius assigned the Eagle exclusively to the Roman legions.

Sometimes the design of the flag revealed too readily the identification of those who bore the standards. In a naval action off Marseilles, in 49 B.C., Brutus was commanding Caesar's fleet against the Massilians who represented Pompey. Brutus' flagship was immediately recognised by his flamboyant standards, and she narrowly escaped being rammed by two triremes simultaneously.

With the growth of Christianity, these standards became sacred, residing in temples and churches. When Colours were presented to a regiment, prayers were offered, solemn services were held. After battle the Colours were returned tattered and scarred to their churches. The custom still survives. In St. Giles Cathedral, Edinburgh, today several score of Colours rest, never to be removed until there is nothing left but the staff on which they were borne.

The eleventh century produced other Standards which, though connected with Christianity, could certainly never have entered a church. These great cumbersome structures appeared in the Crusades. One which bore the Personal Flag of Richard I, in a battle near Acre in 1191 consisted of "a very large beam like the mast of a ship, placed upon four wheels in a frame very solidly fastened together and bound with iron, so that it seems incapable of yielding either to sword, axe, or fire."

As long as everyone saw the banner borne aloft they knew their leader was safe and all was well. The structure was defended by a specially selected bodyguard. In battle it was also a refuge. "Hither the sick were brought and cured, hither were brought the wounded, and even famous or illustrious men tired out in the fighting."

Colours are frequently mentioned in connection with banners and standards. Gold, purple, and red are the most prominent. Early evidence of red being used as a definite signal comes from the voyages of the Cabots. In A.D. 1020 when Karlsefni, Bjarni and Thorbjorn sailed to the westward from Iceland they were probably just as surprised to strike the American coast as the inhabitants were to see them. When the Vikings approached, so long as they displayed white shields all was peace, but the moment red shields were shown it was taken by the Indians as a general signal for a battle.

To the Crusaders, red seemed to have a more gruesome significance. Apart from the mobile standards, personal banners were carried into battle by kings and noblemen. These banners, which were usually white, were attached to sword or spear. The speed at which they changed from white to red gave some indication of how their owners were faring.

So far these historical examples have been more military than naval so let us embark with William Duke of Normandy on board *Mora* at St. Valery, in the estuary of the Somme, late on the afternoon of 27th September, 1066.

As he did not wish to reach the English coast before daybreak, the Duke ordered his ships to anchor round him on making the open sea. At the appointed time the signal to proceed with the invasion of England was made by lighting a lantern at *Mora's* masthead followed by the sounding of a trumpet. This seems worthier of such an occasion than what happened when the next successful invasion across the channel was launched 878 years later, by a nod from a meteorologist.

That important historical monument, the Bayeux Tapestry, which has survived since A.D. 1150, shows William Duke of Normandy's ship after he was promoted to Conqueror. She is distinguished by a blue-bordered white banner with a golden cross. Other ships are shown flying the personal flags of the knights who accompanied him. This gay flourish seems a fitting introduction to the Royal Navy.

The first authority on the subject of signalling in our Navy is the *Black Book of the Admiralty,* which appeared in A.D. 1338, and is still in existence. Before looking at it we must remember that, in those days, this country was a long way behind our contemporaries in the Mediterranean, who were backed by Greek and Roman tradition and encouraged by Mediterranean weather.

Take, for example, the intelligent grasp which Emperor Leo VI had three hundred years previously on the matter of signalling at sea. "Let there be some standard in your ship," he insisted, "either a banner or a streamer or something else in some conspicuous position, to the end you may be able thereby to make known what requires to be done." He then suggests appropriate signals for what does require to be done to control a fleet at sea. He finishes, "And thus, O general, let the exercise of these signals be practised, so that all officers in command of ships under you may have

B

certain knowledge of all such signs, . . . so that well familiarised with the signals, they may readily understand them in time of emergency and carry out the orders indicated."

At least these instructions laid the foundations for reasonable communication between ships, whereas three hundred years later our *Black Book* contained only two single flag signals.

(1) "Also it is to be noted that at whatever convenient time it pleases the admiral to call together the captains and masters of the fleet to take counsel with them he will carry high in the middle of the mast of his ship a banner of council so that in all parts of the fleet, whether in port or out at sea, this may be recognised and perceived, etc., and then immediately the captains and masters of ships are bound to assemble without delay with their boats well manned with seamen to row and go on board the ship of the admiral there to hear and do what the council of the admiral shall have ordained."

(2) "In case any ship or other vessel of the fleet perceive any enemy vessel upon the sea then he shall put a banner aloft by which the ship of the admiral and other ships of the fleet may have knowledge that he has seen one or more enemy vessels and thus afterwards give the best orders they know to encounter it."

This comparison shows that while in the Mediterranean tactics and manoeuvre were understood, and signals existed to implement them, nothing so subtle had occurred to us. Our ships were tougher and less manoeuvrable. If trouble cropped up they closed one another and conferred with their admiral to decide what to do.

In 1420 Mocenigo, Captain General of the Venetian Navy, imposed a fine of ten lire on ships in formation passing their next ahead without orders. In 1575 Antoine de Conflans reported strange ships in more detail by showing as many banners as the number of sails sighted on the side they had been seen. At home the positioning of sails conveyed a particular meaning, and the cannon was used to attract attention. "If by chance the said ships have parted company, which God forbid, and meet again by day, the one to windward shall lower and raise the topsail once and fire one gun. The one to leeward shall lower and raise the said topsail once and fire two guns."

Some of our naval traditions spring from instructions issued at this time. "If the said Lord and his fleet encounter enemy fleets where they must fight, they shall show all the ensigns and banners they have, so that each one may do his duty"; and again, "Let no vessel salute another while it is in sight of the said Lord, on pain of corporal punishment."

In 1530 "Orders to be used in the King's Majestie's Navy by the sea" added, "When and at all tymes the admyrall will anker or disanker, he must shote a pece, that thereby the rest may know to do the same; and that no shippe ride in anothers walke, for in that is greate danger."

". . . If it chance any shippe in the night fall in leake, or breake his maste, he may shote a pece of Ordinance or two to warne the flete he hath harme and in perall, to the extent he may have help, and the rest to tarie."

". . . If in the night there chanceth any enemyes unlooked for to fall into the flete, he that first doth askrie the same shall shote off two peces, and give a token of two fires and by that token shall he understande that they be enemyes that be in the flete. If they do flee, let everie man make after, and that shippe that is nighest beare a light in his stearnye that the rest may know whither the enemye goeth, for otherwise they may lose them; and if he that giveth the chace, see not the fleete follow, let him shote a pece, that they may follow by his shotte, in case they should not see his light."

By this time we had caught up on our Mediterranean contemporaries. Signalling at sea in our Navy had, in fact, advanced about as far as our unwieldy ships allowed. It was up to the constructors and the seamen to make the next move. Ships had reached the same relative stage of development as tanks in the 1914-18 war. They were not used tactically and collectively; they were independent units which fought their own way through. In fact, in July, 1588, when the Spanish Armada was off Plymouth, tactical instructions did not exist in our Navy.

It was not until the 1650's that naval tactics began to take shape, and more signals became necessary. Orders for the line ahead formation were issued over the signatures of Blake, Deane and Monck. In 1653 Admiral Blake used the five most prominent parts of his ship to hoist about twenty-five different manoeuvring signals. Throughout the rest of that century flags of different colours and designs appeared. James, Duke of York, later James II, took a great interest. In 1673 he co-ordinated all the existing signal flags, which by that time were far too numerous to remember, and he issued the first signal book, a copy of which exists today in the Naval Historical library. In 1714 Jonathan Greenwood went one better. He edited a pocket signal book in which, he boasted, he had "disposed matters in such a manner that any instruction may be found in half a minute."

Throughout the eighteenth century the Navy developed rapidly. The increasing flexibility and requirements of the fleet could no longer be dealt with by a few flags in strongly contrasted designs appearing in prominent positions. More signals were needed but there was no room to hoist them. In 1746 there were sixteen flags in use to express 144 signals. In 1780 there were fifty flags expressing about 330.

In 1776 a complete revolution in signalling methods was inaugurated by Admiral Lord Howe. He issued a signal book in which the total number of flags was twenty-one. Many of these were of new design. In this book he grouped and numbered each instruction and numbered each page so that any instruction could be signalled by quoting its number and the page on which it appeared. The idea was opposed by some Flag Officers who thought that several flags on one hoist could not be read at any distance. They maintained the scheme did not compare with the simplicity of single flags in prominent positions. Nevertheless Lord Howe's ideas began to take hold. Improvements and variations in flag design were also introduced by Kempenfelt and Sir Charles Knowles. Great personal interest was taken in the subject. It soon became customary for Flag Officers to draw up and print their own instructions when they took over a command. Each particular operation received a suitable set of signals to go with it. "While you remain in this service you will establish such signals and instructions for the government of the ships under your command as you may think fit," said Howe when he gave Kempenfelt his orders for the command of a detached Squadron on 30th April, 1782.

Howe's interest continued and he revised his ideas periodically. His latest signal code was in use in the fleet under his command on the Glorious First of June, 1794. With amendments, this edition existed up to the Battles of St. Vincent and the Nile.

Perhaps the best testimony to Howe's efforts is given in a letter from Nelson in reply to Howe's congratulations on the victory of the Nile. "By attacking the enemy's van and centre, the wind blowing directly along their line, I was enabled to throw what

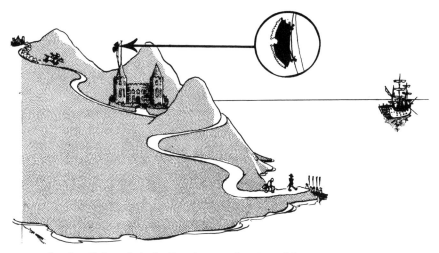

... the simplicity of single flags in prominent positions.

force I pleased on a few ships. This plan my friends conceived by the signals (for which we are principally if not entirely indebted to your Lordship) and we kept a superior force to the enemy."

In 1795, a completely new form of signalling called semaphore, devised by the Rev. Lord George Murray, was introduced into the Navy. To start with it consisted of a screen with six shutters which could be operated to give numerous combinations, and it was used ashore by the Admiralty to communicate with Portsmouth and with the Nore. The semaphore signals were relayed by a chain of signal stations in sight of one another on neighbouring hills.

In 1799 the Board of Admiralty, who hitherto had been content to allow flag officers to make their own private codes, issued the first printed signal book. It was a development of Howe's principles, with some additions from Kempenfelt and others. Its greatest asset was that it was universal, so that a ship joining a fleet need no longer fear that the signals meant nothing until a copy of that particular admiral's private code had been received on board.

By now the offensive spirit and personal skill of officers and men were being welded into squadrons which could manoeuvre, concentrate, and harass with increasing efficiency. They were certainly getting plenty of practice, and each battle brought a lesson; a new manoeuvre, a suggested formation. Each innovation had to be translated into instructions which could be signalled and, once again, our signal system began to feel the strain. An Admiral found he could handle a fleet in a crude fashion but he could not make his intentions clear. The language of signalling was too rigid. Captains were on their own now. Conferences at sea, or closing to trumpet range, were no longer fashionable. Steps had to be taken to make the signal language more realistic to increase its scope of expression from the language of a child to that of an adult. These steps were taken by Sir Home Popham.

His first vocabulary contained 1,000 useful words. These were signalled by using numbers in 3- or 4-flag hoists. For the next twelve years he worked away, printing and circulating his books privately. His telegraphic signals were in use at Trafalgar.

In 1812 Sir Home Popham produced his second, and very much enlarged edition of telegraphic signals. By introducing alphabetical letters as well as numbers he increased the permutations in 3- and 4-flag hoists to a vocabulary of some 30,000 words. These included geographical and technical tables, tables of stores and provisions. The only indication that Sir Home had a sense of humour comes from the two examples he chose for "Private Communications."

(1)	BOE	YOUR
	AC8	SISTER
	852	MARRIED
	85F	TO
C87		A LORD OF THE ADMIRALTY
(2)	FAI	HAVE YOU AN IDEA?
	G647	A CHANGE OF MINISTERS IS ABOUT TO TAKE PLACE

These telegraphic signals went through ten editions before their author's death in 1848. Popham also improved the semaphore of 1795. In 1816 he introduced an instrument with arms working on two separate uprights. At night it was lit by lanterns, and messages from the Admiralty relayed through ten stations could be passed, we are told, in ten minutes.

In 1817, Captain Frederick Marryat showed that as well as being a distinguished and courageous naval officer, he had interests in signalling. He introduced the first code of signals for the Merchant Service, designing his own numeral, and later alphabetical, flags. In spite of the many revisions between his day and ours, thirteen of his flags are still in use.

The next milestone was planted in 1844. In that year the first signal to travel beyond visibility distance made a successful journey of some thirty miles on a wire stretched between Baltimore and Washington. It was propelled by electricity in a code invented by Samuel Morse. Twenty years later the Morse code was introduced into the Navy. This "make-and-break" principle was adapted to artificial light, in 1867 when Captain Colomb's flashing signal lantern appeared.

Thus, a stage had been reached afloat where intercommunication by day and night was practicable within the limits of visibility. But a unit at sea at the end of the nineteenth century was just as isolated from the world as it had been when sailing ships were invented.

Then, out of the air, came wireless.

On 1st September, 1895, Admiral Jackson, who saw great possibilities in wireless telegraphy, met Signor Marconi, who was producing practical results from experiments in that direction. On 7th May, 1898, in Admiral Jackson's presence, the sceptics were severely shaken when Marconi tied an insulated wire to a flagstaff at Bournemouth into which he pumped morse messages which were received at Alum Bay, Isle of Wight, fourteen miles away.

This achievement must have been a setback to those interested in another line of research at this time. The *Handbook of Homing Pigeons for Naval Purposes,* published the same year, began confidently by saying: "Now that the conveyance of messages by homing pigeons for naval and military purposes has become an essential part of war preparation in all European countries . . ."

Another handbook also appeared called *Working Wireless Telegraphic Apparatus.* It did not sound so confident. It explained that when receiving signals various things could happen. The signals might be satisfactory, but this was most improbable. Later on it added, to avoid confusion: "If in doubt about a signal always ask for a repetition of the doubtful words or signs. The very worst thing to do is to keep the sender waiting in suspense, for after waiting for about two minutes for your RD (message read) he will probably make another signal to you, 'Have you got last signal?' And you will probably not yet get this one either, and ask him to repeat, when he will repeat the wrong one, and so on, causing great delay."

But radio had come to stay and everyone in command of H.M. ships was soon clamouring to have it installed. In a certain cruiser the captain in his bath was made to complete the circuit physically when dockyard workmen were looking for a suitable "earth." But

PRIVATE SIGNALS for knowing each other by DAY.

Day of the Month	N°	*These Signals are all to be made by Flags*	Main-Top-Maft-Head.	Fore-Top-Maft-Head.	Mizen-Top-Maft-Head.
1 11 21 31	1	The first Signal made is —— Anfwered by a ——	Red & White Union to Common Pendant over	Red	White
2 12 22	2	The first Signal made is —— Anfwered by a ——	White	Yellow & Blue White & Red	Red
3 13 23	3	The first Signal made is —— Anfwered by a ——	White & Red Dutch	Blue to Common Pendant over	Red & White
4 14 24	4	The first Signal made is —— Anfwered by a ——	Red & White	Red White	White & Red
5 15 25	5	The first Signal made is —— Anfwered by a ——	Union to Common Pendant over Dutch	Dutch Yellow & Blue	
6 16 26	6	The first Signal made is Anfwered by a ——	Blue & Yellow	Blue to Common Pendant over 	Yellow & Blue Red & White
7 17 27	7	The first Signal made is —— Anfwered by a ——	Red	Union to Common Pendant over Blue & Yellow	Blue & Yellow
8 18 28	8	The first Signal made is —— Anfwered by a ——	Dutch Yellow & Blue	Blue & Yellow Red & White	
9 19 29	9	The first Signal made is —— Anfwered by a ——	Red	White Dutch	White & Red
10 20 30	10	The first Signal made is —— Anfwered by a ——	Blue & Yellow White	Red	Red & White

N:B. The declaratory Signals and answers by Day & Night which
are to be shewn to and from a Ship on meeting again other ships here
or on joining the Fleet at Sea, will be found in the several ... ...
of the Month opposite to the first Column; where the day of the month
at the time of meeting is to be looked for; and such declarations ...
to be respectively made accordingly and the nautical day of ...
... at noon is to be used with these Signals

PRIVATE SIGNALS for His Majesty's SHIPS by NIGHT.

Day of the Month.	
	N.B. The Lights are to be shewn where they can be best seen by the Ship to which the Signals are respectively made.
1 4 7 10 13 16 19 22 25 28 31	The Ship making the firft Signal *is to shew* 2 Lights *of equal height & burn* 2 False Fires *together* ——— The other Ship is to anfwer by *burning* 2 False Fires *in fucceffion* ——— Then the Ship which firft made the Signal is to shew 3 Lights *of equal height.* ——— Which the other is to reply to, by *burning* 1 False Fire *and shewing* 2 Lights *of equal height* ——— The Ship that is firft hailed is to anfwer *Northumberland* ——— And the Ship which hailed is to reply *Warwick* ———
2 5 8 11 14 17 20 23 26 29	The Ship making the firft Signal *is to shew* 3 Lights *one under the other* ——— The other Ship is to anfwer by ——— 2 Lights *of equal height.* ——— Then the Ship which firft made the Signal is to shew *burn* 2 False Fires *together* ——— Which the other is to reply to, by *shewing* 1 Light *and burning* 1 False Fire ——— The Ship that is firft hailed is to anfwer *Great Britain* ——— And the Ship which hailed is to reply *Ireland* ———
3 6 9 12 15 18 21 24 27 30	The Ship making the firft Signal *is to shew* 3 Lights *of equal height* ——— The other Ship is to anfwer by ——— 2 Lights *one under the other* ——— Then the Ship which firft made the Signal is to shew 2 Lights *of equal height and burn* 1 False Fire ——— Which the other is to reply to, by *burning* 2 False Fires ——— The Ship that is firft hailed is to anfwer *Hanover* ——— And the Ship which hailed is to reply *Brandenbury* ———

To

Commander of His Majefty's

Given under my Hand on Board His Majefty's Ship

By Command of the

Private signals delivered to Horatio Nelson in Agamemnon.

nothing mattered so long as the equipment was installed before the ship sailed on manoeuvres.

Stepping stones of radio achievement followed one another further and further into the ionosphere. The flagship of the West Indian Squadron, eighty miles from Bermuda received R-CKS--D five minutes after ROCKSAND won the Derby. By 1904 Gibraltar was reading the Admiralty. Out of sight at sea would never again be out of mind.

By the early 1900's the Royal Navy was still wading into its fabulous legacy from Nelson's achievements. Wooden hulls, masts and snatching sails had already been replaced by smoking chunky flatirons, sprouting swivelling guns. Nelson would have been staggered at the speed, manoeuvrability and power of this, the most formidable sea-borne fortress the world had ever seen, but he would hardly have been so impressed by that umbilical fuel cord which so restricted the operational limits of these juggernauts. And at this stage in our navy, ninety years after his last battle and ten years before our next, Nelson might also have thought we were getting soft and complacent. How could such an Armada, manned by generations who had never seen a shot fired at anything more belligerent than a defenceless target, train for a war no-one could visualise?

"Let the strategic impact of the speed and gunpower sort itself out" the admirals cried. "Sharkskin, burnish, polish, everything that can't move. Burnish brightest of all the word DISCIPLINE. Let it shine from foretops to bilges; let smartness and ceremony march hand in hand". Included in this fanatic cult were of course the signalmen. On every flag deck those twenty-five gay signal flags introduced by Admiral Blake in 1653, joined by others over the years, leapt and fluttered from and back to their signal lockers. Forked tongues goaded their manipulators; hot eyes glued to polished telescopes checked them, all in mortal combat for promotion. Before raw signalmen aspired to the flag deck, they spent hours on parade grounds ashore, pretending they were battleships, cruisers or flotillas, where they were formed, deployed and chivvied around by flags hoisted by Signal Yeomen pretending to be admirals.

Afloat, the contraptions designed to decant semaphore and morse were handled with the precision and speed of field gunners at Royal Tournaments. It was normal to see a flagship with four pairs of mechanical semaphores spinning, a few searchlights and signal lamps blinking, festoons of bunting bobbing up and down the signal halyards, while the Chief Yeoman supervising it all calmly read the latest test match score by buzzer from the main radio office.

The lower deck wasted no time in differentiating between the two aspects of communication by dubbing the visual signalman "Bunts" and the radio telegraphist "Sparks". At that time and for many years to come it was Bunts who stole the limelight, for he was both visual and visible. Not only was he in the picture, he was painting it. So was Sparks, but he was hidden down below the armour belt, wrestling with tuning knobs and morse keys. But neither evaded the discipline cult. Bunts was kept moving and thinking at the speed of light by the Signal Bos'un, the Sergeant Major of the signal deck, carrying instead of a persuasive cane a truncheon disguised as a telescope. Sparks might be warm and dry, but he had to keep on the alert. There were plenty of earphones around which would pick up the first suspicion of a snore.

Wireless telegraphy—which refused to be called radio for half a century—also introduced the backroom electronic boffin. To the uninitiated sailor, radio was witchcraft, highly suspect because there was nothing to polish. But before the century was very old this new wireless magic had spun its communication web between the Admiralty and every ship afloat. The whole operational picture had suddenly leaped from arms length to world wide.

Sitting there with helmet, shield and trident polished and shining fit to dazzle the whole world, Britannia held these ever-lengthening reins of communication; as well as the ocean, she now ruled the wireless waves. A touch on those reins and massive fleets ploughed forth, frightening everyone who saw them into awesome humility. Wherever temperatures rose, a cool breeze fluttered the white ensigns of a cruiser squadron as it appeared over the horizon. Round corners of tropical rivers popped glistening gunboats just in time to rescue missionaries from the hot pot.

Fearing God, honouring Queen or King, and demanding obedience, stood Britannia's minions, the admirals, who in this era had taught the Royal Navy to do everything except fight. There was no reason to believe these admirals were not brave and competent leaders in battle, but there were no battles. Nelson had arranged all that.

Where did these peacetime admirals start? What were the qualifications for joining the Navy in those days? One candidate, on nomination in 1847, was ordered to Woolwich, told to write out the Lord's Prayer, asked if he could drink a glass of sherry, then told to strip by his examiner who promptly struck him in the chest. When and if the youngster squared up to fight, he was passed. It seens logical that some graduates grew into colourful characters. The immaculate "Pompo" Heneage, for example, who flew his flag in Queen Victoria's reign. Every day he wore a clean white piqué shirt (selected from a wardrobe of some twenty dozen, laundered in England wherever he was serving). His daily toilet also included breaking two eggs over his head. He was a religious man, but when praying, the thought of an admiral kneeling was so incongruous that he removed his jacket and prayed as a civilian. Coming alongside his flagship once in a loppy sea, when assisted from his barge by a seaman, he arrived on his quarterdeck shaking, white with rage, squealing "that man *touched* me,"

At the other end of the colour spectrum, and a generation later came Sir Robert Arbuthnot, Bart., killed at the battle of Jutland. He was immaculate in a different way. A stickler for physical fitness—himself a remarkable athlete—he set a tirelessly efficient example often painful both to superiors and subordinates. But everyone respected him. Commanders write their own order books. Some are short. I remember one with a single sentence: "I expect my officers to fear God, honour the King and keep their bowels open". Commander Arbuthnot's order book covered 303 pages. Once two seamen brought up before him left the defaulters' table muttering threats which Sir Robert overheard. That evening they were summoned to the quarterdeck, given boxing gloves whereupon he knocked the living daylights out of them both.

Then there were the Prothero brothers. 'Prothero the Good' passed through the Navy unnoticed. 'Prothero the Bad' passed nowhere unnoticed. A distinguished admiral once described him as "quite the most terrifying man I ever served with. Eyes like a hawk, a great hooked nose over a bristling black beard down to his waist, terrific shoulders, nearly as broad as he was long. If a midshipman got in his way on the bridge he would pick the lad up, one great fist grasping his collar, the other the seat of his trousers, and drop him over the bridge screen onto the deck below."

In spite of the lively eccentricity of our leaders, there is no doubt that our fighting efficiency was slowly coming to a burnished halt, when suddenly there appeared another one of two distinguished brothers who, as First Sea Lord, fired a shot which hit the Navy plumb in the arm. The impact of Admiral Jacky Fisher in 1904 was terrific. Here in one dynamic container was the intelligence, vision and drive that the Service was waiting for. Up went the stockades of protest, only to be blasted to smithereens by the shock waves of Jacky's personality. Our next war, he prophesied, would be against Germany, so he set about preparing a Navy to fight it. Although encouraging new innovations like the torpedo and submarine he set his sights on speed and gunpower in the battle fleet. Thumping, oozing reciprocating steam engines were uprooted and replaced by purring turbines taking up a fraction of the space and pushing the speedometer from 16 to 25 knots. Twin 12-inch gun turrets ditched all the untidy "pin-cushion" armament overboard. Gunfire became concentrated, with its effective range stepped up from 3,000 to 16,000 yards. "Hit first, hit hard, and keep on hitting" roared Admiral Fisher, drowning all those around him who seemed quite content not to hit at all.

Although this marine earthquake had no immediate effect on the current signalling methods in the Fleet, it certainly introduced inter-communication to armament. In the last sea battle off Cape Trafalgar, the flagship's Master Gunner had no time to bother about who the ships around him were firing at. In the next sea battle it was the First Sea Lord's intention that the guns in each battle squadron would concentrate and work as one battery under the orders of the flagship's Gunnery Officer. Signalmen and Telegraphists were accordingly trained to implement this new technique of aiming the squadron's guns and controlling its fire.

Incidentally the other Fisher brother, also an admiral, and Jacky's junior by ten years, was known to bevies of little girls as "Uncle". To no-one's surprise he took no interest in the earthquake.

The international shop window for the Royal Navy has always been Spithead. In 1897 Queen Victoria reviewed her fleet there to commemorate her Diamond Jubilee and to mark the last occasion of mustering such an ornamental display of warships. In long lines they glistened in the sunshine, with their yellow masts and funnels, white upperworks, salmon pink waterline cutting their black hulls by ribbons of white. At the next Spithead Review, which was to celebrate the Coronation of King George V in 1911, the Navy's new look was complete and impressive. Anchored lines of more businesslike sombre grey monsters, which included 42 battleships, stretched over 26 miles. Visiting ships from foreign countries saw for the first time a Navy twice the size of any other navy which had just been saved from expiring with fatty degeneration of its heart by Dr. Jacky Fisher. In three years' time, this fleet, to be commanded by one of the doctor's ex-pupils, would again muster there, prior to plunging into the war prescribed.

The Beginning of World War I

3/8/14	*From Admiralty to destroyer flotilla at sea* British ultimatum to Germany expires at 2300. *From Admiralty* Commence hostilities with Germany. *From Flotilla Leader* Importance of wearing clean underclothes in action is stressed. This may make all the difference between a clean and a suppurating wound.
4/8/14	*From His Majesty King George V to Admiral Sir John Jellicoe, C.-in-C. Grand Fleet* At this grave moment in our national history I send to you and through you to the officers and men of the fleets of which you have assumed command, the assurance of my confidence that under your direction they will revive and renew the old glories of the Royal Navy, and prove once again the sure shield of Britain and her Empire in the hour of trial.

George RI

A lieutenant in command of a refitting destroyer returned from a yachting cruise p.m. 4th August, 1914. On arrival on board he sent for the Signal Log. He waded through all the routine signals about ships' movements, exercise programmes, Sunday church parties, changes in personnel, cricket matches. Slowly he brought his mind back from the limited horizon of his 10-ton yawl. Staring at him from the log was General Signal from Admiralty which read:

Commence hostilities with Germany.

5/8/14   *From Admiralty*
Following are transferred from conditional to absolute contraband: Aeroplanes, Airships, Balloons and aircraft of all kinds and their component parts together with accessories and articles for use in connection with balloons and aircraft.

5/8/14   *From Admiralty to C.-in-C. Med.*
Austria has not declared war against France or England. Continue watching Adriatic for double purpose of preventing Austrians from emerging unobserved and preventing Germans entering.

6/8/14   *From Admiralty to Bacchante*
German Ambassador leaving Harwich today in Great Eastern Steamer *St. Petersburg.*

7/8/14   *From Admiralty to Bacchante*
British Ambassador from Berlin returning Hook of Holland in Great Eastern Steamer *St. Petersburg.* She leaves between 4 and 5 p.m. today.

(It is reassuring to know Great Eastern Steamer *St. Petersburg* ended up on the right side.)

U.S.A. Declares War

7/4/17   *From British Ambassador, Washington*
War Resolution passed by Congress was signed by President this afternoon. Proclamation also issued that a state of war exists between United States and German Government, and establishing regulations to ensure good behaviour of alien enemies.

The End of World War I

7/11/18   *From Chief of Naval Staff to Admiralty*
Am leaving for unknown destination with Marshal Foch this afternoon.

9/11/18   *From German Imperial Chancellor Prince Max of Baden*

The Kaiser and King has decided to renounce the throne. The Imperial Chancellor will remain in office until the questions connected with the abdication of the Kaiser, the renouncing of the throne of the German Empire and of Prussia and the setting up of a Regency has been settled.

11/11/18   *From Admiralty*

The Armistice is signed. Hostilities are to be suspended forthwith. All anti-submarine defensive measures for the security of men-of-war at sea or in harbour are to remain in force until further orders. Submarines on the surface are not to be attacked unless their hostile intentions are obvious.

(As someone pointed out, this meant waiting until you were torpedoed to find out.)

11/11/18   *From Commander-in-Chief, Grand Fleet to Admiralty*

It is not the custom for H.M. ships to dress ship except on ceremonial occasions. . . . The traditional method of celebrating an auspicious occasion is to splice the main brace and I have given orders to that effect.

11/11/18   *From His Majesty King George V to the First Lord of the Admiralty*

Now that the last and most formidable of our enemies has acknowledged the triumph of the Allied Arms on behalf of Right and Justice, I wish to express my praise and thankfulness to the officers and men of the Royal Navy and Marines, with their comrades of the Fleet Auxiliaries and Mercantile Marine who for more than four years have kept open the seas, protected our shores and given us safety. Ever since that fateful 4 August 1914, I have remained steadfast in my confidence that whether fortune frowned or smiled the Royal Navy would once more prove the sure shield of the British Empire in the hour of trial. Never in its history has the Royal Navy, with God's help, done greater things for us, nor better sustained its old glories and the chivalries of the seas. With full and grateful hearts the Peoples of the British Empire salute the White, the Red, and the Blue ensigns and those who have given their lives for the flag. I am proud to have served in the Navy. I am prouder still to be its head on this memorable day.

GEORGE R.I.

12/11/18 *From Admiralty*

The Lords Commissioners of the Admiralty desire heartily to congratulate officers and men of the Royal Navy and Royal Marines upon the triumph of the Allied cause, in realisation of which they have played so splendid a part, adding lustre throughout to the great tradition of the Service to which they belong.

Their Lordships feel that after four years of ceaseless vigilance a relaxation of war conditions cannot but be eagerly desired by officers and men and they may be relied upon to grant leave and modify routine immediately when circumstances permit. For the present however with German submarines possibly still at sea ignorant of the Armistice, with the work of escorting ships to be surrendered or interned devolving largely on British Navy and with the full capacity of the mine-sweepers required for sweeping the seas it is plain that no officer or man can be spared from their duties until the safety of the country at sea is assured.

The Navy had in time of Peace to be ready for War in a sense which land forces cannot be. Now that Peace is again in prospect, it may prove that even after the troops in the field are enjoying a relief from tension the Navy must for a time continue its war routine. If so their Lordships are confident that this will be cheerfully accepted as being at once the burden and the privilege of the Empire's first line of defence.

(in other words—wait for it.)

From Commander-in-Chief, Grand Fleet (Admiral Beatty) after the surrendered German Fleet had anchored in the Firth of Forth.

21/11/18 THE GERMAN FLAG WILL BE HAULED DOWN AT SUNSET TODAY AND NOT HOISTED AGAIN WITHOUT PERMISSION.

From the point of view of furthering our naval communications system, World War One brought little more than the spinning of this ever-extending radio web. For warships at sea, however, radio introduced two built-in headaches. The first was the nakedness, the insecurity of transmitted waves which, unprotected by telegraph cable, could be snatched out of the air by anyone who had

c

the right equipment. Accordingly, radio signals were enciphered by a lengthy complicated process of turning words into figures. Before long a secret radio signal, irrespective of its priority, found itself spending far more time wandering about the cipher book than fulfilling its object. Cipher books themselves, like Old Masters, were safeguarded. They were mustered and checked every watch, day, and night; only officers were permitted to touch them; they were almost sacred, and lost a lot of officers a lot of sleep. To make them more cumbersome to handle cipher books had lead covers so that they would sink if thrown overboard; even so, one dismayed captain serving in foreign waters reported that in the prevailing brine his cipher books floated.

It is all too clear now that the time and effort which went into composing and protecting ciphers could have been far better employed by our enemies and ourselves in devising something quicker and more secure. All those muddled up numbers presented an instant challenge for mathematicians on both sides. They became so skillful at breaking each other's codes that we were soon reading each other's secrets as quickly as if they were in plain language. By the end of the war it was questionable if either side had a secret to call his own. How credulous we were. How insecure our security.

The second radio headache still exists; a ship transmitting on radio can be pinpointed. Very soon the boffins produced electric fingers which pointed to her. Two fingers pointing from different positions could fix that ship on the chart. Henceforth the Captain of a ship had to choose whether what he had to say was worth the risk of giving away his position. To attain surprise necessitated being unheard as well as unseen.

If war is, or was, the only thing that kept men and women apart, then the converse is true. Anyone who looked carefully at Britannia as the German Fleet steamed to its last anchorage on the 21st November, 1918, would not only have noticed that she was relaxed, but that there was a glint in her eye. Peacetime was going to be different. Vive la différence! Suffragettes may have jolted Queen Victoria's strict code of social behaviour, but by 1918, anyway in the Royal Navy the pendulum was swinging. Women's Lib was beginning to loom.

Malta, the centre spot in the centre sea, soon resumed its role as once more the centre of naval attraction. We could still afford quite a fleet. Looking down on Grand Harbour, Valetta, the water lay almost hidden beneath a vast mosaic of teak, stretched awnings, and brasswork; a pattern you could walk across without getting your feet wet. Out came the women; wine and song were there already. Some of the older women became tiresome and started wearing their husbands' gold stripes. Captains' wives, arriving on the spotless quarterdecks of glistening battleships would remind the Officer-of-the-Watch that 'Y' Turret could do with another coat of enamel. Woe betide any wife who in the company of other wives, failed to get in and out of a pinnace in strict order of her husband's seniority.

Social life ashore revolved round one room, the only lounge in the Officers' Club, Valetta, in which ladies were permitted. It was called the Snake Pit. It was invariably draped with members of the "fishing fleet", an industry which flourished in those waters, exclusively manned by young ladies. What had all this to do with making signals? Any bachelor going into the Snake Pit would say it had quite a lot.

Strict Victorian upbringing followed by suffrage produced some pretty formidable females after World War One, some were wives of admirals, called admiralesses.

Apart from family, the nearest human being to an admiral in everything but age was his Flag Lieutenant; it often happened that this young officer's signal and social duties were combined. As it was the conventional dream of admirals' daughters to marry their father's Flag Lieutenants, admiralesses naturally took a great interest in casting. Although it would be going too far to suggest there were male mannequin parades at the Signal School on Graduation Days, there would have been dead trouble in any "flag drawingroom" had an admiral introduced his choice, a young signal genius perhaps, but a non-dancer with wet hands, and no charisma.

Admiralesses were about, so they say, before World War One, and in fact when war came and the Navy shed its social skin one or two admiralesses had inflicted their husbands with flag lieutenants who were nimbler on the dance floor than the signal bridge. Stripped from their ballroom prowess, some of these young standard bearers caused their masters anxiety. Nevertheless, by Armistice, 1918, the ebullient spirit of these young gentlemen emerged to launch the Royal Navy's signal branch's age of glamour. It was an age which the rest of the Navy—who did not particularly mind getting its hands dirty—remembers well.

As swords clicked back into their scabbards, out came ebony canes with glistening silver tops. White cuffs, silken handkerchiefs, protruded. Well-cut monkey jackets hung wide open to reveal brass-buttoned waistcoats festooned with clanking watchchains. A faint whiff of Morny's June Roses emanated from the hand proferring the golden cigarette case with a sliding hinge, packed with Sullivan & Powell's (duty free) Sub-Rosa's.

But underneath it all these young stalwarts were far from decadent. They were smart between the ears as well as clean behind them. A particularly bright star in this naval galaxy was Lord Louis Mountbatten. Between the wars, when Malta bulged with our enormous Mediterranean Fleet, Commander Mountbatten was out there as Fleet Wireless Officer. Monthly meetings to which he summoned the whole fleet radio personnel soon overran the vast naval canteen, so he commandeered the opera house.

At one such meeting the F.W.O. strode on stage relaxed, hands in pockets, no notes, to tell his packed audience that a few days previously when he was having a bath at his house after playing polo, he switched on his bathroom radio (an unheard-of luxury then) and heard a passing merchant ship asking the naval radio guard-ship for a time check. He had no idea, he said, who had the guard that day, but from the way in which the radio operator answered, the way he used his key, it sounded to the F.W.O. like Leading Telegraphist Bloggs, of H.M.S.—— If Bloggs was present, would he please stand up. From the vast sea of faces Bloggs rose. Yes, it was he. Whether or not Bloggs had acted correctly was beside the point; what hit everyone present was that one of them, tucked away in the sanctity of his radio office, had been identified from all the other operators in this huge fleet by his touch on a morse transmitting key. The shock waves bounced off the audience in a reverberating OO-OO-OO-OO!

And so, with steady advance in radio technique, polished by signal discipline, and still with money enough to build and maintain fleets at home, in the Mediterranean, North America, West Indies, South Atlantic, East Indies, and China, Britannia continued to rule the waves without lifting a finger.

The same old Admiralty, so long content to sit and wait for ships' captains to report their remote proceedings was now in instant operational control at the centre of that web, whose spokes were made of radio waves. What a chance for an imaginative sculptor to replace all those tangled aerials sprouting from the Admiralty's green dome by Britannia herself, holding them aloft on her trident.

The threat of World War Two found the Navy with fewer, better ships than in 1914. Fighting power above, on and beneath sea level had advanced considerably, so had radio signal communication, but visual signalling hadn't budged an inch. On signal bridges pretty flags still huddled breathlessly in their private pigeonholes awaiting the harness of the halyards. On the wings of bridges the same gaunt mechanical semaphores spun their black and white arms. Above stood an assortment of searchlights with hand-worked Venetian–blind shutters strapped across their gaping faces. Never pausing, the portable little Aldis lamp with built-in triggered mirror aimed its pencil beam, like a sawn-off shotgun. (As well it might have been, from the castigation that often flashed from it.)

But in fairness to the Boffins, at that very moment they were producing something even better than human eyesight, radar. Though not directly connected with signalling at first, who was to know what the superheated incubator of war would hatch it into?

With yet another clanking gear change World War Two began.

3/9/39   *From C.-in-C. Rosyth to all watching W/T stations*
Pass the following to all British vessels with which you may be in touch during the next 24 hours. War has broken out with Germany. You must not repeat not repeat not go into German ports.
Timed: 1210/3/9/39.

The Beginning of World War II

1/9/39   *From Admiralty*
The use of sirens and hooters is prohibited except for air raid warnings. The sounding of sirens or whistles in ships which might be heard on land is to be restricted to the minimum necessary for the safety of navigation.

3/9/39   *From commander-in-Chief, Portsmouth*
All concerned at Home and Abroad from Admiralty. Commence hostilities at once with Germany.

3/9/39   *From Admiralty*
Winston is back.

3/9/39	*From Admiralty*
	Immediate. Special telegram TOTAL Germany.
3/9/39	*From Admiralty*
	All available destroyers at Rosyth are to proceed to sea and steer NNE with moderate despatch.
3/9/39	*From Admiralty to Admiral Commanding 2nd Cruiser Squadron*
	Steer North East at Full Speed.
5/9/39	*From Admiralty to C.-in-C. Home Fleet*
	A general issue of life-saving belts has not been contemplated but arrangements are now being made to obtain supplies and secure the most rapid production practicable.
5/9/39	*From C.-in-C. Home Fleet to Admiralty*
	Request the latest information as to number of long distance bombers Germany possesses.
6/9/39	*From Admiralty*
	Special telegram FISHING 3 September FORECASTLE all areas PUGILIST WINCH DOVER.
6/9/39	*From Admiralty to destroyers Jackal, Janus, Juno*
	British Embassy party from Berlin will be leaving Rotterdam in S.S. *Batavia V* at 0500 tomorrow Thursday, *Jaackal, Janus* and *Juno* are to rendezvous with S.S. *Batavia V* in position 130 degrees 4 miles from Maas light vessel and escort her to the Tongue light vessel.
6/9/39	*From C.-in-C. Home Fleet to Admiralty*
	At present the navigation lights at Copensay, Pentland Skerries, Stroma and Swona in Orkney Islands cannot be controlled from the base and it is requested that immediate steps are taken to rectify this. . . .This is a matter affecting the safety of H.M. ships and I trust it will receive their Lordships' early attention. My first communication on this subject was dated 27 September 1938.
Autumn 1939	*From Admiralty to Destroyer*
	Proceed with all despatch.
	From Destroyer to Admiralty
	Request destination
	From Admiralty to Destroyer
	Aden, repeat Aden.

From Destroyer to Admiralty
Am at Aden.

9/9/39   *From Admiralty to C.-in-C. Home Fleet*
It is suggested that if practicable the force now in
Icelandic waters might look into Denmark Strait and
report if any considerable quantity of shipping is
avoiding contraband control by using this channel.

The End of World War II

11/9/43   *From   Commander-in-Chief   Mediterranean   to
Admiralty:*
BE PLEASED TO INFORM THEIR LORDSHIPS THAT
THE ITALIAN BATTLE FLEET NOW LIES AT
ANCHOR UNDER THE GUNS OF THE FORTRESS
OF MALTA.
*From: Commander-in Chief Mediterranean to Medi-
terranean Fleet*
I have this day informed the Board of Admiralty that
the Italian Fleet now lies at anchor under the guns of
the fortress of Malta. So ends a chapter of the war. For
just over three years the Royal and Merchant Navies in
close concert with the sister service have fought the
battle of the Mediterranean so that our object has now
been achieved and the Mediterranean is once more
fully in our control. The way has been long. We have
had our great moments and our bad times when the
horizon looked black. During that time except for a
short break it was my privilege and pride to key
synchronise main forces at sea in the Mediterranean.
At this moment for which all of us have worked so
long and which has at last come to pass, I send every
officer and man of the Royal and Merchant Navy who
has contributed to it my thanks and admiration for the
resource and courage which has now made these things
possible. In doing so I address my words to those
whom it is my honour to command but let us not
forget what we owe to the service and in particular the
determination of those in the Royal Air Force to
whose loyal help we owe so much for what has been
achieved.

7/5/45   *From SHAEF, signed Eisenhower*
A representative of the German High Command signed the unconditional surrender of all German land, sea and air forces in Europe to the Allied Expeditionary Force and simultaneously to the Soviet Command at 0141 hours Central European Time 7 May, under which all forces will cease active operations at 0001 hours 9 May.

7/5/45   *From Admiralty*
Cease attack on ALL repetition ALL shipping. Attacks on U-boats should continue as heretofore.

7/5/45   *From Admiralty*
A 3-day course of instruction for resettlement information for officers is being held. . . .

8/5/45   *From C.-in-C. Home Fleet to Home Fleet*
For many months I have watched with admiration and pride the officers and men of the Home Fleet carrying out their many arduous and often monotonous tasks with unfailing zeal and thoroughness. Now at last victory has come without giving the chance of bringing the enemy fleet to action at sea, but the very fact that he has allowed his ships to be put out of action separately in harbour is of great tribute to the way in which the Home Fleet has carried out its task. Ships of the Home Fleet may be called on to carry out tasks to help in the settlement of Europe in the near future and I have no doubt that you will tackle these with similar efficiency and enthusiasm. I wish to convey my congratulations and thanks to all officers and men who have served so well in the Home Fleet.

9/5/45   *From Vice Admiral Lemounier to 1st Sea Lord*
En ce jour qui consacre la victoire totale sur L'Allemagne je vous exprime en mon nom et en celui des officiers et marins français nos sentiments de profonde admiration pour l'oeuvre formidable accomplie par la marine Britannique dans la lutte contre l'ennemi commun, pour la maîtrise des mers et lors des grands débarquements qui ont permis la libération de la France. Les marins français ont été fiers de prendre leur part dans cette lutte aux côtés de leurs camarades des marins alliés. Les succes remportés dans cet hemisphère garantissent le rapide et complet

succes dans la lutte en extrême-Orient contre le dernier
adversaire.

13/5/45 *From Admiralty*
S.S. *Scythia* has been allocated to convey the Norwegian government to Norway. The party will consist
of about 700 men and 150 women.
From C.-in-C. Fifth Fleet to Fifth Fleet Pacific
The war with Japan will end at 1200 on 15th August.
It is likely that Kamikazes will attack the fleet after
this time as a final fling. Any ex-enemy aircraft
attacking the fleet is to be shot down in a friendly
manner.

19/7/45 *From Commander-in-Chief*
Effective upon signing of Japanese surrender terms
propose discontinue all combat areas.
From Admiralty to B.A.D. Washington
In view of the end of the war it is intended to propose
at the conference in September that the whole world
should be declared a non-combat area.

Late 1945. A Trawler passes close to a Cruiser. The Trawler's
crew are in various interpretations of naval uniform and they pay
no attention to the Cruiser whatever.

From Cruiser to Trawler:
Why no marks of respect.
Reply from Trawler:
Release Group 22 (next day).

It was a very different sort of gear change that brought World War
Two to its legendary halt. Many of us just marched through
London in the conventional manner, peeled off our uniforms and
switched off. Not so the Boffin/Scientists. With a bang to end all
wars still ringing in their ears they pressed on to domesticate the
nuclear age, while the heads of state shook their heads and vowed
they would never again drop such a bomb—unless someone else
did.

Peace, who had scarcely settled in, certainly had no chance to
recline and feed her turtle-doves. She sat tense, surrounded by
"hot" telephones. At last someone introduced the word Deterrent,
under cover of which the science of self-destruction proceeded
smoothly and everybody—except Peace—relaxed.

When wars end it is natural for navies to shrink, especially ours
in 1945, for two World Wars had more than burned up the legacy

left us by Nelson. But when has a war-weary navy ever faced such a metamorphosis in the ethics of sea warfare as was triggered off at Hiroshima. For centuries the naval Queensberry rule-book said "seek, find and fight the enemy *within Visibility distance*". The post-war drawing board shattered this concept overnight with the design of a missile which could obliterate *thousands of miles away*.

Down came the curtain on those fighting flatirons, so arduously developed by Jacky Fisher, now they would be more useful transformed into washing machines and razor blades. The six mighty fleets which graced the world between the wars vanished overnight. To replace them there emerged fewer, lighter ships, designed to launch and control these nuclear missiles in co-operation with their NATO consorts on a new strategic network. No more flotillas and close formations, so no more fluttering flags, semaphore or morse; in fact, goodbye to all that signal Victoriana which had cluttered bridges for so long. Even the naval interpretation of the word signal—after its long and colourful life through the pages of our naval history—had to be modernised to compete with the rising volume of information and technical data injected into it.

And yet paradoxically the whole conception of nuclear warfare was being built on, and depending on—signals.

Today's admiral, commanding our one and only fleet, can see what goes on all right, not through his binoculars, but on beam television from wherever he chooses to plug in, ashore or afloat. A private satellite some twenty thousand miles high provides his interference-free, inter-everyone-else-concerned, voice link. Soon subordinates may see their admiral's reaction to their misdemeanours—in colour.

The missile's personal communication problem was more sophisticated. For a start, it had to be conned like a ship. Ships' navigators once calculated their positions by visual observation of known fixed objects. Now the process was being reversed. In other words, fixed objects began observing and tracking ships by exchanging signals. What navigates a missile to a pinpoint thousands of miles away is a steady stream of electronic signals. Imagine the volume of signals passing to and from while the missile is in flight. It is with this problem at this point that the human brain throws up the sponge and calls in the computers, counselling them to keep in touch with one another and sort it all out between themselves.

Missiles come in different sizes for different purposes, but they all depend on radio voice links plus this computer gossip, to con them from launch to bang. Signal communication is their life-blood. When a rating joins what used to be called the Signal and is now the Communication Branch, the first thing he learns is to type. It looks as though this will continue until science can transform the spoken word into print. At present R.A.T.T. (Radio and teleprinter transmission) is the documented end of voice telephony. A message is typed into a teleprinter which scrambles and transmits it by radio to other linked teleprinters, which in turn unscramble and reproduce the message in its original form.

At today's action stations the Signal Officer no longer skips about the bridge, occasionally flinging his telescope at his minions struggling below on the flag deck; instead, he sits in the Operations Room clad in earphones, telling his admiral on a very private line what is happening. The Communication rating, who as a signalman invariably used to be cold wet and miserable, now sits warm and dry, strumming away at the manual of his teleprinter.

What happens if the enemy shoots down our private satellite? That, the Signal School will tell you is not a Good Question. How much of all this I wonder will be solved by tomorrow? It seems that what used to be called progress is now an endless eruption. This chapter opened with our forefathers easing themselves down from the trees they lived in. The age in which we live moves so fast that waking brainwaves are redundant by bedtime. The very word communications is now striding at such speed, uniting human beings on earth or launching them to neighbouring planets, that we ask ourselves where does it end? To which the obvious answer is, when the money runs out, as it did with the American Apollo series of moon flights in December, 1972.

Apollo 17 carrying three human computers streaked to the moon, stretching vital lines of communication some 240,000 miles. Having reached their objective, the astronauts changed from computers back to very human beings for their last romp on the moon's surface. The antics of one of them are still fresh in our minds as he sang:

> We were walking on the moon one day
> In the merry merry month of May , , ,
> May?
> No, not May.
> December's the month, December . . .

Perhaps the extravagance of putting men there was a blessing in disguise. Perhaps what this communication explosion most needs is a breather, for everything else to catch up with front line achievement; a chance for U.S.A. and U.S.S.R. to co-operate as well as compete.

Pioneer travel has always been hazardous and expensive. Even in fairy stories only courageous, well sponsored princes really got around. As centuries rolled by and the horse became mechanised, travel agents started package deals, long journeys were divided into stages. Someone whose name might have been Hilton had an idea. Travelling steadily became quicker, cheaper and more comfortable, providing we kept our heads down and remained in the earth's orbit.

Outer space put travel back into square one. A different breed of prince in a different kind of armour returns from the moon with a different kind of treasure. (Imagine the Fairy King after financing his son's trip getting no more than a few rocks and some dust.) Now it is only a question of time before transport and travel agents step in and take over space travel. Perhaps they have started, for there is already talk of Skylabs for research, possibly followed by sky factories, where weightless men in perfect vacuum and unlimited solar radiation will soon be running up hotels of unheard-of purity. Where would the power come from? Why not harness those electric currents on the ionosphere which flow round the earth? After all, they are doing nothing.

Satellites may soon have us wondering how our world has supported life for so long with such wastage, so much mineral and agricultural wealth untouched. People may even stop talking about the weather; it will now be as predictable as night following day.

The same principle of signal control operates London's surging air traffic at Heathrow. Every day thousands of people in millions of pounds worth of aircraft flutter in and out of that great airport, already the second largest cargo port in Britain. The firm smooth way this skreeling jet-hive functions in such limited air space is fascinating. The controlling reins are not made of leather, they are, once again, the same electronic signals. Every unit in this great miscellany of aircraft approaches and departs along its presignalled airway, flying through separately controlled sectors, spaced, and passed on to the next sector. When the terminal sector receives an incoming aircraft, (there can be as many as 150 queuing at any one time) they each have five horizontal miles or 1000 vertical feet air space around them. When landing space is congested they are stacked in adjacent holding space.

Gone are the days when controllers peered hopefully in darkness into radar screens for "blips". Today they watch electronic maps laid out almost like motorways, in which appear aircraft, each one bearing its own label, height and route. One almost expects to hear the stewardess telling passengers what to do with their seat belts.

Cacophony apart, the procession of jumbo jets peeling off the stack to land in their appointed sequence and intervals conjures up the vision of a string of those great pachyderms whose name they bear, moving majestically by. It is disappointing they don't hold each other's tails in their trunks.

What is mentioned here is but a fraction of what goes on in this communications power-house, with its ever-increasing load, often presenting unforeseeable problems which have to be met "on the nose" with appropriate innovation. One way to keep such a hive alert and buzzing is to have inventive improvisation for ever chasing redundancy and barking at its heels. How relieved bees must feel to know they will never be expected to fly at the speed of sound, or will they? Here is a simple example of tomorrow's equipment. The technical language may be strange, but the music sounds re-assuring.

"This computer room will form the heart of the myriad flight plan proceeding systems, one of the most advanced systems of its type in the world and well ahead of any comparable system in Europe when it goes into operation next year.

This massive computer-controlled system is based on a triplicated Marconi myriad I computer complex made to handle flight plans and control data for all aircraft under Air Traffic Control in the middle air space in the southern half of the country. The myriad computers will automatically process the vast quantity of traffic information in a fraction of the time required by previous methods and eliminate a vast amount of manual calculation. Over 200 man-years of computer programming have gone into the very comprehensive software back-up to this system, in which not·only is failure almost completely eliminated, but the speed of operations is such that the most complex instruction is carried out in less than three microseconds."

And here at last is the answer to all those passengers who wonder what is happening to the radar signals their aircraft are creating:

"Primary radar signals are fed from the radar station over Marconi Multiplex broad-band micro-wave links. Secondary surveillance radar information is converted into digital form and is transmitted by the same links, using free slots in the base band or as a standby by Post Office landlines."

More and faster aircraft = more noise. When Concorde first landed at Heathrow to carry out trials, the Decibel-Deplorers stood by their telephones, ready to complain. At the other end of the line at Heathrow waited the Professional-Pacifiers. A technical hitch delayed Concorde's take-off, but that didn't dissuade a violent protest from an elderly Deplorer. When she had run out of breath, she heard the Pacifier's smooth voice "Concorde hasn't actually left yet, Madam—but don't hang up."

After Heathrow where else may we expect to find such sophisticated signal equipment? It could be almost anywhere. Communication has reached a stage where we can't afford to live alone so we subdivide into groups. However the groups are spread individually, they must have intercommunication. The services, firemen, police, doctors, farmers, stockbrokers, villains, hijackers, all lean on instant voice—and soon visual—communication. So let us return to the sea for a brief look at the Merchant Navy's pilotage problems.

En route from Heathrow to the Port of London Authority Navigation Service, compare these two communication centres. Basically their objects are the same but at the moment they are at very different stages of achieving that object.

The rapid increase of air travel since World War Two has expanded London's airport into a national centre of great importance. Superintending Air Traffic Control is a brilliant figurehead; a man with seven years experience in the Royal Air Force followed by a quarter of a century's study of air traffic, and the setting up of its control, all over the world. To establish this control certain equipment and a fixed routine are rated mandatory. Discipline is rigid. Each aircraft is a unit conforming to a pattern. If a pilot breaks the rules he will soon wish that he had never been airborn.

At one time I was hoping to collect some witticisms from Heathrow voice telephone logs. I need not have bothered. All radio conversation is certainly recorded, but it isn't funny; there's no funny business in air traffic control.

The Port of London Authority Navigation Centre at Gravesend is quite a different story. It has—so to speak—been carved out of the river bank by the Harbourmaster himself, an ex-Commander of the Royal Navy. River traffic from tankers to yachts is monitored onto radar screens placed side by side, making up a mosaic of the river. In the air traffic manner vessels are met by radio in the estuary and then with Trinity House pilots on board, passed up the river (with radar warning what is round the next corner) until they are safely berthed. Similar service aids their departure. A splendid growing service, invaluable in fog, but compared with Heathrow, produced and operated on a shoestring budget. Ships found their way up and down rivers long before aeroplanes were thought of. Unlike Heathrow practically nothing on the Thames is mandatory. Ships/shore communication is by voice radio (VHF) but ships aren't *obliged* to have VHF. The Harbourmaster has no control over Trinity House pilots or tugs. Visiting ships keep contact with their shipping agent but neither the ships or their agents are obliged to pass intended movements to the Harbourmaster. None of this is the Commander's fault. On the contrary, he started this set-up from scratch and like anything new, against opposition. What he has built up is a vast improvement on what he found. Once upon a time Heathrow was at the Gravesend stage. The common factor about this type of communication control is that it can neither shrink, nor for that matter stop growing.

Your attention has already been drawn to the intricate equipment and inflexible standard of efficiency demanded to operate aircraft in and out of London's airport. The following report by a river pilot, which the Deputy Master of Trinity House has kindly permitted me to reproduce here, shows that life is not, and probably never will be, quite so rigid up and down London's river.

Report on Panamanian Vessel *Fair Lady* on passage from Gravesend to Greenhithe. Vessel inward bound from Ceuta with cargo of pulp.

Just prior to boarding the above vessel in the Gravesend Reach the Master of the pilot cutter and I checked the draft, which we found to be 15′6″ aft, although the Master of the vessel had declared 14′6″. When asked about this later he said he failed to understand it but did not check same.

Whilst I was boarding I noticed a bucket being passed to someone on the ship from the Port Health Launch *Humphrey Morris* and was informed by one of the crew of the latter vessel that it was a bucket of fresh water to enable the crew to have a wash.

I relieved the sea pilot and introduced myself to the Master, who was at the wheel. He explained that he did not trust his crew steering and that the vessel seemed to have some slight steering trouble at the moment. The passage from the Reach and round Tilburyness was without incident, but in the North Fleet Hope it appeared to be impossible to hold the vessel on a steady course.

Off the New Granary the vessel started swinging to port and although full starboard wheel was applied it refused to answer. The wheel was placed amidships and the bypass lever lifted and full starboard wheel applied again. At this the vessel answered and course was resumed.

Rounding Broadness Point there was a repeat of the above occurrence and the Master then stated he thought that there was definitely something wrong with the steering. As we passed a large outward-bound cargo liner at this point a collision could easily have resulted. Again control was regained and the vessel steadied up in St. Clement's Reach.

Almost immediately both ship and Reach were illuminated in a bright orange glow and it was observed that the funnel was on fire. No-one appeared to be particularly perturbed, and I asked the Master if anyone was attending to both the steering gear and the fire. I was informed that the steering gear was now all right and would definitely be overhauled the next day. The only information he volunteered about the fire was that he hoped falling sparks would not set fire to the lifeboat covers. No attempt was made to contact the engine room to find out if the fire was under control, and no information was at any time passed from the engine room to the bridge about same. The fire eventually died out and appeared to be under control as the vessel approached her berth.

Just short of the berth the vessel again began to fall off to port, with the wheel hard a-starboard. The engines were placed at Full Ahead but the bow continued to swing to port, in towards the berth. The Master informed me that the steering gear had now definitely ceased to function and the engines were ordered Full Astern. The starboard anchor was dropped and when one shackle was out the Master ordered the cables to be held. The anchor had not held so another half shackle was dropped and held. The vessel brought up at this about fifteen yards off the lower end of the jetty and lines were passed ashore.

The water barge *William Stearing* which was handy and was to attend the vessel with fresh water when alongside was hailed and lashed alongside on the starboard quarter, and with assistance from this craft the vessel was eventually manoeuvred alongside the jetty. I advised the Master to weigh anchor, but this proved to be impossible due to a defect in the windlass. The Master left the bridge and went to the focsle head to supervise the repairs. After thirty-five minutes had passed, I advised the Master to slack down more cable and get the vessel properly secured alongside, as in the present situation there was no way of securing the stern which seemed to me to be in danger of grounding on the falling tide. The Master told me it was impossible to slack down more cable and continued to work on the windlass.

At about this time a man appeared from the engine room and shouted to the Chief Engineer that there was no water in the boilers. The Chief Engineer left the focsle head and went to the engine room. After one hour the windlass was sufficiently repaired to lift the anchor just off the bottom. The vessel was then manoeuvred into her proper berth. The mooring was completed at 2300 hours approximately.

Although the vessel was fitted with VHF radio it was found to be inoperable and no message could be passed to the Thames Navigation Authority or anywhere else. The vessel is equipped with a steam whistle and steam siren. The former is operated by one lanyard on the after end of the starboard side of the bridge structure. The latter has no method of operation that I could find.

Before I disembarked I was given assurance by the Master that all things would be rectified, especially the steering gear, before the vessel sailed from this port.

(Signed) J. A. J.

Report on Panamanian Vessel *Fair Lady* on passage from Greenhithe to Gravesend (Two days later)

Further to my previous report on the above vessel I have to advise you that I was also the pilot appointed to assist the Master on his outward passage from Greenhithe to Gravesend. Due to the rather eventful inward passage of this vessel, I approached the duty officer of the P.L.A. (Port of London Authority) in the T.N.S. (Thames Navigation Service) building and requested his advice with regard to assistance available should we have a repeat of any of the failures on the inward passage. I received wonderful cooperation from both this officer and all the P.L.A. staff involved. It was agreed that a P.L.A. officer should accompany me on board the vessel and endeavour to discover if all the equipment was now in satisfactory working order so as to ensure a safe passage to the vessel's next port of call.

We received assurances from the Master that the steering gear had been repaired by Telemotor specialists and was now functioning correctly. But when requested by myself as to whether the boilers would now maintain water he informed me that there had never been any trouble with water in the boilers. I reminded the Master of the conversation I had overheard between someone I believed to be the Second Engineer and the Chief Engineer two days previously, and was immediately told that I shouldn't take any notice of the Second Engineer as he had just been released from a mental institution and was quite unreliable.

With the Master's further assurances that all was well, we commenced passage, but the P.L.A. Officer and I agreed that the Harbourmaster's launch should remain handy in case of accident or failure of equipment.

As the vessel swung from the jetty I attempted to blow the requisite signal on the whistle but this was found to be inoperative and eventually rectified by sending the Bosun from the focsle head to the Engine Room. To blow the whistle meant facing aft, thereby obscuring the whole of the port side from vision. Full Ahead was rung on the telegraph and answered by the engine room. When the vessel was abeam the upper buoy of Swanscombe Tier it became obvious that the vessel was stopped and drifting with the tide. No notice had been received from the engine room and when I questioned the Master he asked me to take the wheel while he went down to the engine room to see what was the matter. He returned to the bridge saying there was difficulty in maintaining the water level in the boilers. He told the Chief Engineer to keep going at slow speed as it was impossible to anchor. We discussed berthing to effect repairs. The P.L.A. launch made arrangements for us to secure to Denton No. 2 swing buoy if we could make it that far.

On entering Gravesend Reach the Chief Engineer came onto the bridge and informed us that there was no water in the boilers and we would have to stop soon. We decided it would be unwise to proceed beyond Gravesend Lower Swing Buoy, to which we moored. Ropes and wires were hauled taut by hand, no effort being made to use the windlass which, according to the Second Engineer, was still not working satisfactorily. The Master assured us that repairs could be effected and the vessel ready to proceed with its voyage within two hours. The Second Engineer was dispatched ashore to an ironmonger's to obtain spare parts. When I disembarked shortly afterwards I noticed the pilot's ladder was in bad shape. I instructed one of the crew to inform the Master.

Again I cannot praise too highly the cooperation received by all the P.L.A. staff involved. Without their assistance and understanding things would have been far more difficult.

Special Flags and Customs

When Empires disintegrate new countries form, each — as of old — with its own personal banner. Before World War I a new national flag was a rarity. How many new national flags have appeared since World War II?

Three British flags with long lives and great character are the Royal Standard, the Banner of the Federation of the Cinque Ports, and the Jolly Roger.

The first has kept its dignity through many changes in colour and design for over 700 years. The second which had great significance when it floated from our Channel bastions is now, as we weld ourselves to the Continent of Europe, no more than a page of history. The third, with its brilliant, sinister design, belongs for ever to the High Seas and fiction, although it is liable to reappear occasionally in fact.

THE ROYAL STANDARD

A herald is a forerunner, one who bears tidings.

A flag is a good background for the display of heraldry, it gives the herald a chance to reveal interesting facts about the character who owns the flag. It becomes a signal illustrated with recognisable symbols. The frequent appearance of the symbolic lion and the absence of the louse shows that heraldry, generally speaking, builds up its subjects.

Highest in dignity among all our flags is the one signalling the presence of the Monarch which used to be flown at sea by the Lord High Admiral.

The Royal Arms first appeared on a flag in 1189 in the form of a golden lion, the first Great Seal of King Richard I. This seal was lost during Richard's captivity, and replaced by three lions one above the other. Those heraldic beasts have appeared on every Royal Standard since.

They have had many associates, for the Royal Standard is a personal banner combining the federation of the realm with the ancestry of each succeeding ruler. In 1340, when Edward III acquired the throne of France, the British lions were joined—and for a while dominated—by the Fleurs de Lys. On Edward III's death the design shrank to make way for the Cross of Edward the Confessor. Perhaps Henry IV found that he could not live up to such piety, for, in his reign, the Cross disappeared.

Then came the Stuarts, with the Scottish lion extremely rampant at being placed in the second quarter. The Irish harp, which first appeared at the funeral of Queen Elizabeth, was added to represent a Kingdom which, in historical fact, had never been under one King.

After a period of Cromwellian austerity, William III added his own private lion of Nassau to the Stuart banner, raising the Pride of heraldic lions to fourteen on one Standard. Queen Anne reverted to the Stuart design and after the union with Scotland, the Scottish lion was more amiably housed in the same quarter as his English contemporaries.

On the accession of George I one of these quarters had to give place to the arms of Hanover, which introduced three more lions and a white horse. In 1801 this Standard was revised, and the three British lions bade farewell to the golden lilies of France after an association of 461 years, some of which had been spent in armed conflict between the two countries.

Queen Victoria removed the Hanoverian embellishment, and so the Royal Standard remains today, with the three British lions still "passant guardant in pale" in quarters 1 and 4, the Scottish lion still rampant in the second quarter, and the harp, which was never an authentic symbol of Ireland, in the third quarter.

The reason given by a special commission in 1911 as to why Wales is not represented was that Wales is a Principality and not a Kingdom. In that case the harp's position does not look very secure.

Will those restless British lions ever settle down for good?

THE BANNER OF THE CINQUE PORTS

After invading England, the Normans showed their intention of closing the back door, and guarding the south-east corner of Britain by fortifying the towns of Hastings, Sandwich, Dover, Romney and Hythe.

As far back as Edward the Confessor a charter was issued, and granted by successive sovereigns, calling upon the Barons of these towns to maintain the fortifications, and to provide "their full service of 57 ships at their own cost for 15 days, when summoned by Ourself or Our Heirs." In return they received certain enviable privileges which set them free from the general legal system of the realm, and granted them a handsome cut on the price of wine.

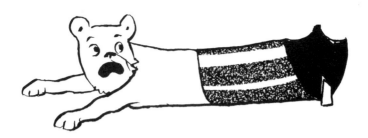

This banded the Cinque Ports together under one banner, and they have remained so ever since. Chief of the Barons was the Lord Warden who also became Admiral of the Cinque Ports fleet.

Today the flag of the Cinque Ports only flies from Walmer Castle, and never at sea. From 1941 until his death Sir Winston Churchill, K.G., was the Lord Warden.

In the original banner the three British lions suffered severe heraldic treatment. The banner shows them emerging into a scarlet void from a blue one. In crossing over, the poor creatures have been dimidiated and their sterns have become the sterns of ships. Today, the lions are there, still naturally looking rather surprised. Four castles, a ship, a crown and an anchor have been added.

THE JOLLY ROGER

Thieving in the open started as soon as people began carrying valuables about. Piracy started when they took their valuables to sea. No ocean has been free from pirates. They have appeared, thrived, and been suppressed on every seaboard. Years ago Piracy passed as maritime adventure. The Phoenicians combined piracy with enterprise. In Homeric days it was a reputable, even a dignified calling. Gradually it came to be frowned upon. From the eighth to the eleventh centuries the Norsemen became the terror of our western coast. In the Mediterranean, Algiers became a pirate stronghold. The racket spread. The Corsairs struck out towards our shores. Lundy Island became a pirate's nest. On they came, up the Channel to Ireland, to Iceland and across the Atlantic. For three centuries they infested the High Seas.

The exact moment when pirates were banded together under one distinguishing flag is obscure. So is the date that the Skull and Cross-bones on a Black ground were accepted as the design for this flag. As far as heraldry is concerned, however, one must congratulate the designer. It seems to convey the whole calling in a flash. It seems appropriate to fly over gentlemen like Captain Teach, with "that large quantity of hair like a frightful Meteor," covering his face, which "frightened America more than any Comet." It seems to blend with Captain Edward Low's treatment of the master of a whale-boat whom he captured off Rhode Island — he cuts off his ears and made him eat them with pepper and salt — "which hard injunction he complied with without making a word."

The early part of the eighteenth century was a colourful time in the history of pirates. In the West Indies especially there was plenty of shipping and valuable cargoes. Merchantmen in that area had a grim gauntlet to run.

The Pirate technique was to fly some national colours and approach a merchant ship. At the appropriate moment the bogus colours would be struck and replaced by the Black flag—and the merchant ship's number was generally up.

Occasionally the pirates did not have it their own way; sometimes they got a shock. Pirate Captain Charles Vane "fell upon a ship, which 'twas expected would have struck as soon as our black colours were hoisted; but instead of that she discharged a Broadside, and hoisted Colours, which shewed her to be a French Man of War." Vane desired to have nothing further to say to her, but trimm'd his sails and stood away from the Frenchman; "but Monsieur, having a mind to be better informed who he was, set all his sails and crowded after him. During the chase the Pyrates were divided in their resolutions what to do, Vane the Captain, was for making off as fast as he could, alledging the Man of War was too strong to cope with . . . so the Brigantine having the heels, as they term it, of the French man, she came clear off".

Periodically there was a big clean up. On Monday, 5th February, 1721, H.M.S. *Swallow* found the pirate ships *Ranger* and *Royal Sovereign.* Having forced them to submit she took some 300 prisoners, who later stood their trial, and 52 were executed.

But, on the whole, the Black Flag Industry at that time flourished, and the design upon the flag varied with the different pirate leaders. They each had their own house flag. The rascal Captain Bartho Roberts, for example, had a flag "with his own figure portrayed standing upon two skulls and under them the letters ABH and AMH, signifying A BARBADIAN'S HEAD and A MARTINICAN'S HEAD." The flag which the *Swallow* captured had—"the figure of a skeleton on it, and a man portrayed with a flaming sword in his hand, intimating a Defiance on Death itself." On promotion, Pirate Captain Spriggs had "a black Ensign made which they called Jolly Roger, with a white Skeleton in the middle of it, with a dart in one hand striking a bleeding heart, and in the other an Hour-glass." The hour glass was a symbol of the time allowed for victims to choose between joining the pirates or taking the consequences. Chains and Battle-axes appeared on other flags. The nearest approach to the design we know today belonged to Pirate Chief Worley, who had "a black Ensign with a white Death's Head in the middle of it," but no cross bones. When those thigh bones were added is not clear.

Neither is it clear why this awe-inspiring flag should have such a cheerful name; though the derivation of Jolly Roger is probably not so gay as it sounds. Jolly could be taken as meaning "to flatter with intention of deceiving"; Roger could be connected with the word Rogue.

In both World Wars the Jolly Roger has reappeared. With great personal pride, and with official tolerance if not blessing, it has flown from our submarines returning from their patrols. A wartime submarine, like a pirate, was nobody's friend, but what a fine bunch of British submarine pirates World War II produced! The 10th Submarine Flotilla, for example, operating from beseiged Malta, under their great leader Captain 'Shrimp' Simpson must have been a permanent headache to Rommel as they ceaselessly menaced the life-lines to his desert army. Distinguished amongst the distinguished were the Captains of H.M. Submarines *Upholder* and *Urge*, Lieutenant-Commander Wanklyn VC. DSO** (Wanks) and Lieutenant-Commander Tomkinson DSO** (Tommo). They were great friends, and between them they sank thousands of tons of very important shipping. Wanks never returned after his 25th patrol. Tommo survived him by 2 weeks.

SIGNAL FLAGS

There are other flags which appeared singly or in groups in those colourful days of flag signalling and acquired characters of their own.

Private signals with private meanings were not permitted as in Lord Howe's day, yet they appeared occasionally to meet special circumstances. Between the wars a certain destroyer had the frequent task of steaming through a practice area in which submarines attacked her with dummy torpedoes. After each attack the submarine surfaced in the destroyer's wake anxious for a quick assessment of her attack. To give this assessment without wasting time the destroyer hoisted a large raspberry fashioned in basket work. If it appeared the right way up it meant the attack was a failure. The position in which it appeared indicated how it had failed. An inverted raspberry at the masthead meant a successful attack.

General Drill had a signal routine of its own. These drills were tasks, initiated by signal, carried out competitively between ships in a squadron or flotilla. The tasks naturally had to suit the ships

Lieutenant-Commander Tomkinson DSO** and Lieutenant-Commander Wanklyn VC, DSO**. Tommo survived Wanks by only two weeks.

Wanklyn's personal Jolly Roger.

Bird's-eye view of the happy return.

taking part, so private signals were allowed. In the signal book
there was a general drill table, where suitable tasks were entered
against the flags initiating them. The tasks, which demanded
prodigious feats of seamanship from large bodies of men, were
carried out at full speed and full pressure. Ships and crews were
tied in knots.

The general drill signal table was designed to cater for all tastes.
Here are some examples:CHIEF COOK TO REPORT ON BOARD
   FLAGSHIP WITH FRIED EGG.
   CHAPLAINS PADDLE ROUND THEIR SHIPS ON CARLEY
   RAFTS.
   SECURE CAPTAIN IN STRAIT JACKET AND SEND HIM
   TO FLAGSHIP.
   LAND ALL HEADS OF DEPARTMENTS. NEXT SENIOR
   TAKE OVER.

AT THE SIGN OF THE STORK; by Wing-Commander E. G. Oakley Beuttler. A picture which appeared in The Tatler *embroidering on a true story. Lt. J. C. Y. Roxburgh, commanding the submarine* United *was expecting news from his wife about a highly important event, and arranged with base staff to signal the result while he was at sea. A few days later he sank an Italian warship, picking up the commander and some of her crew. The Italian C.O.'s chief concern was for the safety of his wife—she too was expecting a baby. That night* United *surfaced and the signal from base came through—a daughter. On returning to base* United *flew, in addition to the Jolly Roger (with symbols denoting enemy ships sunk), a white flag emblazoned with a stork in its beak and one bar in the corner to denote the successful arrival of Miss Roxburgh.*

SPECIAL CUSTOMS

Many customs have grown up round our national colours.

Saluting them at sea, for example, has had an historic background.

In 1201 King John decreed that if his Admiral should meet any ship at sea which refused to lower their sails at command, their crews should be reputed as enemies and their ships and cargoes should be forfeited.

Many decrees and incidents followed before this practical method of demanding submission changed into a signal of respect. Eventually the seafaring community of all nations submitted ungrudgingly to the Royal Navy by dipping their colours whenever they met on the high seas. But the Navy earned that respect the hard way.

In 1554, for example, a Spanish Fleet of 160 sail was escorting their King Philip on his way to England to marry Queen Mary, when he was met by an English Fleet commanded by Lord William Howard, Lord High Admiral. When the Spaniards passed without paying the customary honours, Lord Howard signalled his twenty-eight ships to prepare for action, and fired a round shot into the hull of the Spanish Flagship. The Spaniards immediately saluted.

In 1652 Admiral Blake met a Dutch Squadron under Admiral Van Tromp in the Channel. As the latter did not salute, Blake fired two shots across his bow. A third followed which Van Tromp declared struck his ship and wounded a man. Battle ensued and the first Dutch war was launched. When it was over the Dutch agreed to strike their flags and lower their topsails on meeting our ships in the British seas.

Our stubborn demands rankled with the French. Louis XIV did his best to induce Charles II to dispense with this compulsory salute to British men-o'-war. Charles II seemed surprised at the idea. Writing to his sister, the Duchess of Orleans, at the French Court, he says, "I extremely wonder at that you writ to me, for certainly never any ship refused to strike when they met any ships belonging to the Crown of England. That is right well known, and never disputed by any King before."

In the eighteenth century, the decree still ran—"when any of His Majesty's ships shall meet with any ship or ships belonging to

On a particular occasion during the Royal Australian Tour of 1953/4, the Australian Naval Commander-in-Chief arranged to have the ship's company of the aircraft carrier Vengeance fallen in on the flight deck to form an aerial view of the Queen's signature as the Royal Aircraft flew overhead. In due course came the following signal:

From Flag Officer Royal Yacht to Flag Officer Commanding the Australian Fleet

I have to convey the following message from the Queen. Thank you for your original forgery.

any foreign Prince within His Majesty's seas (which extend to Cape Finisterre) it is expected that the said foreign ships do strike their topsail and take in their flag, in acknowledgment of His Majesty's Sovereignty in those seas; and if any shall refuse or offer to resist it is enjoined to all Flag Officers and Commanders to use their utmost endeavours to compel them thereto, and not suffer any dishonour to be done to His Majesty." The Merchantmen also had to toe the line— "And if any of His Majesty's subjects shall so much forget their duty as to omit striking their topsail in passing by His Majesty's ships, the name of the ship and master, and from whence and whither bound, together with affidavits of the fact, are to be sent up to the Secretary of the Admiralty, in order to proceed against them in the Admiralty court." After Trafalgar,

British naval power stood at such a height that no loss of prestige could possibly arise from easing these regulations, so the salute was no longer demanded. Today Merchant ships dip their Colours to warships and to each other as an act of courtesy.

Half-masting of Colours does not seem to have gone back as far as saluting. After the Restoration it was a custom in the Navy to observe the anniversary of the execution of Charles I by lowering Colours to "halfe staff high" but in 1586 the *Black Pinnace* which brought the body of Sir Philip Sidney from Holland is shown with a black flag at the main top masthead.

Striking Colours as a signal of submission seems also to be comparatively modern. In the olden days, before the gun, when fighting was hand-to-hand at close quarters, the battle raged till one side gave in. Everyone was much too busy to notice whether their Colours were flying or not. It was not until sea battles were fought by gun at a distance that a ship hauled down her colours to show that her internal state was beyond hope and that further loss of life seemed pointless.

During the French wars it was customary to hoist our own Colours above those of a captured enemy, either at the peak or ensign staff.

More recently, a German trawler was captured off the Danish coast by a destroyer in 1915 and was steaming into an East Coast harbour with a prize crew. The custom had obviously been forgotten by the local fishermen for they fired on the German Ensign, although the White Ensign flew above it.

Captured Colours at sea, as on land, are treated with reverence. The flags of many Spanish Galleons were paraded at a Thanksgiving Service attended by Queen Elizabeth after the defeat of the Armada.

In the seventeenth century it was considered a proper thing to decorate a ship with the flags of captured enemies. A certain Captain Heaton supported this custom. He was in command of H.M.S. *Sapphire*. . . . "in which ship he took so many prizes that on a festival day the yards, stays, backstays, and shrouds being hung with Dutch, French, Spanish, and Burgundian Colours and pennants variously intermixed, and the English Colours and pennants spread, made a beautiful show and raised the courage of all belonged to her."

Successful racing yacht owners of today still follow in the footsteps of Captain Heaton.

A diagramatic sketch of the flagstaff of the Royal Albert Yacht Club, Southsea, on 4th July, 1968, showing the hoists which greeted Sir Alec Rose on completion of his sail round the world. The flagstaff was, of course, dressed overall with gaily coloured flags.

The Broad Pennants numbered 1, 2, and 3 belong respectively to the Commodores of the Royal Albert Yacht Club, the Royal Naval Sailing Association, and the Eastney Cruising Association. International flags spell out the word BRAVO in plain language. Flag S, under International Sailing Rules means: DONT GO ROUND A SECOND TIME.

E

THREE DECK LINE-OF BATTLE SHIP 100 GUNS

Three-deck-line-of-battle-ship.
QUEEN CHARLOTTE · 100
(Flagship)
ROYAL SOVEREIGN · 100
ROYAL GEORGE · 100

BARFLEUR · 98
IMPREGNABLE · 98
QUEEN · 98
GLORY · 98

TWO DECK LINE-OF-BATTLE SHIP · 74 GUNS

Two-deck-line-of-battle-ship.
GIBRALTAR · 80

CAESAR · 80
BELLEROPHON · 74
MONTAGUE · 74
TREMENDOUS · 74
VALIANT · 74
RAMILLIES · 74
AUDACIOUS · 74
BRUNSWICK · 74
ALFRED · 74
DEFENCE · 74
LEVIATHAN · 74
MAJESTIC · 74
INVINCIBLE · 74
ORION · 74
RUSSELL · 74
MARLBOROUGH · 74
THUNDERER · 74
CULLODEN · 74

FRIGATE · 32 GUNS

Frigate.
PHAETON · 38

LATONA · 38
NIGER · 32
SOUTHAMPTON · 72
VENUS · 32
AQUILLON · 32
PEGASUS · 32

Naval History by Signal

THE BATTLE OF
THE GLORIOUS FIRST OF JUNE
1794

As the eighteenth century drew to a close Admiral Lord Howe, who had personally revolutionised naval signalling, was rewarded by being the first British Admiral to control a fleet in action by signal flags.

After two weeks' cruising, his Channel Fleet, consisting of 26 ships-of-the-line, looked into Brest. On 17th May, 1794, he learnt that the French Fleet had sailed to protect a large convoy from North America and the West Indies. Lord Howe immediately followed them on the course they had taken out into the Atlantic.

A few ships previously captured by the French were met and recaptured. From these and other sources the Admiral estimated the whereabouts of the French Fleet. Ploughing into heavy seas, fading hopes were revived when, soon after daylight on Wednesday 28th May, the enemy fleet was sighted.

The following presentation of the operation which unfolded comes from the original signal log of H.M.S. *Queen Charlotte,* the 100-gun Fleet Flagship. The narrative is supported by extracts from deck logs, and reports made by ships taking part.

Wednesday, 28th May
A.M.
4.00   *Queen Charlotte* logged strong winds from S.S.W. Cloudy sky. All Fleet in sight. Course E.S.E.
Dawn   *Bellerophon,* Flagship of the fast sailing squadron, sent the frigates out ahead of the Fleet to scout.

5.00   From *Latona*
        STRANGE SAIL BEARING S.E.

6.30   *From Russell*
       STRANGE SAIL BEARING S.E.

7.35   *From Latona*
       STRANGE FLEET BEARING S.S.W.

8.00   H.M.S. *Queen* sighted strange fleet of large ships standing towards her. At first the ships seemed to be coming down in a confused manner, as though not expecting it to be the British Fleet they had in view. It was some time before they formed into any regular line of battle.

8.25   *From Queen Charlotte to Bellerophon*
       RECONNOITRE ENEMY SHIPS IN VIEW AND REPORT TO THE ADMIRAL

8.34   *From Queen Charlotte—General*
       ENEMY IN SIGHT

8.39   Flagship sighted enemy fleet 12 to 15 miles to windward on Easterly course, forming line of battle.
       Phaeton, cleared for action, carried away her fore topsail yard, which she threw overboard, together with a hencoop, a binnacle, a pantry, and a bulkhead, in order to clear ship.

8.45   *From Queen Charlotte—General*
       PREPARE FOR BATTLE

9.45   *Queen Charlotte to Bellerophon*
       SHORTEN SAIL

9.46   *From Russell*
       ESTIMATE 22 SHIPS OF THE LINE

When *Bellerophon* had shortened sail, as ordered by signal, and called in the frigates, she noted the Enemy Fleet in line ahead with our fleet, 3 or 4 miles to leeward in the order of sailing, under a press of sail.

10.22   *Majestic* observed by Flagship with 3 reefs in her topsails, her fore topsail yard bending like a bow.

10.28   *Queen Charlotte—General*
       WEATHERMOST SHIPS TO TACK FIRST, REMAINDER IN SUCCESSION

11.13   THE PEOPLE HAVE TIME FOR THE NEXT MEAL

11.14   Some of the Enemy ships observed changing station in the line

11.50   *Queen Charlotte* counted 31 sail of the Enemy

Noon   Fleet estimated to be W. by S. 350 miles from Ushant.

P.M.
1.00   Fresh gales. Squally. A great head sea. Double reefed topsails. Flagship split jib in a squall.

1.40   *Queen Charlotte—General*
          ATTACK AND HARASS ENEMY'S REAR

1.50   Enemy altered course to Southward

1.52   *Queen Charlotte—General*
          CHASE

1.56   *Queen Charlotte—General*
          TAKE SUITABLE STATIONS FOR MUTUAL SUP-
          PORT AND ENGAGE THE ENEMY AS ARRIVING UP
          WITH THEM IN SUCCESSION

2.00   The whole Fleet in chase of the French, hoping to bring on a general action by attacking the rear with our fast-sailing ships.

3.03   *Russell* hoisted her colours and opened fire on the rear of the Enemy's line. Fire was returned.
          Bellerophon tacked before the rear enemy ship was on her beam, which brought her immediately into action.

4.37   *Queen Charlotte—General*
          EACH SHIP IS TO CARRY A LIGHT THE ENSUING
          NIGHT AND REPEAT SIGNALS MADE BY THE
          ADMIRAL

6.00   *Bellerophon* still closely engaged. She had received considerable damage and had to break off to repair masts and rigging.

7.19   *Queen Charlotte—General*
    KEEP THE ENEMY IN SIGHT. MAKE THEIR
    MOTIONS KNOWN BY DAY OR NIGHT TO THE
    ADMIRAL.

7.25   *Queen Charlotte to Russell and Marlborough*
    ASSIST BELLEROPHON ALREADY IN ACTION

7.30   *Queen Charlotte General*
    FORM LINE OF BATTLE AHEAD AND ASTERN OF
    THE ADMIRAL AS MOST CONVENIENT WITHOUT
    REGARD TO ESTABLISHED FORMATION

7.33   *Queen Charlotte to Marlborough, Bellerophon, Leviathan*
    LEAVE OFF CHASE

8.03   *Audacious* engaged 3-decked Frenchman *Revolutionnaire*
    until 9.50 when Frenchman ceased fire and struck her
    colours, but *Audacious* was too disabled to take
    possession. *Thunderer* coming to *Audacious'* assistance
    hailed Frenchman and asked if he had struck. He assured
    Thunderer that he had, and that he would follow during
    the night. No more was seen of this ship.

9.00   Firing ceased on both sides.
    British ships carried a stiff sail all night in pursuit of the
    enemy.

Midnight The enemy's lights were visible 5 miles to windward.

Thursday 29th May

Dawn   *Queen Charlotte* noted a fresh wind still, and a heavy
    swell. She also noted that *Audacious* had disappeared.
    (Nothing further was heard of that disabled ship until she
    reappeared in Plymouth Sound on 4th June.)
    By daylight the Admiral had made enough advance on
    the Enemy to go about and menace his rear ships.

6.57   *Queen Charlotte—General*
    TACK IN SUCCESSION

7.23   *Queen Charlotte—General*
    SHIPS ARE AT LIBERTY TO FIRE ON THE ENEMY
    THOUGH NOT MEANT TO BRING HIM TO GENERAL
    ACTION IMMEDIATELY.

7.48   The Enemy, now in line of battle, course South, began to wear and shape Northerly course, to protect his rear.

8.06   *Queen Charlotte to Caesar*
       MAKE MORE SAIL.

8.15   *Caesar* and *Queen* in action with enemy's rear.

8.30   *Queen Charlotte to Caesar*
       MAKE MORE SAIL.

10.50   Vans engaging each other at long range.
Noon   Wind S. by W. Fresh gales. S.80°W, 300 miles from Ushant.

1.08   *Queen Charlotte to Caesar*
       ENGAGE ENEMY'S CENTRE

1.13   Flagship observed *Caesar* did not answer the signal which was flying.

1.13   *Queen Charlotte—General*
       THE ADMIRAL INTENDS TO PASS THROUGH THE ENEMY'S LINE TO OBTAIN THE WEATHER-GAUGE

1.30.   The Flagship tacked, closed the enemy, and cut through his line ahead of the 5th ship. Other ships followed but only *Bellerophon* succeeded, passing between 2nd and 3rd ship. *Queen Charlotte* tacked and chased a 3-decker wearing an Admiral's flag, flooding her own lower deck through her gun ports.

2.50   *Queen Charlotte—General*
       CHASE
3.00   *Queen Charlotte—General*
       ACTION OVER CLOSE ADMIRAL

3.00   Fog coming down.
       Having outsailed and confused the enemy, the Admiral broke off action to repair damaged ships.

Friday, 30th May

    Fog. Fleets occassionally sighting. No action.

Dawn Fog still thick. Ships making good defects.

    Culloden. Punished Richard Alfred and Dan Malone with 18 lashes for fighting.

4.00pm Fog cleared. Enemy forming line of battle 5-6 miles to leeward.

4.49   *Queen Charlotte to Van Squadron*
    PREPARE TO ENGAGE ENEMY'S VAN.

4.57   *Queen Charlotte to Centre Squadron*
    PREPARE TO ENGAGE ENEMY'S CENTRE.

5.14   *Queen Charlotte to Rear Squadron*
    PREPARE TO ENGAGE ENEMY'S REAR.

6.27   *Queen Charlotte to Latona and Southampton*
    PASS WITHIN HAIL.

7.07   Flagship hailed *Southampton* and desired Captain Forbes to circulate that the Admiral intended to carry same sail all night, letting as many reefs out of topsails as possible without endangering masts.

Sunday, 1st June

4.00   Fresh breeze. Cloudy. Fleet visible from Flagship.

6.00   Flagship counted 26 Enemy line-of-battle ships, 6 frigates.

7.16   *Queen Charlotte—General*
    FORM IN ORDER OF BATTLE

7.35   *Queen Charlotte—General*
    INTEND TO PASS THROUGH ENEMY'S LINE AND ENGAGE HIM TO LEEWARD

8.00   Fleet turned away from the wind and bore down on the enemy, singling out their adversaries. It was the first time in naval history that Seniors could tell their Juniors by signal to get out of the way.

    Once more *Queen Charlotte* broke through, throwing the enemy into confusion. This time she was supported by most ships, except *Caesar.*

8.38   *Queen Charlotte—General*
EACH SHIP TO STEER INDEPENDENTLY FOR AND ENGAGE HER OPPONENT IN THE ENEMY'S LINE.

8.55   *Queen Charlotte to Marlborough and Caesar*
MAKE MORE SAIL

9.12   *To Brunswick, Gibraltar, and Culloden*
MAKE MORE SAIL

9.30   In luffing up alongside the French Admiral, *Queen Charlotte* lost her fore topmast and promptly dismasted an enemy ship. *Brunswick's* duel with *Vengeur,* with anchors hooked, lasted four hours, then *Vengeur* drifted clear and sank.

9.32   *General*
ENGAGE THE ENEMY CLOSER

9.40   *General*
MAKE MORE SAIL

10.00   *To Gibraltar and Culloden*
MAKE MORE SAIL

10.20   *General*
CHASE

11.15   *General*
CLOSE ROUND ADMIRAL

11.25   *General*
FLEET FORM IN LINE OF BATTLE AHEAD AND ASTERN OF ADMIRAL AS CONVENIENT

12.50 pm   *Queen* hailed *Pegasus* and desired Captain Barlow to take her in tow.

1.00   12 dismasted ships in sight. *Marlborough, Defence,* and 10 enemy ships.

3.00   Action ceased, enemy having had enough.
Extensive damage to masts and sails of our ships.
Flagship alone lost fore and main topsail yards, topmasts, rigging, and all signal halyards.
Somehow, enemy managed to tow away 4 or 5 disabled ships.

3.33   *Queen Charlotte—General*
KEEP IN THE ADMIRAL'S WAKE

3.52   *General*
       LEAVE OFF CHASE
4.15   *General*
       STAY BY PRIZES

4.22   Enemy making off to leeward shattered and disabled. Took possession of 7 Enemy ships.

4.50   *From Caesar*
       UNABLE TO STAY BY PRIZES
6.00   *Queen Charlotte to Caesar*
       ARE YOU IN CONDITION TO TAKE SHIP IN TOW

8.00   Enemy Fleet out of sight.
10.00 Course of British Fleet E.N.E.
       Light airs.
       Prizes in tow.

It is hardly surprising that the Captain of H.M.S. *Caesar* was later tried by Court Martial and dismissed his ship for not having done his utmost to bring his ship into close action with the enemy.

The operation is summarised more concisely in a letter written by an officer in the Queen's Regiment on board H.M.S. *Royal George* on 2nd June.

Dear Mother,

After a smart and most decisive action we have, thank God, gained one of the most splendid victories ever fought at sea. The French fought with desperate bravery. We have taken 6 sail-of-the-line. A 3-decker was likewise taken on Wednesday last. Two French 3-deckers and a 74 were towed off by their fleet dismasted, but we hope to catch them before they can gain Brest. Our ship and the *Queen* are greatly distinguished and much damaged. I am quite untouched. Our foremast and main and mizen topmasts are gone. The *Queen Charlotte's* main and fore topmasts are gone. Admirals Graves, Bowyer, and Pasley are wounded, Captain Montague killed. Lord Howe is safe. It was a desperate business and the victory was gained by our breaking the line. The *Royal George* went through first. You must understand that there have been two actions; one on 29th May, in which we were in the van, and suffered much; another on 1st June, when we were in the rear. The first was only partial, the second decisive. We are now 150 leagues to the West of Ushant, but are returning home as fast as our shattered condition permits.

(*Navy Records Society, 1899.*)

THE BATTLE OF COPENHAGEN
2nd April, 1801

When Denmark joined Russia and Sweden in an armed neutrality against us, the Baltic was sealed.

Early in 1801 Britain decided that this seal must be broken, and on 7th March a Fleet of some 50 sail left Yarmouth for the Kattegat. Admiral Sir Hyde Parker commanded the Fleet with Vice Admiral Lord Nelson as second in command.

Delayed by gales the Fleet eventually arrived off Elsinore on 24th March. Terms were offered to the Danes which were promptly rejected. When Sir Hyde Parker sought to enter the sound the Governor of Elsinore regretted that "he was not at liberty to suffer such a fleet—whose intention was unknown—to pass."

This we regarded as an act of war, and on 30th March the Fleet weighed and Nelson, flying his flag in H.M.S. *Elephant,* took station in the van. Our ships passed out of range of an uninterrupted bombardment from the guns of Kronenburg Castle, and anchored about 10 miles from Copenhagen.

The Danes, meanwhile, were taking full measures to defend their capital. They removed the channel buoys, and built up a formidable defence of moored ships and floating batteries.

After inspecting these defences the C.-in-C. held a council of war on board H.M.S. *London,* his Flagship, on the afternoon of 31st March.

Nelson favoured immediate action. He paced the cabin "mortified at all remarks about intervention by Russia or Sweden which savoured of alarm or irresolution." He calmed down when he was given command of the Attacking Squadron. Sir Hyde Parker allowed him twelve line-of-battle ships and all available small craft.

By dark that evening the British pilots had replaced the channel buoys and the Attacking Squadron had moved in. By 1 a.m. the following morning Nelson's detailed operation orders were complete.

The events which took place and the signals which were made that day are taken from the logs of H.M. ships *London* and *Elephant.*

2nd April 1801
A.M.
  7.15 *From Elephant to attacking Squadron*
        CAPTAINS REPAIR ON BOARD FLAGSHIP
  7.45 *From Elephant to attacking Squadron*
        PREPARE FOR BATTLE
  7.57 *From Elephant to attacking Squadron*
        ARTILLERY   OFFICERS   REPAIR   ON   BOARD
        FLAGSHIP
  9.00 *From Elephant General*
        ARMED BARGES AND PINNACES PROCEED TO
        FLAGSHIP
  9.10 *From London General*
        MEN INTENDED TO BE LANDED ARE TO BE
        HELD IN READINESS TO LAND
 10.00 *From Elephant to attacking Squadron*
        WEIGH
 10.05 *Edgar* weighed and led the Squadron to the attack of the
        Danish line.
        Agamemnon grounded on middle. *Russell* and *Bellona*
        also grounded on shoal, within range of enemy.
 10.20 *From London to Agememnon*
        WEIGH
 10.40 *London* observed southern batteries open fire on *Edgar*.
        The ships of the Squadron followed in succession and
        anchored and opened fire as they arrived on their stations.
 10.53 *From Elephant to attacking Squadron*
        ENGAGE THE ENEMY MORE CLOSELY
 11.30 *From Bellona*
        AM STUCK ON A SHOAL
 11.40 *From Bellona*
        REQUIRE ASSISTANCE

The situation at noon from the Commander-in-Chief's point of
view was gloomy. The *Agamemnon* was hard and fast on the
middle ground flying the signal of inability. Distress signals flew
from *Bellona* and *Russell*, also grounded. Only three out of the
fourteen gun brigs and bomb vessels had managed to get into
position. Our ships seemed to be getting better than they gave.
The strong current which prevented the smaller craft getting into

position also prevented him joining the Attacking Squadron. With the enemy always able to reinforce, the odds seemed to be against his second-in-command, and there was nothing he could do to help.

P.M.
12.15 *From London to Elephant*
DISCONTINUE THE ENGAGEMENT

On board *Elephant,* Nelson had been pacing the quarterdeck since the action, began. He was tense and alert. When a few splinters fell from the mainmast he remarked to those around him, "It is warm work, and this day may be the last to any of us at a moment, but I wouldn't be elsewhere for thousands."

At that moment the signal lieutenant reported the Commander-in-Chief's signal to him. At first he did not appear to take any notice. When the signal officer asked if he should repeat the signal he answered, "No, acknowledge it." As the officer returned to the poop, Nelson asked, "Is No. 16 still flying?" The officer answering in the affirmative, Nelson said, "Mind you keep it so." (No. 16 was the signal for close action hoisted at 10.53.)

The Admiral then became agitated, which he always showed by moving the stump of his right arm. After a turn or two he said, "Do you know what is 'shown on board of the Commander-in-Chief—No. 39? Why, it's leave off action. Leave off action," he repeated. "Now damn me if I do." Then turning to his Flag Captain, "You know, Foley, I have only one eye, I have a right to be blind sometimes." Putting his telescope to his blind eye he exclaimed, "I really do not see the signal."

So signal No. 39 was received and acknowledged, but it was never repeated to the Attacking Squadron.

2.00   General Battle raged at close range. The greater part of the enemy line, being subdued, ceased fire. *Dannesbrog* (Danish flagship) struck her colours and later blew up. Lord Nelson sent a Flag of Truce to the Danish Government to arrange the landing of wounded prisoners. His Lordship's terms were accepted and all firing ceased.

3.15   Flag of Truce flying in *Elephant* observed from *London.*

4.00   *Elephant* cut cables and made sail for the outer harbour.

4.10   *Elephant* grounded on shoal.

9.30   *Elephant* refloated and rejoined fleet.
        The Danes then agreed to grant maintenance facilities and
        our Fleet proceeded into the Baltic.

NELSON'S SIGNAL AT TRAFALGAR
21st October, 1805

About fifteen months before the Battle of Trafalgar the signal
book became compromised. *Redbridge,* a frigate commanded by
Lieutenant Lempière, was captured by some French frigates off
Toulon. Confidential signal books were not supplied to
lieutenants, but Lempière had his own hand-painted edition which
he failed to throw overboard when captured. When one of
Nelson's scouts looked into Toulon later, she was told by signal
from *Redbridge* to anchor. Fortunately the commanding officer
was quicker witted than Lempière, and he hastened back to report
the matter to his Admiral. Nelson told the Admiralty that the
code had been compromised, and on 4th November, 1803, Their
Lordships directed all C.'s-in-C. to alter their numeral flags in
accordance with a painted copy enclosed. They also frowned
heavily on all junior officers who made manuscript copies of secret
documents. They still do.

The amended signals were in use at the Battle of Trafalgar. It
was from them that the message of exhortation, which was to
become the most famous signal in our Naval history, was made.

Lieutenant Pasco, signal officer to Lord Nelson in H.M.S.
·*Victory,* describes this occasion on the morning of Trafalgar, in a
letter written after the battle.

"His lordship came to me on the poop, and after ordering
certain signals to be made, about a quarter to noon he said, Mr
Pasco, I wish to say to the Fleet, 'England confides that every
man will do his duty,' and he added, 'You must be quick for I
have one more to make which is for Close Action.' I replied, 'If
your Lordship will permit me to substitute "Expects" for
"Confides" the signal will soon be completed, because the word
"Expects" is in the vocabulary and "Confides" must be spelt.'
His lordship replied in haste and with seeming satisfaction,
'That will do, Pasco. Make it directly.' "

The word "Duty" was also missing from the vocabulary and had to be spelt. While it seems strange that "Duty" was not included, there is no intention here to improve upon the selection of the 1,000 words which an admiral would find most useful.

And so, but for the change of one word, the signal was read by all ships present in a matter of minutes from the time Nelson composed it. Had he wished to send it six years before Trafalgar it would have had to be circulated by voice trumpet or boat.

One previous signal had already been sent that morning by Nelson, "Prepare to anchor after the close of day." As the 33 flags which made up the famous message were hoisted, Collingwood, Nelson's second in command, showed his distaste for any form of signal verbiage by exclaiming, "I wish Nelson would make no more signals, we all understand what we have to do." Later on, however, when he was shown the immortal words he repented with, "Great man, I forgive him."

To continue from Pasco's letter—No sooner had this signal been answered by a few ships in the van than, "he ordered me to make the signal for close action and to keep it up, accordingly I hoisted No. 16 at the top gallant masthead, and there it remained until shot away."

Neither did this signal escape the sincerest form of flattery from Napoleon himself, for when he heard about it later he ordered ships of the French Navy to place in a prominent position the inscription:

LA FRANCE COMPTE QUE CHACUN
FERA SON DEVOIR.

Again, a few months short of a century later, a signal flew from the halyards of the Japanese Flagship MISAKA, as Admiral Togo, a great admirer of Nelson, led his fleet to annihilate the Russians at the battle of Tsushima. The signal:

ON THIS BATTLE RESTS THE FATE OF OUR
NATION. LET EVERY MAN DO HIS UTMOST.

Nelson's signal at Trafalgar has been hoisted annually on board H.M.S. *Victory* on the anniversary of the Battle of Trafalgar ever since she sailed into Portsmouth Harbour for the last time. At first it was hoisted by men who had fought in the ship and knew the flags by heart; but, after some years, someone who knew nothing of the *Redbridge* incident said the flags were wrong, and they were changed. For the next twenty-three years the signal was hoisted incorrectly. In 1908 the mistake was discovered and rectified, but there is still some doubt about one of the flags.

MEDITERRANEAN MANOEUVRES
1893

On a bright sunny Mediterranean afternoon in June, 1893, in clear, calm weather, two battleships of the world's crack fleet were leading their respective division at nine knots on parallel courses, prior to anchoring off the port of Tripoli. One of these battleships, H.M.S. *Victoria,* flew the flag of Admiral Sir George Tryon, K.C.B., Commander-in-Chief of the Mediterranean fleet. Leading the port line was H.M.S. *Camperdown,* temporarily flying the flag of Rear Admiral A. H. Markham, Admiral Tryon's second in command.

At 3.27 *Victoria* hoisted a signal ordering the two divisions to turn towards one another. *Camperdown* hesitated, then made her turn and about four minutes later she struck *Victoria* on her starboard bow almost at right angles. At 3.44 *Victoria* sank, drowning Admiral Tryon, 22 officers and 336 men.

The Admiral was a tall, burly figure of a man with a masterful personality. He had seen war service in the Crimea and he had proved his ability at the Admiralty. With plenty of practical experience behind him, he had a flare for handling ships. He enjoyed carrying out complicated manoeuvres. That very morning on sailing from Beyrout, he had surprised his captains with a brilliant manoeuvre which depended upon his judgment and timing. He was undoubtedly in every way suited to this important Command.

About noon on this ill-fated day he decided to anchor the fleet off Tripoli at 4 p.m. in a particular formation. Shortly after noon he signalled this formation so that all ships would know how and where they would finish up.

At 2.20 he formed the fleet into two divisions. Captains probably began to speculate with their officers as to how their Admiral would manoeuvre them to arrive at the anchorage in that

F

particular formation. They knew it would be neatly done. It always was with Admiral Tryon.

A certain detail was, however, puzzling at least one Captain. At the subsequent Court Martial, Captain Noel, of H.M.S. *Nile,* stationed astern of *Victoria,* said: "As a rule, after the anchoring signal has been made, I have always found that I could foretell how the fleet was to be got into the necessary formation for anchoring. On the fatal 22nd June, 1893, the anchoring signal was made soon after noon. About half past two the columns were closed to six cables (1,200 yd.). It then occurred to me that there was some error, and we might have taken it wrong, so at 2.55, I made a signal, 'Please repeat third hoist of anchoring signal.' This was done, repeating the former signal. I still thought there was something wrong, but of course it was impossible for me to say where the mistake might have been."

There was, indeed, something very wrong.

The ships present were not all of one class. They varied in size and shape—and consequently in turning power. To ensure uniformity in manoeuvre, it was necessary for all ships to use such helm as would make their turning circles equal; that is, equal to the ship with the largest turning circle, which was about 800 yd. diameter.

To Captain Noel a solution to the problem would be for the leading ships of divisions to turn inwards 16 points (180 degrees) and, when this was completed, for all ships to turn together towards the anchorage. This would be simple if the divisions were more than twice their turning diameter apart—but six cables was not enough. At six cables their turning circles would overlap.

Before stationing the divisions at six cables, the C.-in-C. had discussed the matter in his cabin with his Staff Commander and his Flag Captain. On explaining his intention the Staff Commander suggested that eight cables would be a better distance apart than six, to which the Admiral replied, "Yes, it should be eight cables." When the signal was hoisted however the Staff Commander (who survived the tragedy) noted the distance given was six cables, so he sent the Flag-lieutenant down to the Admiral to have it corrected.

The Cpatain (who also survived) was with the Admiral when the Flag-lieutenat entered. The Admiral now said the distance was to remain at six cables. At the Court Martial, the Captain said, "After the Flag-lieutenant left, I reminded the Commander-in-Chief that our turning circle was 800 yards. The interview I am referring to did not take more than a minute. To the best of my belief the

Commander-in-Chief said to me, rather shortly, something to the effect of 'that's all right, leave it at six cables,' and then I left the cabin."

At 3.27, when the Commander-in-Chief, Captain, Staff Commander and Flag-lieutenant were on top of *Victoria's* chart house the Flag-lieutenant was ordered to hoist two signals—one to each division—ordering it to turn in succession 180 degrees inwards, towards its opposite division.

It did not take the Captains long to work out that the manoeuvre they were being called upon to perform was dangerous, yet every ship except one acknowledged these signals, indicating that they were both seen and understood.

That one ship was *Camperdown*. When the signal was reported to Admiral Markham, he said at once, "It's impossible. It's an impracticable manoeuvre," and directed his Flag-lieutenant to keep the repeat hoist "at the dip" indicating that the signal had been seen, but was not understood. He then made to the Commander-in-Chief by semaphore.

DO YOU WISH THE EVOLUTION TO BE PERFORMED AS INDICATED BY SIGNAL

But before this message got through, *Victoria* signalled to *Camperdown*,

WHAT ARE YOU WAITING FOR

Markham was no yes-man, but he readily acknowledged his Chief as his superior in manoeuvre. He had followed him blindly before now. Besides, he thought, with these two separate hoists the divisions could be turned one at a time. Relieved at seeing a solution and not wishing to hold the fleet up any longer, Admiral Markham added his testimony that he understood the signal, and round went the two leaders.

When this incredible blunder eventually dawned on Admiral Tryon he stood, speechless, watching *Camperdown* approaching, heedless of the repeated urges of his Flag Captain to take avoiding action. After the collision he was heard to mutter "It's all my doing—all my fault," later he said to his Staff Commander, "I think she's going," and his last recorded words were to a midshipman, "Don't stop here, youngster—go to a boat."

The two signals hoisted by the Fleet Flagship at 3.27 were:

FIRST DIVISION ALTER COURSE IN SUCCESSION 16 POINTS TO PORT PRESERVING THE ORDER OF THE DIVISION.

SECOND DIVISION ALTER COURSE IN SUCCESSION 16 POINTS TO STARBOARD PRESERVING THE ORDER OF THE DIVISION.

(16 points is 180 degrees.)

The orders they conveyed were dangerous to every ship. Everyone trusted the leader, and his personality was such that his own officers and the Captains of other ships preferred to believe he had some trick up his sleeve than to challenge him on a matter of elementary arithmetic.

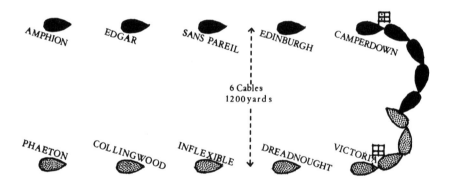

SHORT WEEK-END

In the winter months shortly before World War I Commodore Sir Robert Arbuthnot's destroyer flotilla was at Bantry Bay calibrating guns. Bad weather had considerably delayed the programme; in fact, his own ship had not even made a start. But the weather was improving and the experts prophesied that it would be possible to begin on Saturday. Unfortunately, they were twenty-four hours out in their reckoning and no guns could be fired that day; but Sunday held out still more promise.

The Gunnery Lieutenant asked the Staff Commander whether he could persuade the Admiral to allow firing to take place on the Sabbath. The Staff Commander, knowing Sir Robert pretty well, thought the Admiral would have no personal feelings on the matter, but said he would have to remind the Admiral about possible repercussions from the Roman Catholic population on shore.

The Admiral gave permission to go ahead with the plans to calibrate irrespective of the day of the week, but added cryptically that the guns would not be fired on a Sabbath day.

At one minute before midnight on Saturday the Admiral made the following signal:

TOMORROW WILL BE MONDAY

Calibration went on uninterruptedly throughout daylight hours the following day.

At one minute past midnight on Monday morning, the Admiral signalled:

YESTERDAY WAS SUNDAY

Despite Episcopal protests from ashore and subsequent questions from the Admiralty, Sir Robert blandly maintained that no guns had been fired on the Sabbath.

A SIGNAL WHICH EXPLODED
1907

A signal made in Weymouth Bay in November, 1907, had almost the same effect as a spark in a petrol tank. The explosion which followed rumbled away for many years.

The detonation was caused by the conflicting temperaments of Admiral Lord Charles Beresford on one hand, and Admirals Fisher and Percy Scott on the other. Sir John Fisher was First Sea Lord, Lord Charles was Commander-in-Chief Channel Fleet. Rear Admiral Percy Scott was commanding a Cruiser Squadron.

Lord Charles was a nobleman. Jacky and Percy Scott were brilliant men whose creed at that time was Strength through Gunnery. All three had strong personalities.

The Channel Fleet was at Portland; the Cruisers in Weymouth Bay; Percy Scott flew his flag in H.M.S. *Good Hope.*

The Cruisers were carrying out their annual gunnery competitive firing, an affair of great importance to Percy Scott. Bad weather had held up the firing and by the end of the week when the competition should have been completed, one Cruiser, the *Roxburgh,* had not finished.

Kaiser William II was about to pay a State visit to this country and, at the end of the following week, the Fleet was to assemble at Spithead to greet him. This meant that all ships must look their smartest. Accordingly, the Commander-in-Chief had given orders that ships were to start painting on Monday.

On the previous Friday, Percy Scott asked the Commander-in-Chief if *Roxburgh* could go out in the Channel and complete her firing before she started painting on Monday.

Lord Charles made the following reply:

NOT APPROVED. ROXBURGH MUST GET READY FOR THE REVIEW AND REMAIN IN HARBOUR WITH THE REMAINDER OF THE FLEET.

Between Portland Harbour and Weymouth Bay, it was necessary to station a ship to repeat signals. H.M.S. *Illustrious,* flying the flag of Rear Admiral Foley was fulfilling this task. When *Illustrious* passed on the Commander-in-Chief's refusal to *Good Hope,* the explosion occurred.

When Percy Scott was shown the signal, he took a signal pad, and wrote. When his Flag Lieutenant saw what he had written he urged that the wording should be modified. The Flag Captain did the same. Their advice was scorned. The only concession the Admiral granted was to defer sending the signal until after lunch.

In desperation the Flag Lieutenant contacted his opposite number in *Illustrious.* Together they vowed they would do all they could to stop the signal being read by the Fleet. But after lunch the signal was duly passed to *Roxburgh.* It read as follows:

SINCE PAINTWORK APPEARS TO BE MORE IM-
PORTANT THAN GUNNERY YOU MUST REMAIN IN
HARBOUR AND MAKE YOURSELF LOOK PRETTY.

During the afternoon officers foregathered as usual afloat and ashore and by evening everyone in the Fleet was discussing *Good Hope's* signal to *Roxburgh*. They did not have to wait long for developments. In due course *Roxburgh* was ordered to send her signal log to the Fleet Flagship. Rear Admiral Percy Scott was ordered to put on his frock coat and sword and personally to bring *Good Hope's* signal log to the Commander-in-Chief.

The C.-in-C. interviewed him on his quarter-deck before his staff and all the Captains of the Fleet. It must have been one of the most unpleasant sessions two Flag Officers have ever had. Having accepted the responsibility of making the signal, Percy Scott was told that the Admiralty had been requested to order him to haul down his flag. Percy Scott stated afterwards he was never given a chance to state his case. It seems that Lord Charles Beresford did all the talking.

Shortly after this distressing scene the following signal was made by semaphore to the whole fleet, thus ensuring the widest possible publicity.

From Commander-in-Chief—General.

THE LORDS COMMISSIONERS OF THE ADMIRALTY HAVING DIRECTED ME TO PREPARE THE CHANNEL FLEET TO DO HONOUR TO HIS IMPERIAL MAJESTY THE GERMAN EMPEROR AN ORDER WAS GIVEN TO ALL VESSELS UNDER MY COMMAND TO BE OUT OF ROUTINE AND PAINT SHIP AFTER THE MAN-OEUVRES. WITH REFERENCE TO MY ORDER ON MONDAY, 4TH NOVEMBER, THE ADMIRAL COMMAND-ING THE FIRST CRUISER SQUADRON FORMING PART OF THE CHANNEL FLEET MADE THE FOLLOWING SIGNAL TO THE CAPTAIN OF THE ROXBURGH. SINCE PAINTWORK APPEARS TO BE MORE IMPORTANT THAN GUNNERY YOU MUST REMAIN IN HARBOUR AND MAKE YOURSELF LOOK PRETTY. IN REGARD TO MY ORDER MADE TO THE FLEET TO PAINT SHIP THIS SIGNAL MADE BY THE REAR ADMIRAL FIRST CRUISER SQUADRON IS CON-TEMPTUOUS IN TONE AND INSUBORDINATE IN CHARACTER. THE REAR ADMIRAL IS TO ISSUE ORDERS TO GOOD HOPE AND ROXBURGH TO EX-PUNGE THE SIGNAL FROM THEIR SIGNAL LOGS AND

TO REPORT TO ME BY SIGNAL WHEN MY ORDERS HAVE BEEN OBEYED.

The episode certainly did not end there. Admiral Sir John Fisher at the Admiralty, declined to order Percy Scott to strike his flag on the grounds that the Commander-in-Chief had already dealt with the matter by taking the unprecedented step of censuring the Rear Admiral in a general signal to the whole Fleet. This ruling showed clearly which side Sir John was on.

The incident didn't seem to affect the career of Percy Scott, who finished his brilliant, if tactless career as a full Admiral and a knight. The Battle, however, continued after retirement.

In 1912 Lord Charles Beresford wrote in his autobiography:

"It is now four years since I had occasion to appeal to the Admiralty with reference to a grave instance of indiscipline in which my authority as Commander-in-Chief and also my personal character were involved. The matter having passed out of my hands and having become known to the public at the time, the Admiralty and the Admiralty alone could have set it right.

". . . During my tenure of the Command of the Channel Fleet, two incidents occurred of which highly misleading accounts appeared in the Press. The first occurred in November, 1907. The breach of discipline was so grave a character and was committed in so public a manner that it was my duty to make strong representations to the Admiralty with regard to the offender. Those representations were so far disregarded that the officer in question was permitted to retain his position without having proffered a public apology for a public offence.

"I appealed to the Admiralty in the interests of discipline to take such measures to put a stop to these nefarious proceedings as I was myself debarred by King's Regulations from adopting. The only response of the constituted authorities to my request was a brief statement made in the House on March 9th, 1908, many weeks after the event, by the Civil Lord of the Admiralty in answer to a question. By that time the mischief was done."

Here Lord Charles goes on to describe the second incident which, it relates, refers to a signal concerned with the manoeuvring of *Good Hope* and *Argyll.* As Percy Scott did not leave *Good Hope* until January, 1909, it could well be related to the bitterness which still existed over the "Paint Ship" incident.

". . . In January, 1908, there was sent to every officer under my command in the Channel Fleet, a copy of a newspaper containing a violent attack upon myself.

"On Thursday, July 9th, an account of a signal said to have been made by me was published in the Press, together with a statement to the effect that had the signal been obeyed, a disaster comparable with the accident which befell the *Victoria* and the *Campberdown* must have occurred. The incident could only have been reported by an officer in the Fleet."

Lord Charles goes on to say that he showed the Civil Lord, Mr. McKenna, the written evidence in his possession with regard to the person who sent the account of the signal to the Press.

"On July 30th Mr McKenna said in the House that the signal was not dangerous, but that if the officer to whom the signal was made thought it was, he was quite justified in disobeying it. But ... he had no knowledge who sent the message and it was impossible for him to find out."

In 1913 Sir Percy launched *his* attack. He maintained in *his* autobiography, that, "neither contempt nor insubordination was shown in my conversation with the Captain of the *Roxburgh*. Lord Charles publicly labelling it as such was a gross injustice to me and an act highly prejudicial to the maintenance of good order and discipline in H.M. Fleet. A further deplorable example to the officers and men under his command was Lord Charles Beresford's order to me not to speak to him, but only to communicate with him in writing. Such an act was extraordinary and fatal; it made him the laughing stock of the Fleet. ... Such a state of affairs as the Commander-in-Chief of our Channel Fleet not to be on speaking terms with the Rear Admiral in Command of his Cruisers was nationally dangerous."

Then Sir Percy really warms up to his work. ". . . Lord Charles rightly says that a sailor can only learn his trade at sea, that his true education can only be gained at sea; the corollary of this is that if the sailor does not go to sea he can not learn his trade. In point of view of his education, I have always thought that the Admiralty treated Lord Charles very badly by not giving him sufficient opportunity at sea to acquire the necessary knowledge for establishing a reputation as a seaman. Out of the twenty-one years of his service in the Navy as Commander and Captain he only served in a ship of war for five years. This could not and did not make a seaman of him."

A POSSIBLE SOLUTION
1917

This incident contains a signal the text of which, as far as can be ascertained, has never been revealed. No mention is made of it at the Court of Inquiry which was held after the disaster. The incident is related here as it was told to the author.

"At the time in question I was serving as Signal Officer to Commodore (F) who commanded the five Destroyer Flotillas attached to the Grand Fleet. He flew his Broad Pennant in *Castor.*

"Attending the Destroyers was the *Sandhurst.* She was the largest Destroyer depot ship at that time. She was commanded by Captain English, a retired navigating officer recalled for the war. He had a fluent knowledge of the German language.

"*Sandhurst* was accommodating a number of Gunnery Artificers. They had been sent to carry out alterations to the magazines of certain ships. These alterations were found necessary after the explosions which sank three of our Battle Cruisers at the Battle of Jutland.

"I was walking up and down *Castor's* quarterdeck when at 11 p.m. precisely I saw *Vanguard* go up into the air in two quite distinct portions. It required no ballistical expert to realise that the explosion could have been the result of simultaneous time bombs.

"At daylight the next morning the following signal was received in *Castor*:

Captain of Sandhurst to Com. F.
AM SATISFIED I HAVE ARRESTED THE ENEMY AGENT RESPONSIBLE FOR BLOWING UP VANGUARD. WHEN MAY I COME AND SEE YOU.

"At the subsequent interview it transpired that on hearing the explosion, Captain English had promptly mustered every Gunnery Artificer on deck and had them brought down to his cabin one at a time.

"To each man he spoke—very slowly—a short sentence in

German making him repeat it back as best he could. In three cases his suspicions were aroused. It seemed as though the ratings in question were familiar with the language, in spite of their assurance to the contrary.

"Captain English then turned up the history sheets of these three suspects. He noted that one had worked onboard *Bulwark* (previously sunk by explosion at Chatham) and onboard *Natal* (previously sunk by explosion at Cromarty). He had been onboard *Vanguard* up to 8 p.m. on the day she exploded.

"Later that morning I was ordered to detail one'of the Duty Destroyers to take this Artificer under armed guard to Thurso. He went on by train to London to be interviewed by Admiral 'Blinker' Hall, the famous head of Naval Intelligence in World War I."

Nine months after this incident when the narrator was serving at the Admiralty he asked the Admiral what eventually happened to this Artificer. He was told politely to mind his own business.

TOP SECRET SCIATICA

In time of war, secrecy in operational signals is paramount. Secrecy also enshrouds personal signals about officers, their behaviour, their physical condition. The higher the rank, the deeper the secret. Think what might have happened to morale in the Grand Fleet in World War I for example, if everyone knew their Commander-in-Chief had backache.

The following sequence of signals, all stamped PERSONAL and SECRET, passed between the First Sea Lord, the First Lord (Winston Churchill), the Commander-in-Chief, Grand Fleet (Admiral Jellicoe), and others intimately concerned, a few months before the Battle of Jutland.

> *From First Lord of the Admiralty to Commander-in-Chief Grand Fleet*

1650/17   I am sorry to learn you have sciatica. While the good information continues the Fleet and you should rest. Consider whether you should not take four or five days' holiday on shore at some comfortable Scotch house. We will take full responsibility for your absence. Keep fit it will last a long time.

1605/18   *From First Lord*
Pray let us know your wishes and make your own arrangements. We attach importance to your having a few days' holiday.

1058/27   *From Commander-in-Chief*
Medical Officer is very anxious for me to keep quiet for four days. If you consider it important to see me I will of course come.

1930/27   *From First Lord*
Your health and rest are first consideration. If possible I will come to you Friday night reaching you Saturday morning.

0905/28   *From First Sea Lord to Commander-in-Chief*
I earnestly entreat and urge you to take complete rest on shore as I can assure you that no present anxiety exists as to the Fleet being required and it is very urgent indeed you should completely re-establish your health by a long stay on shore without any Fleet work of any kind.

1050/28   *From Chief of Staff to Commander-in-Chief*
Request all Admiralty telegrams for Commander-in-Chief except personal telegrams may be repeated to Vice-Admiral Commanding 1st Battle Squadron until return of Commander-in-Chief.

1545/28   *From Commander-in-Chief to First Lord*
Doctors in consultation from Hospital Ship *Drina*

today. They inform me it will be risky for me to be out of bed for four or five days. I am at Caledonian Hotel Inverness. Admiralty Mail Officer can decode telegrams sent to me direct. Much regret my temporary incapacity.

1843/28   *From Chief of Staff to Commander-in-Chief*
Doctor informs me it is essential Commander-in-Chief remains in bed for three or four days. I have informed Vice-Admiral Commanding 1st Battle Squadron. Submit I may be authorised to take Flagship to sea if such eventualities become necessary.

2340/28   *From First Sea Lord to Chief of Staff to Commander-in-Chief*
IMMEDIATE. Following has been sent to Vice-Admiral Commanding 1st Battle Squadron. In the event of Grand Fleet being required to proceed to sea during temporary indisposition of Commander-in-Chief you are authorised to take full command in his absence.

0915/30   *From First Lord*
Good to hear such favourable report. Inform C.-in-C. that there is nothing to cause him anxiety in anything that is occurring.

2157/1   *From Chief to Staff*
Doctor reports, patient's condition most satisfactory. Could not be better.

1155/2   *From Chief of Staff to Medical Director General*
Patient thoroughly well and Doctors propose to go south at 3 p.m. today but if you think Sir . . . should wait he will do so for another day. On the other hand Sir . . . thinks it would be better for him to go now and return later in order to make sure that patient is all right before assuming duty.

1630/11   *From Chief of Staff to Medical Director General*
Patient is very anxious he should be allowed to attend to important correspondence and see his staff. Sir . . . considers this permissible for one hour daily. Meanwhile he has had another motor drive and is feeling much stronger.

1343/12   *From Medical Director General of the Navy to Chief of Staff*
One hour's work approved.

1915/17 *From Chief of Staff*
Doctor reports patient's convalescence. Steadily pro-gressing. Yesterday and today he had been on board the Flagship transacting business. Tonight he is tired but well.

1845/19 *From Chief of Staff*
Doctor reports patient continues very well. He was on board Flagship four hours and afterwards played a round of golf.

1510/22 *From Commander-in-Chief to Admiralty*
I have returned to full duty. Ship will probably sail tomorrow afternoon.

SCHARNHORST AND GNEISENAU,
MUTTER UND TOCHTER

In the Naval history of the last two wars the names of *Scharnhorst* and *Gneisenau* are so closely associated that one would imagine the characters whose names they bear were twins. In historical fact Gerhard Johann David von Scharnhorst was five years older than August Wilhelm Anton Gneisenau. They had, however, many things in common. They were both eminent soldiers. They were both decorated with the envied *Pour le mérite*. Gneisenau actually worked under Scharnhorst in reforming the Prussian Army in

1809. Scharnhorst had Clausewitz as a pupil at the Berlin War Academy. Gneisenau had him later as his Chief of Staff. Scharnhorst was Chief of Staff to General Blücher after Napoleon's retreat from Moscow. Gneisenau was Blücher's Chief of Staff at Waterloo. But the ships named after them seemed to be operationally inseparable.

In the World War I they were a couple of powerful cruisers completed in 1907, displacing 11,600 tons, with complements of 765 men, mounting eight 8.2 in. guns, six 5.9 in. guns and capable of steaming 22 knots. They did not last long, but 88 of their 166 days of war life were spent at sea, covering 16,000 miles. With three light cruisers they inflicted at Coronel the first defeat the Royal Navy had suffered for over a century. It took a concentration of thirty ships to regain our command of the South Atlantic.

In World War II the daughters of *Scharnhorst* and *Gneisenau* were two mighty Battlecruisers displacing what they declared to be 26,000 tons but which we considered to be a modest underestimation of 10,000, three times as robust as their mothers. They were armed with nine 11 in. guns, eight 5.9 in. and sixteen 4.1 in. They carried two aircraft and could steam 32 knots.

In company they sank the armed merchant cruiser *Rawalpindi,* and the aircraft carrier *Glorious* with her two destroyers *Acasta* and *Ardent.* For sixty days they evaded opposition in the Atlantic and between them they sank twenty-two merchant ships totalling 115,622 tons. A year later they shocked us by steaming up our Channel from Brest to their own dockyards.

There the partnership ended. Royal Air Force bombs put *Gneisenau* out of the war for good. *Scharnhorst* sailed for Norway once more and reached Altenfjord. In September, 1943, she ventured with *Tirpitz* on a one-sided raid on Spitzbergen. Finally she was pounced on and sunk by ships of the Home Fleet while threatening a Russian bound convoy on Boxing Day, 1943. By then her crew of about 1,900 substantially unchanged throughout the war, were a proud team with great faith in the fighting qualities of their ship.

One battleship, four cruisers and four destroyers were immediately responsible for their end, but the total sum of our ships ranged against these two in their lifetime must be unique.

Here is the story of those two *Scharnhorsts* and two *Gneisenaus* retold in signals which shaped their lives.

World War I—Mutter

Scharnhorst was Admiral Graf von Spee's flagship on the China Station. With *Gneisenau*, her sister-ship, she had earned a great reputation for smartness and efficiency.

As the relationship between England and Germany became strained in the late summer of 1914, the movements of the two ships became of increasing interest to Vice Admiral Jerram, the British Commander-in-Chief on the China Station.

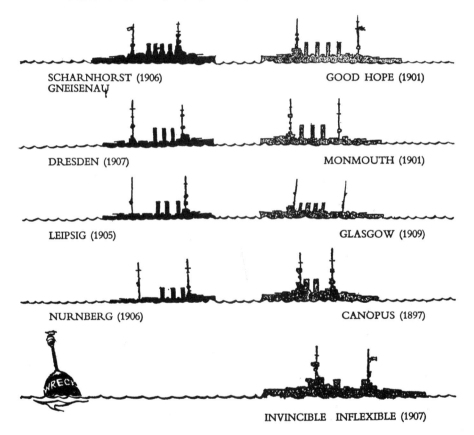

SCHARNHORST (1906)   GOOD HOPE (1901)
GNEISENAU

DRESDEN (1907)   MONMOUTH (1901)

LEIPSIG (1905)   GLASGOW (1909)

NURNBERG (1906)   CANOPUS (1897)

INVINCIBLE INFLEXIBLE (1907)

On the eve of the outbreak of war, von Spee set out into the Pacific, never to return to the China seas.

In those days ships on distant foreign stations were not in direct wireless touch with London or Berlin. Long-distance communication was by cable, and messages were sometimes delayed.

G

October   *From Admiralty to Rear Admiral Christopher Cradock,*
1914   *commanding 4th Cruiser Squadron in the Atlantic*
5th   (*Good Hope,* flagship, *Glasgow, Monmouth, Otranto,*
           auxiliary cruiser, *Canopus,* old battleship).

It appears from information received that *Gneisenau* and *Scharnhorst* are working across to South America. *Dresden* may be scouting for them. You must be prepared to meet them in company. *Canopus* should accompany *Monmouth* and *Otranto* and should search and protect trade in combination.

8th   *From Cradock to Admiralty* (*received 12th*)

Without alarming, respectfully suggest that in event of enemy's heavy cruisers and others concentrating West Coast of South America it is necessary to have a British force on each coast strong enough to bring them to action. For otherwise, should the concentrated British force sent from South-East coast be evaded, which is not impossible, and thereby get behind the enemy, the latter could destroy Falkland, English Bank and Abrolhos coaling bases in turn with little to stop them, and with British ships unable to follow up owing to want of coal enemy might possibly reach West Indies.

8th   *From Cradock to Admiralty* (*received 11th*)

Following Intelligence re *Scharnhorst* and *Gneisenau* has been received. Evidence found by *Good Hope* revisiting Orange Bay on 7th October that *Dresden* had been there 11th and there are indications that *Scharnhorst* and *Gneisenau* may be joined by *Nurnberg, Dresden* and *Leipsig.* I have ordered *Canopus* to proceed there, and *Monmouth, Glasgow* and *Otranto* not to go further north than Valparaiso until German cruisers are located again. Does *Deence* join my command.

26th   *From Cradock to Admiralty* (*received 27th*)

With reference to orders to search for enemy and our great desire for early success, I consider that owing to slow speed of *Canopus* it is impossible to find and destroy enemy's squadron. Have therefore ordered *Defence* to join me. ... Shall employ *Canopus* on necessary work of convoying colliers.

27th   *From Cradock to Admiralty* (*received 1st November*)

Have seized German mails. *Monmouth, Good Hope,*

Otranto coaling at Vallemar. *Glasgow* patrolling vicinity Coronel to intercept German shipping, rejoining flag later on. I intend to proceed northward secretly with squadron after coaling and to keep out of sight of land. Until further notice continue telegraphing to Montevideo.

27th *From Rear Admiral Stoddart (East Coast) to Admiralty (arrived 29th)*

I have received orders from Admiral Cradock to send *Defence* to Montevideo . . . submit I may be given two cruisers in place of *Defence* as I do not consider force at my disposal is sufficient.

28th *From Admiralty to Cradock*

Defence is to remain on East Coast under orders of Stoddart. This will leave sufficient force on each side in case the hostile cruisers appear there on the trade routes. . . . Japanese battleship *Hizen* shortly expected on North American Coast. She will join with Japanese cruiser *Idzumo* and *Newcastle.*

(This signal and subsequent signals sent from Admiralty to *Good Hope* were never received.)

Night Frequent German wireless transmissions noted in
31/1 *Glasgow's* signal log.
Nov.
1st

0200 *From German Mechant ship Gottingen to Scharnhorst*
English light cruiser anchored in Coronel Roads 1900 31 October.

1620 *From Scharnhorst to ships in company*
Clear for action.

1628 *From Scharnhorst to Gneisenau*
Take station astern. Raise steam for full speed.

1647 *From Glasgow to Good Hope*
Enemy protected cruisers in sight steering between SE and South.

1818 *From Good Hope to Canopus (300 miles South)*
I am now going to attack enemy.

1834 *From Scharnhorst to Gneisenau*
Open fire.

1839 *From Good Hope to Otranto*
There is danger proceed at your utmost speed (message unfinished).

2015   *From Glasgow to Monmouth*
Are you all right.
From Monmouth to Glasgow
I want to get stern to sea. I am making water badly forward.
From Glasgow to Monmouth
Can you steer north west. The enemy are following us astern.
(There was no answer from *Monmouth*).

Nov.   *From Consul General, Valparaiso to Admiralty (arrived 3rd)*

2nd   Master of Chilean merchant vessel reports that on 1st November 1 p.m. he was stopped by *Nurnberg* 5 miles off Cape Carranza. . . . Two other German cruisers lay west. . . . Master believes one of these was *Scharnhorst*. . . .

Nov.   *From Admiralty to Stoddart, Defence*

3rd   *Defence* to proceed with all possible dispatch to join Admiral Cradock on west coast of America. Acknowledge.

November 3rd. *Scharnhorst* sent full report of Coronel action to German Consul, Valparaiso, for onward transmission by cable to Naval Staff, Berlin, where it arrived on 6th November.

    From Consul General Valparaiso, to Admiralty (arrived 4th)
Have just learnt from Chilean Admiral that German Admiral states that on Sunday at sunset, in thick and wicked weather his ships met *Good Hope, Glasgow, Monmouth* and *Otranto*. Action was joined and *Monmouth* turned over and sank after about an hour's fighting. *Good Hope, Glasgow* and *Otranto* drew off into darkness. *Good Hope* was on fire, an explosion was heard, and she is believed to have sunk. *Gneisenau, Scharnhorst* and *Nurnberg* were among the German ships engaged.

Nov.   *From Admiralty to C.-in-C. Grand Fleet*

4th   Order *Invincible* and *Inflexible* to fill up with coal at once and proceed to Berehaven with all dispatch. They are urgently needed for foreign service. . . .

From Admiralty to Kent (Sierra Leone)
Urgent. Proceed to Abrolhos Rocks with all dispatch. It
is intended you shall join Admiral Cradock's Squadron.
From Admiralty to Rear Admiral Stoddart (Carnarvon)
In view of reported sinking of *Good Hope* and
Monmouth by *Scharnhorst* and *Gneisenau* off Coronel
November 1st, armoured ships on SE coast of America
must concentrate at once. *Carnarvon, Cornwall* should
join *Defence* off Montevideo. *Canopus, Glasgow,
Otranto* have been ordered if possible to join you there.
Kent from Sierra Leone also has been ordered to join
your flag via Abrolhos. Endeavour to get into
communication with them. Enemy will most likely
come on to the Rio trade route. Reinforcements will
meet you shortly from England. Acknowledge.
*From German Naval Staff, Berlin to Von Spee (Scharn-
horst)*
*It is left to your discretion to attempt to return home
with all your ships.*
From Admiralty to Canopus
In view of reported sinking of *Good Hope* and
Monmouth by *Scharnhorst* and *Gneisenau* on 1st
November you should make the best of your way to
join *Defence* near Montevideo. Keep wide of track to
avoid being brought to action by superior force. If
attacked, however, Admiralty is confident ship will in
all circumstances be fought to the last as imperative to
damage enemy whatever may be consequences.
From Admiralty to Glasgow, Otranto
You should make the best of your way to join *Defence*
near Montevideo. Keep wide of track to avoid being
brought to action by superior force.

Nov.
5th

From Admiralty to Japanese Admiralty
In consequence of unsuccessful action off Chile and
definite location of German Squadron, we have ordered
concentration off Montevideo of *Defence, Kent,
Carnarvon* and *Cornwall.* These will be joined with all
dispatch by *Inflexible* and *Invincible,* Battle cruisers
from England, and *Dartmouth*, light cruiser from East
Africa, and remainder of defeated squadron from Chile.
This assures the South Atlantic situation. We now desire
assistance of Japan in making equally thorough arrange-

ments on Pacific side. We propose for your consideration and friendly advice the following. *Newcastle* and *Idzumo* to go south in company to San Clemente Island off San Diego, California, there to meet *Hizen* from Honolulu. Meanwhile *Asama* will be able to effect internment or destruction of *Geier*. We also propose to move *Australia* battle cruiser from Fiji to Fanning Island. By the time these moves are complete, probably by November 17th we may know more of *Scharnhorst* and *Gneisenau* movements, and a further concentration of *Australia* and *Asama* with *Hizen*, *Idzumo* and *Newcastle* will be possible either at San Clemente or further to the south, further movements depending on the enemy. We should also like a Japanese Squadron to advance to Fiji to take the place of *Australia* and so guard Australia and New Zealand in case the Germans return. . . .

From Admiralty to C.—in—C. Grand Fleet (Personal from First Lord)

From all reports received through German sources, we fear Cradock has been caught or has engaged with only *Monmouth* and *Good Hope* against armoured ships *Scharnhorst* and *Gneisenau*. Probably both British vessels sunk. Position of *Canopus* critical and fate of *Glasgow* and *Otranto* uncertain. Proximity of concentrated squadron of five good ships will threaten gravely main trade route Rio to London. Essential recover control. Sturdee goes Commander-in-Chief, South Atlantic and Pacific.

Note: *Extract from orders to Vice Admiral Sturdee.*

On leaving Devonport with H.M. ships *Invincible* and *Inflexible* under your orders proceed to St. Vincent, Cape Verde Islands and complete with coal on arrival there and thence proceed to South American waters.

On passage to St. Vincent it is possible you may receive orders by W/T to proceed to West Indies, should information be received that *Scharnhorst* and *Gneisenau* are proceeding northward on Pacific Coast. Your presence in the West Indies would be necessary to provide for the contingencey of the German Squadron pasing through the Panama Canal.

Your main and most important duty is to search for the

German armoured cruisers *Scharnhorst* and *Gneisenau* and bring them to action. All other considerations are to be subordinated to this end.

From Admiralty to Governor, Falkland Islands

German cruiser raid may take place. All Admiralty colliers should be concealed on unfrequented harbours. Be ready to destroy supplies useful to enemy and hide codes effectively on enemy ships being sighted. Acknowledge.

Nov. 7th

From Captain Von Knorr (German Naval attache San Francisco) to Von Spee (Scharnhorst)

Information received that British cruisers Defence, Cornwall, Bristol, Glasgow, Canopus assembling Falkland Islands. Japanese ships approaching from north on west coast. If it is your intention to return Germany suggest you do so now.

From Japanese Admiralty to Admiralty

Japanese Admiralty give their consent generally to strategical scheme proposed. . . .

Nov. 9th

From Admiralty to Canopus

You are to remain in Stanley Harbour. Moor the ship so that the entrance is commanded by your guns. Extemporize mines outside entrance. Send down your topmasts and be prepared for bombardment from outside the harbour. Stimulate the Governor to organize all local forces and make determined defence. Arrange observation posts on shore by which your fire on ships outside can be directed. Land guns or use boats' torpedoes to sink a blocking ship before she reaches the Narrows. No objection to your grounding ship to obtain a good berth. Should *Glasgow* be able to get sufficient start of enemy to avoid capture, send her to the River Plate, if not moor her inside *Canopus*. Repair your defects and wait orders.

From Commander-in-Chief, Plymouth to Admiralty

The Admiral Superintendent, Devonport, reports that the earliest possible date for completion of *Invincible* and *Inflexible* is midnight 13th November.

From Admiralty to C.-in-C. plymouth

Ships are to sail Wednesday 11th. They are needed for war service and dockyard arrangements must be made to conform. If necessary dockyard men should be sent

away in the ships to return as opportunity may offer.
You are held responsible for the speedy dispatch of
these ships in a thoroughly efficient condition. Acknowledge.

*From German Naval Staff, Berlin to German Consul,
Valparaiso*

*Instruct cruiser squadron that coaling from colliers in
harbour Argentine and Brazil is not possible owing to
embargo on coal export.*

Nov. *From German Naval Staff to Von Spee (Scharnhorst)*
16th *What are your intentions. Report amount of ammunition remaining.*

*From Scharnhorst to German agents, River Plate and
New York.*

*Send German ship with 10,000 tons coal and sufficient
provision for 1,000 men for three months to arrive
Panta Santa, Elena (Argentine coast) December 15th.*

Nov. *From Von Spee to German Naval Staff.*
17th *Intend breaking through with my squadron. Ammunition remaining Heavy class. Main armament 445,
secondary armament 1,100. Smaller cruisers 1,860.*

Nov. *From Invincible to Inflexible.*
18th The utmost harm may be done by indiscreet use of
0345 wireless. The key is never to be pressed unless absolutely
necessary.

November 20th. German Agents, La Plata, had information for
Von Spee that *Canopus'* guns had been mounted ashore, Falkland
Islands.

November 23rd. German Agents, Montevideo, had information
for Von Spee that ten English ships had been sighted 300 miles
east of Montevideo.

November 24th. German Agents, La Plata, had information for
Von Spee that *Invincible* and *Carnarvon* were at Abrolhos Rocks.

(None of the above information ever reached Von Spee.)

Dec. 6th *From German ship Amasis to Von Spee (Scharnhorst)*
*Naval base Port Stanley, Falkland Islands, empty of
British warships.*

From Port Stanley to Invincible

Following message received from Montevideo by W/T.
Rio de Janeiro reports on 24th November there were

rumours *Scharnhorst* and *Gneisenau* rounded Cape Horn 22 November.

Dec. 7th   *From Sappers Hill (observation station, Falkland Island) to Canopus*
British battlecruisers approaching.

Extract from *Canopus* signal log between 0700 and 0800 on Tuesday, 8th December.

0707   *From Ordance Point to Canopus*
Submit is Yeoman Brooks still on compensation as there are 21 ratings here at present and rations for only 20 have been sent.
Reply: Brooks must be rationed additional. Rations for full numbers will be sent.

0750   *From Sappers Hill*
There is a four funnel and two funnel man of war coming from the southward.

0803/8   *From Invincible to Glasgow*
Where is Sappers Hill.
From Glasgow to Invincible
Sappers Hill is shore station above the town.

0805   *From Invincible to Glasgow, Cornwall*
Raise steam for full speed. Prepare to weigh.

0815   *From Invincible—General*
Raise steam for full speed and report when ready to proceed.

0830   *From Invincible—General*
Strange men-o'-war reported from southward. *Bristol* cast off collier and weigh immediately. Ships are to report when they have steam for 14 knots.

0935   *From Glasgow to Invincible*
There are three more cruisers in sight.

0945   *From Invincible to Glasgow*
Join *Kent* and observe enemy's movements.

1015   *From Invincible*
Follow Flagship out of harbour.

1030   *From Invincible—General*
CHASE.

1100   *From Bristol to Invincible*
Three enemy ships are standing off Port Pleasant. Probably colliers or transports.

1130   *From Invincible to Bristol*
Take *Macedonia* under your orders and destroy transports.

1140   *From Invincible—General*
          Optional. Ships' companies will have time for the next
          meal.
1245   *From Scharnhorst*
          Light cruisers detach and endeavour to escape.
1302   *From Invincible—General*
          Open fire and engage enemy.
1545   *From Scharnhorst to Gneisenau*
          If engines are intact endeavour to escape.
              (This was the last signal from *Scharnhorst*.)

1830   *From Invincible—General*
          Scharnhorst, and *Gneisenau* sunk. Where are the re-
          mainder.
Later   *From Invincible to Admiralty*
          Scharnhorst, Gneisenau, Leipsig sunk. 2 colliers cap-
          tured. All cruisers now looking for *Dresden* and *Nurn-
          berg* who spread and escaped during action.
Dec. 9th *From Admiral Sturdee to Senior surviving German
          Officer from Gneisenau*
          We sympathise with you in the loss of your Admiral and
          so many officers and men. Unfortunately the two
          countries are at war and officers of both navies who can
          count friends in the other have to carry out their
          country's duties, which your Admiral, Captain, and
          officers worthily maintained to the end.
1820/9   *From Canopus to Invincible*
          Message recieved from Admiralty through Montevideo
          begins: From His Majesty. I heartily congratulate you,
          your officers and men on your most opportune victory.
          George.

World War II—Tochter

Here starts the longer lives in the Second World War of the two
descendants of Von Spee's squadron. They were launched in
October and December, 1936. *Gneisenau* lived for five-and-a-half
years. *Scharnhorst,* unlike the general she was named after,
survived *Gneisenau* by twenty months. Their first adventure after
the outbreak of war was a tame affair. They could have done more

damage than sinking one armed merchant cruiser and we could possibly have brought them to action. Nevertheless the German naval staff were extremely pleased that our northern sanctuaries had been penetrated without German loss so soon after the outbreak of war.

Sinking of H.M.S. RAWALPINDI (Armed Merchant Cruiser)

1325/21 Nov. 1939   *Gneisenau*, flying flag Admiral Marschall, with *Scharnhorst* in company sailed from Wilhelmshaven.

23rd Nov.   *From Rawalpindi (on patrol between Faroes and Iceland)*

1605   1 enemy Battle Cruiser bearing 280°, 4 miles. My position (given).

1607   *From Scharnhorst to Gneisenau*
Merchant ship at long range on starboard beam.

1612   *From Gneisenau to Scharnhorst*
Ascertain course of Merchant ship. What type of vessel.

1613   *From Scharnhorst to Gneisenau*
Merchant ship on roughly parallel course.

1618   *From Scharnhorst to Gneisenau*
Am closing merchant ship to observe further details. Apparently a large ship. 2 masts one funnel.

1624   *From Delhi (on northern patrol)*
Am coming to your assistance.

1633   *From Scharnhorst to Gneisenau*
Large Merchant vessel, course 180°, vessel turning away. I am closing her.

1635   *Scharnhorst to Rawalpindi*
(In German) *Heave to. Do not use radio. Where from and where bound.*
(In English) *What ship. Do not use wireless.*

Rawalpindi acknowledged the message, turned away and increased speed. *Scharnhorst* followed and noted a gun, mounted aft, and also that smoke floats were being dropped.

1655   *From Vice Admiral Northern Patrol to Cruisers*
Subject to other orders from Commander-in-Chief

Home Fleet, *Delhi* and *Newcastle* shadow *Deutschland.*
Calypso, Ceres concentrate 5 miles north of Kalso light.
Act as striking force for night attack.

(Note: Identity of German ships was mistaken throughout. At this time *Deutschland* was in Kiel.)

1704   *Scharnhorst* opened fire on *Rawalpindi.* Range 4 miles.

1740   *From Gneisenau to Scharnhorst*
        Close the enemy.

1745   *From Gneisenau to Scharnhorst*
        Pick up 2 boatloads of survivors.

1746   *From Newcastle*
        Gun flashes bearing O50° my position (given).

1750   *From Newcastle*
        Ship indicated is on fire.

1815   *From Rawalpindi* (Ship is now blazing. Signal made from stern)
        Please send boats.

1817   At 13,000 yards range *Newcastle* read the following from *Scharnhorst* made by flashlamp:
        UM UM GO GO FOLGEN.

1819   *From Newcastle*
        2 unknown vessels bearing 060°, 6 miles, course unknown, position (given).

1821   *From C.-in-C. Home Fleet to Newcastle*
        Your 1746. *Rawalpindi* is in action with German armoured ship of *Deutschland* class.

1900   *From Newcastle*
        My 1819. Vessels were hostile. Have lost touch.

1912   *From Gneisenau to Scharnhorst*
        How long do you require to pick up survivors. Make all haste.

1913   *From Scharnhorst to Gneisenau*
        About 15 minutes.

1914   *From Gneisenau to Scharnhorst*
        Cease picking up survivors immediately. Follow Gneisenau.

1920   *From Scharnhorst to Gneisenau*
        Vessel bearing 150° showing no lights.

1932   *From Gneisenau to Scharnhorst*
        Make smoke

1934   *From C.-in-C. Home Fleet to Newcastle*
        Your 1900. Consider that German armoured ship

Deutschland class is homeward bound. Make every endeavour to
regain touch.

1937   *From Scharnhorst to Gneisenau*
Unknown vessel no longer in sight.

1959   *From Scharnhorst to Gneisenau*
Prisoners state sunken enemy ship was merchant cruiser Rawalpindi, armament 8 6-in. guns, 2 A.A. guns, Crew approximately 700 men. Scharnhorst hit on quarter deck but deck not penetrated.

2005   *From Newcastle*
Nothing in sight, my position (given).

1300/27   *Gneisenau* and *Scharnhorst* anchored Wilhelmshaven.

Came the German sea invasion of Norway in the spring of 1940, there was obviously a booking here for this double-turn, and indeed in the first week of April they set off to the northward escorting Invasion Group 1, consisting of 10 destroyers carrying 2,000 troops destined for Narvik.

According to plan they slipped their charges at Vestfiord who proceeded unchallenged to their objective, while *Scharnhorst* and *Gneisenau* carried on north into the Arctic on a diversionary cruise.

In the early hours of 9 April *Scharnhorst* and *Gneisenau* were sighted in appalling weather against the dawn light by H.M.S. *Renown*. A long range gun-duel followed in which both *Renown* and *Gneisenau* received flesh wounds. When the German pair increased speed to 28 knots into the gale, the weather stepped in and put their forward turrets out of action, but they got away to complete their mission.

Sinking of GLORIOUS
8th June 1940

In early June, 1940, the two battlecruisers were at sea again with Admiral Marschall flying his flag in *Gneisenau*. This time they were accompanied by *Hipper* and four destroyers and they were on a more ambitious mission. If the admiral had obeyed his orders to attack Harstadt, our Norwegian base, there is no knowing what they might have run into, for we were busy evacuating at that time. But instead he decided to attack shipping, and on 8th June he and his force had quite a busy day.

At 0605 *Scharnhorst* sighted the tanker *Oil Pioneer,* escorted by the trawler *Juniper.* By 0717 the tanker and trawler were sinking. At 1002 their aircraft reported a transport (*Orama*) and a hospital ship (*Atlantis*). By 1206 *Orama* was sinking. The hospital ship was not molested. *Hipper* and the destroyers were then detached, and the redoubtable pair struck out towards Jan Mayen Island, in quest of a reported aircraft carrier.

Glorious at that time was proceeding home independently, escorted by destroyers *Acasta* and *Ardent. Veteran* and *Vanoc* were on their way from Harstadt to supplement the escort. One would imagine *Glorious* would have been flying a defensive air patrol but she was not. Everyone onboard was tired out after prolonged round-the-clock flying operations. She thought she was clear and safe. Beneath the smoke which *Scharnhorst* sighted at 1700 probably about 70 per cent of the officers and men were asleep. The German plan to close quickly and disable the flight deck before aircraft could be flown off was successful. From the start *Glorious* never had a hope. The action cost the German battlecruisers a mere 400 rounds of ammunition, and two hours of their time.

The two destroyers fought back magnificently. The Germans were amazed at their courage. *Ardent* shielded *Glorious* for a while by laying a smoke screen, *Acasta* closed and attacked *Scharnhorst* and scored a fine torpedo hit which was to put her out of action for several months. The bravery of those two captains, especially *Acasta's,* was of the highest. One still wonders why it was never officially recognised.

At 1808 Admiral Marschall had signalled to Gruppe North:

ENEMY AIRCRAFT CARRIER IN POSITION(GIVEN) PROCEEDING AT FULL SPEED ON A SOUTH EASTERLY COURSE.

With wireless telegraphy as it was at that time, news of an engagement should have reached the authorities while it was in progress or soon afterwards. The tragedy of the *Glorious* was an exception. Our first official report of the engagement was passed to Commander—in—Chief Home Fleet from hand to hand a week or so later, as it might have been brought by a frigate in the days before wireless was thought of.

When *Scharnhorst* and *Gneisenau* had replied to *Ardent's* signal challenge with salvoes of 11in., an enemy report was immediately initiated by *Glorious's* Captain. An aircraft carrier is a network of wireless installations and aerials. With all this equipment available, however, the Warrant Telegraphist who was handling this signal and trying to get it away, soon found himself in a race with the German gunners. Wherever he turned the apparatus was smashed by enemy shells.

No signal was sent by either of the destroyers. Whenever an enemy was sighted simultaneously by destroyer and big ship, it was conventional in those days for the big ship to make the reporting signal. No allowance was made for the big ship not being able to do so.

As the situation in *Glorious* became desperate, the Warrant Telegraphist fell back on an improvised wireless set rigged on the bridge for the purpose of communicating with aircraft. It was the last hope. Believing that the first reporting signal had been sent and that it would have been read (which, sad to say was not the case) he managed to send this amplifying report:

MY 1615. TWO POCKET BATTLESHIPS

This signal was read by only one ship, and that ship unfortunately could neither retransmit it nor act upon it. The cruiser *Devonshire* received it at 1720. She had sailed the previous day from Tromso for England with the King of Norway onboard. She was therefore keeping strict wireless silence and could only hope that someone else had read it as well.

Returning to the *Atlantis*: in return for not being attacked, she had played her international part as a hospital ship by not reporting the enemy by wireless. She remained silent until contacted by the battleship *Valiant* the following day. So by the time it was safe for *Devonshire* to pass on the brief signal from *Glorious* the evidence we had was: this brief signal, the report from *Atlantis* to *Valiant,* our inability to contact *Glorious* by wireless, and the German radio. The only British naval men who knew the full story were now struggling in the cold water on rafts and wreckage with their ships sunk deep beneath them.

Some of these survivors were picked up by a ship and taken to Norway where they became prisoners of war. About thirty others were found by another ship and taken to the Faroes. Here they were collected by *Veteran* and *Vanoc,* the destroyers who had been on their way to supplement *Glorious's* escort.

As the destroyers left the Faroes the weather was bright and sunny and arrangements were made for the survivors to recline on the upper deck. But no, they had had enough unrelieved daylight in the latitudes of the midnight sun. They had had 56 hours in the water, uncertain whether the enemy would return and find them. All they wanted now was food, warmth, some light music from the BBC and—darkness. The tragedy of the *Glorious* was extracted from them as they lay in the dark. By torchlight notes were made from which a report was drawn up. As *Veteran* passed through the Pentland Skerries on her way to Rosyth this report was shot across by rocket gun-line to another destroyer waiting outside Scapa Flow. The second destroyer returned to the Fleet Flagship and so the grim facts were eventually placed before the Commander-in-Chief Home Fleet.

But the sad incident has a shining postcript. A Leading Seamen Carter, manning *Acasta's* torpedo-tubes was picked up, and his story eventually found its way into Winston Churchill's history of World War II. *Ardent* received a direct hit early on which sank her, leaving *Acasta* on her own. Brilliantly handled in and out of home-made smoke by Charles Glasfurd, her imperturbable Captain, she scored a magnificient torpedo hit on *Scharnhorst* before being sunk. "When I was in the water" Carter ends his report, 'I saw the Captain leaning over the bridge take a cigarette from his case and light it. We shouted to him to come on our raft, he waved "Goodbye and good luck" — the end of a gallant man.' By a strange shuffle of events *Scharnhorst's* gunnery officer on that occasion was plucked out of the water by *Vanoc* when he was later serving in a U-boat which *Vanoc* sank. The German officer confirmed the damage to Scharnhorst and described in glowing terms *Acasta's* skill and bravery.

This sortie marked a split between Admiral Marschall and his Commander-in-Chief, Admiral Raeder. Marschall's report on the operation was one long grumble about the risks he was forced to take and the inadequacy of his weapons. On one page of this report Rear Admiral Fricke, Chief of Naval Operations, writes in the margin "To hell! What is needed is a grasp of this new tactical role and a determination to take opportunities, if results are to be achieved."

Needless to say, Admiral Marschall did not remain in this command.

Operations in the Atlantic
22nd January—22nd March 1941

In the winter of 1940—41 the German naval staff supplemented their U-boats with surface ships. *Hipper* operated to the southward as one unit, and on the 28th December *Gneisenau* hoisted the flag of Admiral Lutjens and sailed with *Scharnhorst* to harass the north Atlantic convoy routes. They ran into exceptionally vicious weather off Norway which damaged *Gneisenau's* foc's'le beyond the resources of Norwegian dockyards, and, back they came.

On 22nd January they set out once more from Kiel. The Admiral hoped to break through into the Atlantic south of Iceland but very soon he sensed that the Home Fleet was barring his way. On the night of 28th/29th in seasonable weather the Germans brushed against a line of cruisers, and were extremely lucky in managing to slip round them. These three signals show how lucky they were.

1445/28 *From C.-in-C. Home Fleet to Admiralty*
> Am discontinuing search. Intend to return to Scapa Flow with my force arriving a.m. 30 January if no further information is recieved.

Just as they were turning for home:
0140/29 *From Naiad to C.-in-C. Home Fleet*
> Am chasing two unknown ships approximate course 070°, my position (given).

The contact was lost and nothing further was reported. The C.-in-C. summed up as follows:
0027/31 *From C.-in-C. Home Fleet to Admiralty*
> Investigation of (*Naiad's*) report of sighting unknown ships produces evidence that is far from conclusive. Snow squalls made visibility and Radar conditions patchy and liable to be misleading. There is a small possibility that, if a fast enemy vessel was present she could have worked round to northward and then to westward without being detected. I consider it unlikely that an enemy ship was present.

There was no doubt about the contact with *Naiad* in Admiral Lutjens' mind. His summing up was that either they had not been seen or they would run into stronger opposition concentrated ahead. It was a great relief therefore when they found a hole in the

H

ice and in their opponents' defences, through the Denmark Strait twenty miles from the coast of Iceland. At noon on 3rd February the Admiral expressed his relief in this signal:

> *For the first time in the history of German warfare German battleships have succeeded in safely breaking through to the Atlantic. Go to it.*

Later that day they had additional reassurance that they had not been spotted breaking through.

2217/3   *From Gruppe North*
> *Air reconnaissance of Scapa Flow at 1530 shows following ships present. 7 battleships and heavy cruisers, 4 light cruisers.*

Having fuelled from their auxiliaries south of Greenland they turned their attention to the northern convoy route on which vital war material was passing in the big HX convoys from Halifax to England. They did not have to wait long.

0835/8   *From Gneisenau to Scharnhorst*
> *Convoy in sight (position given) probably HX 108* (it was HX 106).

0841   *From Gneisenau to Scharnhorst*
> *Enemy steering 045°. Intend to attack from the south. Expect you to attack from the north at 1030.*

0928   *From Scharnhorst*
> *One battleship Ramillies class (position given).*

0947   *From Gneisenau*
> *Break off engagement taking avoiding action to southward. Assemble (position given astern of the convoy)*

1050/8   *From Ramillies to Admiralty*
> *At 1000 in position (given) had brief glimpse of mast and top of warship possibly German Hipper class. . . .*

When *Gneisenau* and *Scharnhorst* met astern of the convoy the Admiral learnt that *Scharnhorst* had deliberately shown herself to *Ramillies* in the hope of drawing her away from the convoy and leaving it on a plate for *Gneisenau*. This was not at all according to the Admiral's plan—a fact which he expressed in some heated visual signals which unfortunately are not recorded. The Admiral knew the British could not afford a battleship with every convoy. He therefore decided to leave HX 106 well alone, without revealing his presence, and wait for the next. *Scharnhorst* had spoilt the whole thing. Gruppe West would have to be told. Breaking wireless silence on this sort of operation was an unpleasant risk but now it had to be accepted.

0800/9   *From Gneisenau to Gruppe West*
        Operation has been identified by the enemy.

Gruppe West acted on this by throwing out a hint to *Hipper* who was operating against our Atlantic trade further south.

0100/10   *Gruppe West to Hipper*
        Gneisenau reports operation has been identified by the enemy Hipper now able to operate.

Hipper interpreted this correctly as a suggestion that she should cause a diversion in her area.

        From Hipper
        Have attacked convoy south east of Azores. 13 ships sunk.
        Returning to Brest. Expect to arrive 14 February.

This was splendid news for Lutjens. If only another less heavily escorted HX convoy would turn up. But he saw nothing except one or two independently routed ships which he sank.

Gneisenau again broke wireless silence, this time with short transmissions at short intervals. In these signals she told Gruppe West that no convoy had appeared since the heavily guarded HX 106 fourteen days ago. She added that their oiler had not turned up at the appointed rendezvous, and that they were running short of fuel. Also that the score, to date, was 25,000 tons of shipping sunk. To dispel any feeling of disappointment in his Squadron the Admiral handed out a bouquet:

27/2   *From Admiral Lutjens*
        Battleships have covered in this operation up to now over 11,000 miles which is equal to half way round the world. I express my full appreciation to the engine room personnel of my battleships for this record efficiency.

But the area was not productive enough, and the Admiral decided to move.

28/2   *From Gneisenau to Gruppe West*
        I am shifting my operational area to area Madeira and Cape Verde Islands.

On the way south he was reported by a U-boat, whose Commanding Officer did not seem very efficient at recognising men-o'-war.

2307/6/3 *From U-124*
        Two unidentified battleships in position (given).

The Admiral, noting he was in the position signalled, lost no time in telling the U-boat who she was reporting.

On 8th March their luck changed.

0920/8   *From Scharnhorst*
             Convoy in sight (position given).

0930/8   *From Scharnhorst*
             Enemy battleships Malaya class in sight on westerly course.

This time the Admiral advanced more boldly to sound the strength of the escort. Mistaking a destroyer for a cruiser he considered this Sierra Leone convoy was also too tough a proposition. He therefore reported it, for the benefit of the U-boats, and once again retired with *Scharnhorst*. This is what was seen from the convoy

1600/8   *From Malaya*
             One large vessel, uncertain whether battleship or battle-cruiser (position given) distance 40 miles.

1745/8   *From Malaya*
             Enemy in sight. Battlecruiser *Scharnhorst*. My position (given).

1748/8   *From Malaya*
             Enemy retiring westward.

Malaya eventually reported the affair as follows:

             From Malaya to Admiralty

             During afternoon 8 March *Forester* was sent 10 miles west of convoy to keep down submarines if shadowing. at 1331 she reported ship, apparently warship and was ordered to investigate. At 1410 she reported by W/T sighting top and 1 funnel, and at 1442 possibly *Gneisenau*. *Malaya* and *Faulknor* proceeded clear of convoy to west. *Cecilia* remained with convoy which turned north-east. Further reports showed enemy altering course at high speed. *Malaya* and *Faulknor* continued to close and at 1515 aircraft was catapulted. At 1645 sighted enemy *Scharnhorst* class distance 15 miles. At 1648 enemy altered course to south-west and increased speed. He appeared to have turrets trained fore and aft. Being unable to close range *Malaya* and destroyers turned at once to regain convoy before dark. At 1659 aircraft reported 2 *Scharnhorst* class, confirmed at 1703. *Malaya* rejoined convoy at 1900. Aircraft lost *Malaya* and forcelanded after dark.

In the meantime the U-boats made contact.

0142/9   *From U-124*

Have contacted convoy.

0225/9 *From U-105*
Convoy in sight.

Between them they sank five ships. In the meantime the Admiral was feeling the call of the HX route once more.

2055/9 *From Gneisenau to Gruppe West*
Proceeding to fuel from Erinland. After provisioning proceeding at end of week with supply ships to HX route.

But the German naval staff made reservations.

2100/11 *From German Naval War Staff to Gneisenau*
Operations on HX route permitted only up to 17/3. While still remaining at sea concentrate on causing diversionary action by effective reappearance in Azores and Cape Verde area as soon as possible after 17/3 to facilitate the homeward passage of Hipper and Scheer through Iceland Strait during new moon period. Undue prolongation of current operations not desirable in view of Bismarck and Prinz Eugen being ready for action at end of April and in view of efforts being made to have Gneisenau and Scharnhorst ready for action at the same time. Also possible to divert enemy from passage of Hipper and Scheer through Iceland Straits by a well timed entry into French coast port.

13/3 *From Gneisenau*
Estimate Gneisenau will need 4 weeks and Scharnhorst 10 for repairs.

Again no HX convoy was contacted. Spread out with their auxiliary ships, however, they swept the shipping lanes with the following formidable results.

2157/15 *From Admiralty*
Following intercepted from S.S. *Simnia*. Am being attacked by surface raider in position (given). *Simnia* being shelled.

0308/16 *From Admiralty*
S.S. *Athel Foam* reports being shelled by warship raider in position (given).

0430/16 *From Admiralty*
My 2157/15 and 0308/16. It is possible these attacks were carried out by *Scharnhorst* and *Gneisenau*.

1858/16   *From Admiralty*
S.S. *Metirton* being attacked by surface raider in position (given).

1858/16   *From Admiralty*
S.S. *Demerton* being attacked by surface raider.

2055/16   *From Admiralty*
Following has been intercepted. S.S. *Chilean Reefer* being attacked and shelled by surface raider in position (given).

2129/16   *From Rodney*
One unknown vessel in position (given).

2159/16   *From Rodney*
Enemy almost certainly warship disappeared to north eastward in darkness. One large vessel presumed tanker also seen but lost during darkness. Am rejoining convoy HX 114.

2355/16   *From Rodney*
Captain and Chief Officer of *Chilean Reefer* picked up with 24 survivors, both stating quite clearly enemy warship was *Gneisenau*. Also state she altered course to south eastward after initial retirement to north east. Ship observed by survivors signalling with red and green lights in front bridge to another vessel thought to be tanker referred to.

Once again, a battleship frightened the Germans away, but not before they had accounted for sixteen ships between them. By now Admiral Lutjens knew he had been reported; he believed Force H, consisting of *Renown* and the aircraft carrier *Ark Royal*, was searching for him to the southward. It seemed that the Atlantic was getting a bit hot. So:

0100/19   *From Gneisenau to Gruppe West*
Am returning to Brest.

Gneisenau and *Scharnhorst* anchored at Brest at 0750 on 22nd March, after their greatest combined achievement. In the sixty days they had been at sea together they had steamed 17,800 miles, sinking twenty-two ships totalling 115,622 tons. Admiral Raeder showed his appreciation by means of the following signal:

21st   *From German Naval Commander-in-Chief to Admiral*
March   *Lutjens*
On completion of the first occasion in German naval history on which a squadron of our Battleships has operated successfully in the wide spaces of the Atlantic,

I congratulate you and your subordinates for the fine resolution you have shown and the splendid results you have achieved. I appreciate the vital part played by supply and escort ships, who also receive my fullest praise. I hope before long to be able to put an even stronger force under your command for a similar operation on the high seas.

Escape from Brest
12th February 1942

After the *Bismarck* action *Scharnhorst* and *Gneisenau* were joined at Brest by *Prinz Eugen*. During 1941 the three ships were attacked by 1,875 aircraft. 1,962 tons of bombs were hurled at them, and each ship was only hit once. But this could not last. By the beginning of 1942 the ships were obviously doomed if they stayed much longer. At a conference on 12th January Hitler likened them to someone suffering from cancer. Without an operation they would die. An operation might save them.

Against all advice he decided that they should return to Germany by the Channel route. He was convinced the British were incapable of reacting quickly enough to such a bold plan.

The whole operation depended on surprise. It hinged on how far east the ships could get before they were discovered. This meant secrecy in its strictest sense. Apart from secrecy in planning the operation it must be carried out without a whisper. Here are Admiral Cilliax's signed orders for the operation:

"Destroyers are to take into account that changes of course and speed will not be transmitted, as there are no secure means of signalling. THEREFORE VIGILANCE. . . . The compulsory route provided must be sufficient guide for the course to be followed by the formation.

"Wireless is to be used only when there is definite contact with the enemy or if it has first been used by the Officer Commanding the formation or if from an independent observation it is thought that there is acute danger to the formation which can not be averted or indicated by any other means."

Anything involving co-ordinated movement undertaken by people separated from one another is better achieved if it is carried out in silence. The silence suggests those taking part are sure of themselves and their confederates. But this needs practice and more practice. Those concerned must know one another. Here was an operation which demanded this high quality of cooperation but offered little or no practice beforehand, and probably all taking part were strangers.

Nevertheless, by making full use of the gaps between the Royal Air Force bombs, sporadic trials were carried out, and by 4th February the three ships were ready for the fray.

On the morning of 11th February came the signal from Gruppe West to Flag Officer *Scharnhorst*. It was one of the five code words given to this operation, and it was the warning for the operation to begin that night. Shortly before casting off there was an air raid which delayed the ships getting off the mark.

This was a moment of naval history when a signal of any sort might have brought disaster. Nevertheless one cannot help sympathising with Admiral Cilliax's desire to make a signal at midnight when the formation was 72 minutes astern of schedule. The needle timing planned for contacting his air and surface forces ahead must stand. There was nothing he could do about it except hope that the delay had been observed and checked all the way through. But he always had one consolation. The longer the silence lasted the nearer he was to home.

When 10 o'clock and 10.30 came and went on the following clear morning, there was, to every German's astonishment, NO indication that the formation's presence was known. By 11 the formation had appeared on a British radar screen, 27 miles south-west of Gris Nez, but it had not been taken very seriously. The first sighting, the manner in which they were first reported, is unique and certainly worth a place in this collection.

At the time R.A.F. Fighter Group was engaged in making offensive sweeps, beyond the range of radar, to harass enemy sorties from Northern France. Their long range requirements precluded the planes from carrying wireless or even radio telephone equipment. They were cut off from the world immediately they were airborne. The weather on the morning of the 12th was poor for their job, so the experienced Station Commander, Group Captain Victor Beamish, and Wing Commander Boyd, had taken a hand. They set out on a sweep about 10.00. Off the French coast they sighted two German fighters which they chased at full speed. When they looked down they were amazed to find themselves above two large warships surrounded by escort vessels. Barely had they recognised the ships than they were set upon by a swarm of enemy fighters. They managed to disentangle themselves and streaked for home to report the news by word of mouth at 1.09 as soon as they landed.

The tidings of this alarming affair were, in fact, delivered on foot, as they would have been in the Old Testament.

There was, indeed, a British plan to counter such an operation. The Admiralty had foreseen the likelihood of the enemy breaking eastwards, and had ordered six destroyers and six MTB's to be at immediate readiness. Vice-Admiral Dover signalled the orders to the destroyers:

> If signal "Proceed in execution of previous orders" is made, destroyers are to proceed forthwith at best speed to NE Hinder Whistle Buoy. You will be kept informed of movements of enemy ships through Dover Strait, and you should endeavour to intercept in the approximate (position given). Motor Torpedo Boats will not operate north of (latitude given). Acknowledge.

On the fateful night of 11th/12th February this precaution had been signalled to the destroyers.

2017/11 *From Vice-Admiral Dover to Captain of 21st Destroyer*
Feb./42 *Flotilla*
> Come to 15 minutes notice at 0400/12 and revert to 4 hours notice at 0700/12 unless otherwise ordered.

But to be effective, any plan of attack by us needed more time to develop than was given by an announcement that the enemy was passing Le Touquet at high speed. At 11.45 Vice Admiral Dover directed his only available cat towards the pigeons.

1145 *From Vice-Admiral Dover to Destroyers*
> Proceed in execution of previous orders.

At 12.22 the Motor Torpedo Boats attacked, at 1245 torpedo carrying aircraft attacked, around 1600 the Destroyers attacked. *Scharnhorst* struck two mines, *Gneisenau* one. Admiral Cilliax transferred to a destroyer, it broke down. The formation became separated. But all three ships arrived in German ports, afloat, and the following day brought this signal:

1420/ *From German Naval Commander-in-Chief to Admiral Cilliax.*

> *The transfer of the Brest Group into the German Bight, having been carefully planned by Staffs and Escort groups, was carried out with exemplary dash and skill. I convey to you, your commanding officers, your officers and crews my congratulations in recognition of this operation. I have asked the Commander-in-Chief Air to*

convey my thanks to all those who took part.

With this well-deserved congratulatory signal from their Commander-in-Chief, so ended probably the most formidable partnership in naval history, spread over 2 wars and 36 years.

The fate of *Gneisenau* is thus described in the history book. "After the German Battle Cruisers reached their home bases Bomber Command renewed its effort to destroy them. The *Gneisenau* was hit twice by heavy bombs while in the floating dock at Kiel on the night of 26/27 February 1942. Though the British authorities could not, of course, be aware of it, the cumulative effect of the damage received at Brest, of the mine explosions while on passage, and the latest bomb hits was so serious that it was estimated that a year under repair was necessary. in fact her refit was finally abandoned in January 1943, and this fine ship, which had many times caused us trouble and anxiety, thereafter gradually decayed into a disarmed and useless hulk."

But her sister fought on.

The Sinking of SCHARNHORST
26th December 1943

On Christmas Day, 1943, *Scharnhorst* lay anchored up a fjord on the north coast of Norway. The damaged *Tirpitz* lay there too, but no *Gneisenau*. After all the adventures they had been through together their partnership had ended. Down south *Gneisenau* burned for three days after R.A.F. bombers had pounded her in a German dockyard. Her fighting days were over.

It was sad, but it had no effect on the morale of *Scharnhorst*. She was a proud ship. She had a ship's company who believed in her. At that particular moment they also believed they were set for an enjoyable and relaxed Christmas.

The Christmas mail had been distributed, Captain's rounds were over. They had been quite informal. So far the men liked Captain Hintz, but he had only taken over command in October and had not yet taken the ship to sea. Before him had been Captain Hueffmeier. It was not difficult to be an improvement on him. He was unpopular and, worse still, he was no seaman. He had put the ship ashore, he had collided with a U-boat. Why on earth did they ever have to promote his predecessor, Captain Hoffman, to Admiral? Captain Hoffman was worshipped by everyone. He was the man who had built up their morale and made the ship unsinkable. So much for her Captains. There lay the ship, peaceful and majestic in a setting appropriate for a Christmas card.

And it was peaceful, at least it was up to 1 p.m. Then, through the ship's loudspeakers, came the jarring warning to prepare for sea. Throughout the afternoon came other tiresome and disturbing messages. At five, Rear Admiral Bey and his staff bundled on board from *Tirpitz*, for their own Admiral Kummetz was on leave. At seven *Scharnhorst* slid through the Arctic gloom down the fjord accompanied by five destroyers.

Ahead of them, up in the Barents Strait steamed their objective, a Russian-bound convoy. This had just been made clear in a signal from Admiral Doenitz.

> *From German Commander-in-Chief to Scharnhorst*
> *Attack and destroy the convoy to alleviate the struggle*
> *of your comrades on the Eastern front.*

Escorting the convoy were fifteen destroyers and two corvettes, led by the captain of the 17th Destroyer Flotilla in *Onslow*. Supporting the escort were the cruisers *Sheffield*, *Norfolk* and their flagship *Belfast*. In the background lay the Commander-in-Chief, Home Fleet in *Duke of York*, with the curiser *Jamaica*, and four destroyers.

In latitudes where no daylight relieves the night at that time of year, and in brutal, raw weather, the situation on Boxing Day, 1943, developed thus:

0652   *From C.-in-C. to Belfast*
       Close convoy for mutual support.

When the crew of *Scharnhorst* went to Action Stations at 0700 she was struggling into the teeth of an Arctic gale. The peace of the anchorage they had left had faded completely.

0720   *From Scharnhorst to Destroyers*
       Seek and shadow convoy.

0825   *From Z29 (destroyer leader)*
       Silhouette sighted distance 4 miles.

The German destroyer crews were new and inexperienced and probably very seasick. Most of the signals which passed between them and *Scharnhorst* were too garbled to be intercepted and recorded. Nevertheless inexperience alone hardly explains why the German flotilla took such a small part in the action which follows.

0844   *From Belfast*
       Unidentified Radar contact on bearing 295°, 16 miles.

0906   *From Sheffield*
       Unidentified Radar contact on bearing 258°, 10 miles.

0906   *From Norfolk*
Unidentified Radar contact on bearing 261°, 12 miles.
From Belfast
Enemy in sight bearing 222°.
    (Cruisers passed reports of enemy continuously until 1044.)

0927   *From Belfast to Norfolk*
Open fire.
    (About 0930 a shell, probably from *Norfolk*, disabled Scharnhorst's Radar equipment which, in this visibility, virtually "blinded" her.)

0946   *From Belfast*
Enemy's speed 28 knots.

0955   *From Scharnhorst*
Have been fired on (position given) by what appeared to be cruiser using radar-controlled firing apparatus.

0958   *From C.-in-C. to Onslow (repeated Belfast)*
Send 4 destroyers to join *Belfast*.

1001   *From Scharnhorst*
Check fire.

1012   *From Scharnhorst*
Aircraft reported unidentified vessel in (position given) thought to be Commander-in-Chief, Home Fleet.

1013   *From Z29*
Am advancing into immediate vicinity of convoy, according to plan. Course 230° speed 12 knots.

1020   *From Onslow to C.-in-C. (repeated Belfast)*
Musketeer, Matchless, Opportune, Virago detailed.

1044   *From Belfast*
Have lost touch with enemy who is steering north. Am closing convoy.
    (By steering north at high speed, *Scharnhorst* hoped to work round behind the cruisers and attack the convoy.)

1055   *From Scharnhorst to Destroyers*
What is your position, course and speed.

1103   *From C.-in-C. to Belfast*
Unless touch can be regained by some unit there is no chance of my finding enemy.

1125   *From C.-in-C. to Onslow*
Use your discretion regarding mean course of convoy.

1131   *From Onslaught (with convoy) to Onslow*

Have obtained Radar contact bearing 150°, 6½ miles.

1134   *From Onslow to Onslaught*
Investigate.

1135   *From Belfast*
Onslaught's contact is me.

1205   *From Belfast*
Unidentified Radar contact bearing 075°, 13 miles.

1220   *From Belfast*
Enemy in sight bearing 090°.

1220   *From Belfast to Cruisers*
Open fire.

1230   *From Norfolk to Belfast*
Norfolk hit aft.

1240   *From Scharnhorst*
Scharnhorst in action with several units in position (given) and being fired on by one heavy unit using radar-controlled firing apparatus.

In this encounter *Sheffield* had a near miss from *Scharnhorst*. She reported later that bits of shell up to football size came inboard.

1253   *From C.-in-C.*
Enemy aircraft is shadowing me.

1256   *From Gruppe-North*
All aircraft withdrawn on account of weather.

1318   *From C.-in-C. to Belfast*
Report composition of enemy.

1325   *From Belfast*
One heavy ship.

1418   *From Scharnhorst to Destroyers*
Break away, put into harbour.

1435   *From C.-in-C. to Belfast*
Have you destroyers in company.

1442   *From Belfast*
No, they are following.

1449   *From C.-in-C.*
If practicable, intend to engage from the westward on a similar course.

1450   *From Belfast*
Enemy position course and speed (given).

1551 *From C.-in-C. to Home Fleet in Company*
The estimated bearing and distance of the enemy from me are 025°, 25 miles.

1551   *From Norfolk*
        I have a fire in my wing compartment oil fuel tank.
        Cannot be controlled unless ship stops rolling.
1612   *From Belfast to Sheffield*
        Come on.
1620   *From Sheffield to Belfast*
        Am following you. My maximum speed is 23 knots.
1635   *From C.-in-C to Belfast*
        Prepare to fire star-shell over enemy.
1636   *From C.-in-C.*
        Unidentified Radar contact on bearing 020°, 13 miles.
1640   *From C.-in-C. to Destroyers in Company*
        Take up advantageous positions for firing torpedoes but
        do not attack until ordered.
            (At 1645 *Duke of York* opened fire, by Radar, on
        Scharnhorst.)
1646   *From C.-in-C. to Belfast*
        Open fire with star-shell.

After the second engagement with the cruisers *Scharnhorst*
seemed to abandon the idea of attacking the convoy. The crew
relaxed. Some were allowed to leave their Action Stations where
they had been for nine cold hours. Except for the Radar the ship
was undamaged. With their speed, and nothing opposing them
heavier than cruisers they could withdraw when they chose. The
heavy gun flashes of *Duke of York* followed by the arrival of
armour-piercing shell was therefore a very unpleasant surprise.

1656   *From Scharnhorst*
        Am in action with heavy Battleship.
1657   *From Scharnhorst*
        My position (given) maintaining contact.
1700   *From Admiral, Norway*
        U-boats form a new patrol line (given).
1702   *From C.-in-C. to Belast*
        Any further news.
1713   *From C.-in-C. to Destroyers in Company*
        Destroyers close and attack with torpedoes as soon as
        possible.
1720   *From Belfast*
        Out of touch.
1723   *From C.-in-C. to Belfast*
        Steer south to get between enemy and his base.

1724   *From Scharnhorst*
        Am surrounded by a strong force.
1724   *From C.-in-C. to Belfast*
        Steer 140° and join me.
1808   *From C.-in-C.*
        By Radar enemy bears 070°, 9 miles.
1810   *From C.-in-C. to Scorpion* (destroyer)
        Can you report my fall of shot.
1813   *From Scorpion*
        Your last salvo 200 yards short.
1815   *From Admiral, Norway*
        U-boats close Scharnhorst at full speed.
1816   *From Scorpion*
        Can only see occasional splashes owing to smoke.
        (After 52nd salvo, about this time, *Duke of York*
        checked fire to allow destroyers to press home torpedo
        attacks.)
1828   *From C.-in-C.*
        By Radar enemy bears 069°, 10 miles.
1847   *From C.-in-C. to Belfast*
        I see little hope of catching *Scharnhorst* and am pro-
        ceeding to support convoy.

At 1830 *Scharnhorst's* speed was still undiminished and she was
drawing out of range of *Duke of York,* still confident of escape.
Then grey shadows emerged which turned into British destroyers.
At this stage there was an argument between the 1st and 2nd
Gunnery Control Officer on account of which the vital secondary
armament barrage was delayed. This allowed our destroyers to
creep relentlessly into their attacking positions.

1852   *From Savage* (destroyer)
        Am proceeding to attack.
1852   *From Scorpion*
        Attack completed.
1853   *From Stord* (destroyer)
        Attack completed.
1853   *From Savage*
        Attack completed.
            (There were several underwater explosions heard in
        Belfast at 1858.)
1900   *From Scharnhorst to The Fuehrer*
        We shall fight to the last shell. Scharnhorst onwards.

In a broadcast from the bridge Captain Hintz said to ship's company:

> *I shake you all by the hand for the last time.*

1906   *From C.-in-C. to Jamaica*
Finish her off with torpedoes.

1944   *From C.-in-C.*
All destroyers without torpedoes join me.

1954   *From C.-in-C. to Home Fleet in Company*
Clear the area of the target except for those ships with torpedoes and one destroyer with searchlight.

1956   *From Scorpion*
A lot of wreckage on sea, am closing now.

2012   *From Scorpion*
Am picking up German survivors.

2015   *From C.-in-C.*
Please confirm *Scharnhorst* is sunk.

2018   *From Scorpion*
Survivors are from *Scharnhorst.*

(It was a coincidence that the Captain of the destroyer *Scorpion* bore a strong physical resemblance to the German Admiral Bey. This was almost too much for the German survivors.)

2019   *From C.-in-C.*
Has *Scharnhorst* sunk.

2032   *From Belfast*
Satisfied that *Scharnhorst* is sunk. Where shall I join you.

2100   *From C.-in-C. to Admiralty*
Scharnhorst sunk.

2153   *From Admiralty to C.-in-C. (repeated Belfast)*
Grand. Well done.

SCHARNHORST

GNEISENAU

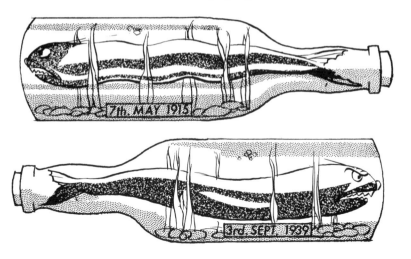

TWO HISTORIC TORPEDOES

Of all the British merchantmen sunk by enemy action in the two World Wars, the sad fate of *Lusitania* in the first, and *Athenia* in the second war will be remembered for ever, not only because they were passenger ships but because many of the passengers who were drowned were Americans. U.S.A. had not entered either war when these sinkings occurred, but such ruthlessness to their men, women, and children must have slanted many minds of many citizens of the United States towards doing so.

The mighty 30,393 ton Cunarder, *Lusitania*, approaching the south coast of Ireland from the Atlantic, had made her landfall when Kapitan Leutnant Schweiger's patience on U-boat patrol, some 10 miles south of the Old Head of Kinsale, was rewarded. A glance through U-20's periscope confirmed that the smudge of smoke which had made him dive had solidified into the prize he had been waiting for. Manoeuvring U-20 on to the starboard bow of his target, at 2.10pm on 7 May, 1915, he fired a single torpedo at a range of about 800 yards, which struck *Lusitania* abaft her bridge. She sank in 18 minutes. 1,021 men, women and children were killed. As she heeled over to starboard her radio officer managed to transmit one emergency broadcast, shortly after 2.15:

LUSITANIA SOS SOS. COME AT ONCE. BIG LIST.

I

Kapitan Leutenant Schweiger's object had been to sink the *Lusitania*. He identified her at the outset, achieved his object, and on his return to Germany he was commended by his superiors.

The sinking of the *Athenia* was a very different story.

This Donaldson Atlantic liner of 13,000 tons—a mere shadow of her illustrious ancestor—had fame thrust upon her by circumstances. In August 1939, as war clouds gathered over Europe, it became increasingly probable that by the time she was ready to sail from Glasgow she would be the only passenger liner facing the Atlantic on schedule. Others, including the *Queen Mary,* were due, but had either been cancelled or taken out of service, and every day Americans, Canadians, and mothers anxious to get their children well clear of Europe turned hopefully to *Athenia*.

She left Glasgow on 1 September, called at Belfast and Liverpool to squeeze in more passengers, and by 4am on that fateful 3 September she was dropping the Inishtrahull light astern and facing 2,5000 miles of Atlantic at 15 knots, with 1,2000 passengers packed tight.

When Oberleutnant Fritz Lemp took his 650-ton Submarine U-30 out of Wilhelmshaven at 4am on 22 August, she was one of 18 U-boats heading for their waiting areas in the Atlantic, from which they would either be ordered to take up prescribed patrols if war was declared or recalled if it wasn't. By 2pm on 3 September he was in his patrol area with a broken seal on the envelope of his orders telling him to wage war in accordance with the rules of International Law which restricted his attention of merchant shipping to those carrying troops, war material, or escorted by warships.

At about 7pm he saw a formidable darkened ship approaching from the eastward at 15 knots. She looked suspicious. Fritz Lemp dived and decided to attack. At 7.40pm, some 250 miles east of the Outer Hebrides, and some 1500 yards from the *Athenia,* he fired 4 torpedoes. The first and second ran wide, the fourth stuck in the torpedo tube, the third made history.

Thanks to a radio operator who kept his head and used auxiliary electric power to call for help, a tanker, a private yacht, and 4 British destroyers rushed to her aid. She floated for 15 hours during which about 1,000 of her passengers and crew were rescued, but the damage was done:
IMPORTANT.
From Malin Head Radio to Admiralty.
INTERCEPTED 2059. JAMMING NEAR. SSSS SSSS SSSS

ATHENIA TORPEDOED (Position given)
(Later)
INTERCEPTED 2207 JAMMING NEAR. ATHENIA 1400 PASSENGERS SOME STILL ABOARD SINKING FAST. BEARING APPROXIMATELY 291 DEGREES FROM MALIN HEAD.

Oberleutnant Fritz Julius Lemp was far from commended by his superiors on his return to Germany.

JUTLAND

The Royal Navy's most resounding clash of seaborne hardware occurred in May 1916, when a total of 50 battleships, 14 battle cruisers, 32 cruisers, 120 destroyers and one seaplane carrier weighed anchor in their respective ports and set forth into the North Sea to dispute whether Britannia or Germania ruled the waves. On the last day of that month they disputed, off Jutland.

Consider a broad comparison between this and the previous major sea-power dispute off Cape Trafalgar, 111 years, 4 months and 21 days previously. Off Trafalgar, the British Commander-in-Chief's pre-ordained tactics were signalled shortly after both fleets had sighted one another, and the British had started closing the enemy at a leisurely walking pace seven hours before the first gun was fired. Nelson's signal to form order of sailing in two columns was one of the three signals he made throughout the operation. We all know the other two. About sixty other signals were made by his frigates reporting enemy movements.

Off Jutland, some 3,000 signals, made between noon 30th May and midnight 1st/2nd June are recorded in an official—and obviously condensed—signal log, bearing on the operation. In the seven hours before the first gun was fired off Jutland, 545 signals are recorded, 67 of which were made by Admiral Jellicoe, the British Commander-in-Chief. Most of these were manoeuvring signals. The only ones which taste of the Nelson spirit were those in which Jellicoe ordered his ships to 'raise steam for full speed with all despatch', to 'assume complete readiness for action in every respect' and for his Flag Officers to 'inform their divisions of the situation', about which, at that particular moment, he wasn't very clear himself. On another occasion he gently admonished the battleship *Revenge* with, 'You must steer a steadier course in action or your shooting will be bad'.

This, our first steam-driven armada, produced new signalling difficulties. Signal flags, always difficult to read 'end on' were frequently being obscured by funnel smoke. 'Attention is called to the smoke issuing from your funnels' (one wonders where else it might issue from before battle was joined) appears repeatedly, and on one occasion, 'Am edging to starboard to keep clear of smoke from *Lion*'. Other signals stimulate the imagination, such as 'Keep a good lookout' followed by 'Keep out of the way'. Also 'Please say what kind of zigzag you are doing'.

The British Commander-in-Chief's vagueness of the situation was no fault of his. History has always pointed an accusing finger at his cruisers who, unlike Nelson's frigates, starved their C.-in-C. of information, even forcing him to ask them for it! Of those 545 signals mentioned above, only ten were enemy reports, most of these were incomplete and they included the reciprocal of one vital bearing. An eleventh was made by the aircraft belonging to our seaplane carrier, *Engadine*, who broke radio silence to pass the first enemy report. Though this signal never reached the flagship, it certainly deserves a monument to commemorate the first enemy warships ever to have been reported from the air. It seems this seaplane was too overcome with her debut into sea warfare to take any further part.

Comparison with Trafalgar now becomes decreasingly realistic with Jellicoe on *Iron Duke's* bridge, surrounded by his mighty fleet, steaming at seventeen knots, seeking action with the enemy. An immediate decision to a vital problem was demanded. Without having seen the enemy, and uncertain exactly where his fleet lay, but with no time to lose, how best could he deploy the British battle-fleet? The decision he made has been generally accepted as tactically correct for, as Naval Historian Arthur Marder says, it enabled our fleet to cross the enemy's 'T', placed our fleet between the enemy and his base and gave us the advantage of the waning light. In the dramatic event, following a tense pause over the compass on the flagship's bridge, the Commander-in-Chief's decision, snapped up by his signal officer, was instantly transformed and implemented to the battlefleet in one raucous, vintage-signalese bellow from the Signal Bos'n to the flag deck, "EQUAL SPEED-CHARLIE-LONDON-HOIST". On this strange pronouncement hung Britannia's shirt.

The battle raged, the light waned, darkness fell, setting—by a glance at the signal log—far too many signal lanterns blinking. One, which wasn't even shaded, bore disastrous results. At 9.32 pm, *Lion* signalled her next-astern, *Princess Royal,* 'Please give me challenge and reply now in use as they have been lost'. Challenge and reply were passed and also read by the enemy scouting forces only two miles beyond. The use of this secret recognition signal was used by the enemy later on, with unhappy consequences.

Any comparison between Trafalgar and Jutland certainly doesn't apply to the results. Jutland left the dispute undecided, and consequently practically everything everyone did has been criticised. Jutland added little to Naval History except tonnage, smoke and everlasting controversy. Even today you only have to mention the subject.

SEND A GUNBOAT—1926

1459/31/8/26 *From: C.-in-C. China to: Admiralty*
Rear Admiral Yangtze reports state of affairs at Wanshien briefly as follows. General Yang Sen has been placing large numbers of troops on board some steamers for passage up and down river, until recently when in presence of gunboats, troops have been turned off British ships.

Yang Sen stated that SS *Wanliu* from whom troops were turned off at Wanshien on 29th August sank a sampan full of soldiers on passage up river and has placed over 300 soldiers on board each of SS *Wantung* and SS *Wanshien* which belong to the same company and is threatening H.M.S. *Cockchafer* from them and from the shore until he receives a guarantee of reparations for the drowned soldiers. Two ships are lying close alongside and have snipers posted behind cover pointing rifles at *Cockchafer*, which is heavily outnumbered. Yang Sen refuses to deal with the Commanding Officer of *Cockchafer* or anyone but the British Consul who has sent vigorous protests and is probably proceeding from Chung King to Wanshien in H.M.S. *Widgeon* today 31st August. H.M. Minister who left here this morning directed Consul General Hankow to take up matter vigorously with Wu Pei Fu, who is at Hankow. If he is unsuccessful the only alternative seems to be to use force as the position is degrading and cannot remain as at present.
1902/2/9 *From C.-in-C. China to Admiralty*
H.M.S. *Widgeon* grounded 31st August and holed returning Chung-

king for repairs. Consul proceeded Wanshien in river steamer, interviewed Yang Sen, who alleged 56 persons drowned and 85,000 dollars sunk with sampan by SS *Wanliu*. He refused to release British officers from the two river steamers unless Consul guarantees ships remain at Wanshien until settlement of the case. Consul declined to accept this proposal and has referred matter to Minister Pekin. Is seeing Yang Sen again today, 2nd September. Master of SS *Wanliu* reported facts are as follows. Whilst discharging passengers at Yungyiang 29th August, 16 armed troops came on board and as another sampan containing troops approached he proceeded Slow Ahead to avoid it. Fire was opened from the banks and troops on board rushed bridge and engine room but were driven off by ship's officers. Meanwhile a sampan tried to come alongside, fouled another and sank. Comprodore was seized and threat made to kill Captain. Armed watch was maintained until arrival at Wanshien, whereupon *Cockchafer* removed troops.

Party of four officers and 60 men from H.M.S. *Despatch*, *Mantis* and *Scarab* have been ordered to prepare steamship *Kaiwo* at Ichang and proceed to Wanshien if required.

0244/4 *From Admiralty to C.-in-C. China*
You should use your discretion using force as a last resort after consultation with Minister Pekin. Foreign Office have telegraphed Minister Pekin in the sense that being on the spot he is in the best position to judge whether force should be used. An act of the British steamer was the cause of incident and this can be made use of to start dangerous anti-British propaganda and possibly lead to a situation even more disagreeable. As no further news received assume the situation has solved itself. If not, make sure that arrangements are made to leave it to his discretion in consultation with C.-in-C. and bearing in mind above considerations to effect solution using force as a last resort.

1215/5 *From C.-in-C. China to Admiralty*
Rear Admiral Yangtze reports consular negotiations at Wanshien have failed.

I have informed R.A.Y. that on arrival of *Kaiwo* at Wanshien I consider that Consul should repeat H.M. Minister's offer of enquiry with *Wanliu* present, provided Chinese troops are withdrawn from British vessels and vessel placed under custody of British gunboat and that if this fails necessary steps should be taken to enforce release of British vessels and *Cockchafer*.

H.M. Minister Pekin has been informed.

From C.-in-C. China to Admiralty
PRIORITY
Rear Admiral Yangtze reports that attempted surprise operation
by *Widgeon, Cockchafer* and steamer *Kaiwo* at sunset yesterday,
5th September, has failed. Very heavy rifle and field gun fire was
opened and eventually their position became untenable.

The city was bombarded and set on fire. Three ships retired
down river and are proceeding Ichang. Casualties believed heavy in
Kaiwo. Commanding Officer and five men wounded in *Cockchafer.* No casualties in *Widgeon.* Captain of SS *Wantung* saved, no
news of other mercantile officers. I am consulting with R.A.Y.
about further action.

1345/7 *From C.-in-C. China to Commodore Hong Kong*
   URGENT
Pass following to Admiralty by cable begins. R.A.Y. reports
following casualties in *Kaiwo*: Officers killed, Commander Darley,
Lieutenant Higgins of *Despatch* Lieutenant Ridge, *Cockchafer,*
wounded and Lieutenant Fogg-Elliott, *Mantis,* wounded. Men
killed, 1 AB *Despatch,* 1 Leading Seaman, 3 AB's *Scarab,* dangerously wounded, 1 AB *Scarab,* 3 AB's *Despatch,* 2 AB's 1 Stoker,
Mantis. Full particulars have been called for. Commander Darley
was S.N.O. of the expedition, which has now returned to Ichang.

2314/8 *From Commodore Hong Kong to C.-in-C. China*
   URGENT
Following has been received from Admiralty begins. Pass to
C.-in-C. China Their Lordships regret to hear of the loss of life and
the number of casualties which occurred whilst carrying out
difficult operation at Wanshien. Request confirmation of statement that five of the six mercantile officers were rescued the other
being killed and that you will forward by telegraph as early as
possible short account of action and full names and official
numbers of casualties.

0143/9 *From C.-in-C. China to Admiralty*
It is confirmed that five mercantile European officers were rescued
and the other was reported wounded presumed drowned. The
following is summary of reports received from R.A.Y. SS *Kaiwo*
manned by officers and men from *Despatch, Mantis* and *Scarab,*
proceed up river from Ichang early 4th September to obtain
release of the European officers and native crew on board SS
Wanshien and *Wantung,* and if possible remove these steamers.
Kaiwo arrived at Wanshien evening of 5th September, went
alongside *Wanshien* but was so heavily fired on that after having

decided it was not possible to proceed SS *Wantung* and *Kaiwo* retired after having removed the European officers. The officers of *Wantung* jumped overboard as previously arranged. Captain was picked up by *Kaiwo*. Chief Officer by French gunboat. Chief Engineer reported wounded and presumed drowned. *Cockchafer* was at anchor at Wanshien and thereupon bombarded the town and as far as is known inflicted considerable damage. *Widgeon* who arrived from Chungkiang also took part. The three ships retired down the river and arrived at Ichang.

1712/11 *From C-in-C. China to Admiralty*

Three gunboats and *Kaiwo* will be ready to proceed from Ichang shortly under R.A.Y. Request early instructions as water will not remain at present suitable height.

Negotiations are going on and there probably will be no necessity to fire another gun but if Yung Sen is not made to accept our terms publicly much more harm will arise in the future. The steamers are reported to have had their cargoes looted and have been moved down river below the town. Presumably with a view to our taking them away and closing the incident. I submit Yang Sen in the presence of an armed demonstration at Wanshien must be made to sign terms on the following lines. (1) Release of steamships *Wantung* and *Wanshien*. (2) Guarantee of complete immunity from interference of all British ships on upper Yangtze. (3) Compensation for cargoes and retention of above. A fixed sum to be paid down. (4) If he complies with the above, offer an enquiry into the *Wanliu* incident.

When this is done *Widgeon* should proceed to Chungking to restore order. *Kaiwo* should be relieved by a gunboat and two should be stationed at Wanshien to enforce compliance with terms until the incident has blown over. I gather from messages received and intercepted that the governing factor in deciding what future steps are taken must be consideration of the amount of anti-foreign feeling that thas been or is likely to be developed. From all information received so far surprisingly little notice has been taken of the incident. Chungking being the only place where reports seem to show that any feeling has been roused and if these reports prove correct, temporary evacuation may become necessary which in view of present foreign gunboats should not be dangerous. But even if anti foreign feeling be aroused by agitation in my opinion it is of secondary consideration and the risk should be accepted. If the Wanshien incident is dealt with firmly ill-feeling will soon die down, but if not it will increase, our prestige will disappear and contempt will be added to ill-feeling. Present position of British, if not foreigners generally, will become impossible on upper river and gunboats will become a farce.

Consul General Hankow has seen this and concurs. Senior foreign naval officers present are acting sympathetically.

1755/14 *From Admiralty to C.-in-C.*

PRIORITY

Reference your signal. In the event of negotiation for recovery of two steamers, *Wantung* and *Wanshien,* you are authorised in conjunction with the British Consular Authority to employ force to effect this, but force is only to be used to attain this object alone. The other three points you propose for terms in your signal will be dealt with later on according to how the situation develops.

1445/18 *From C.-in-C. China to Admiralty*

PRIORITY

R.A.Y. reports after prolonged negotiations it has been agreeed *Wantung* and *Wanshien,* will be returned to Ichang through intermediary of non-British nationality. Yang Sen provides pilot and crew. After return of ships other matters will be considered.

1200/19/9/26 *From C.-in-C. China to Admiralty* (repeated Commodore Hong Kong)

With reference to Article 216 China Station Orders in view of local situation and in order that refits of Yangtze gunboats may proceed propose stationing a sloop at Hankow during the winter, probably *Magnolia* will be detailed.

THE FELLING OF A ROYAL OAK

0200/14/11/39 *From Admiral Commanding Coast of Scotland*
Royal Oak sunk in Scapa Flow after series of explosions.

0210/14 *From A.C.O.S.*

MOST IMMEDIATE

Raise steam for full speed with all despatch.

2047/14 *From Admiralty*

From available evidence it is considered that H.M.S. *Royal Oak* was sunk by submarine which probably obtained entrance to the Flow through Hoxa gate.

1202/16 *From Admiralty*

A Court of Inquiry is to be held at Scapa into the circumstances attending the loss of H.M.S. *Royal Oak.* Officers appointed as

Board. Admiral Drax, President. Vice Admiral Raikes. Captain Muirhead-Gould. They are leaving London by train tonight, 8th October. Board is to investigate (1) whether loss was due to action by an enemy submarine and if so (2) how submarine was able to enter Scapa Flow and how this can be prevented in future. (3) Subsequent sinking of the ship. Request you will make all arrangements for Board to sit as expeditiously as practicable. President has been given terms of reference as stated in this signal. 1202/17 *From Admiralty First Sea Lord*

Hunt is to continue until U-boat is destroyed or Admiralty direct hunt is to be discontinued. The latter would not repetition not be for a week or ten days from now. Report in good time if an adequate number of hunting vessels are likely to be available.

From Admiralty

It must now be assumed U-boat has escaped and hunt may be discontinued.

Note: This was the Royal Navy's seventh *Royal Oak,* the first to be sunk by enemy action.

THE STATE OF DENMARK

Of all the Top Secret Intelligence cypher signals which darted to and fro during World War 2, one which could well have left an indelible print on the ionosphere was made by our Naval Attaché in Denmark, addressed to Admiralty on 8 April, 1940.

As the frozen sea-lanes of the Baltic thawed after the war's first winter, Admiralty remained confident that our naval superiority in the North Sea precluded German invasion of either Denmark or Norway; yet evidence in Denmark challenged this complacency, and the German concentration of force which was busy mounting up to 7 army division, 1,500 aircraft, and 74 warships certainly didn't fool our very alert Attaché. Two days before the storm broke, when he personally identified this German Fleet manoeuvring in the Belts, he drove back to his cypher books in Copenhagen just as fast as his car could carry him. The signal he sent even inferred German seizure of Narvik.

Back in London a few weeks later, this same ex-Attaché of ex-Denmark followed up the course of his signal made on 8 April. On receipt, the Duty Captain had taken it straight to Churchill and got him out of bed to read it. "I don't think so", said Winston.

Some months later in Washington our Prime Minister recalled the occasion with a generous admission of his misjudgment.

TWO POSTHUMOUS V.C.'s
1

On 5 April 1940, Vice Admiral Whitworth, flying his flag in *Renown* sailed from Scapa Flow, screened by destroyers *Greyhound, Glowworm, Hyperion,* and *Hero*. They were joined next morning by *Hardy, Hotspur, Havock, Hunter,* and 4 minelaying destroyers. The Admiral's intention was to sweep in the area of the Lofoten Islands for German forces believed to be invading Norway, and lay mines across the Vestfiord approach to Narvik, the important railhead and harbour of the Norwegian iron ore industry.

In a raging Arctic gale *Renown* sighted and had a brief engagement with *Scharnhorst* and *Gneisenau. Glowworm,* trying to recover a man who had fallen overboard, lost touch with *Renown,* but sighted and engaged two enemy destroyers, presumed to be screening the German Battle Cruisers.

The brief remainder of *Glowworm's* life was pieced together from the following sequence of signals.

0430/8/4 *From Glowworm to Flag Officer—Battle-Cruisers*
> Have been hove to. Now proceeding to join you. My position very doubtful as no fix has been obtained since parting company.
> *From Glowworm to F.O.B.C.S.*
> Am engaging enemy destroyers.
> *From Glowworm to F.O.B.C.S.*
> Enemy course 030.
> *From Glowworm to F.O.B.C.S.*
> Enemy making smoke. Suspect concentrating with another destroyer.
> *From Glowworm to F.O.B.C.S.*
> Am endeavouring to draw enemy to northwards.
> *From Glowworm to F.O.B.C.S.*
> Unknown ship bearing north 6 miles course 180.

1158/8/ *From Admiral Commanding Coast of Scotland to*
4/40 *Admiralty*
> At 0904 whilst Scapa W/T was transmitting, an unknown station was heard with same characteristics and on same adjustment as *Glowworm*. Transmission faded

out and although *Glowworm* was asked for repetition no answer was obtained.

Five years later Germany supplied the grim facts. After a running destroyer fight through driving snow *Glowworm* suddenly found herself sharing a gap in the storm with the heavy German cruiser *Hipper; Glowworm* was overwhelmed, she hadn't got a hope. In her last desperate effort to do all the damage she possibly could, what was left of her launched itself at the cruiser, rammed her, and then sank. A handful of survivors were picked up, but not her Captain, Lieutenant-Commander Gerard Roope.

His was the first deed in World War II of V.C. quality. His posthumous award came later.

TWO POSTHUMOUS V.C.'s
2

On the following morning the Commander-in-Chief in *Rodney* ordered Captain Warburton-Lee in *Hardy* to take his destroyers—*Hotspur, Hunter* and *Havoc*—up to Narvik to prevent German troops from landing. By noon the Admiralty had intervened with a signal direct to *Hardy,* confirming that enemy troops had already landed there. At 1751/9 April Warburton-Lee, having interrogated 2 Norwegian ships made the following signal to Admiralty:

> Norwegians report Germans holding Narvik in force, six destroyers and one submarine, channel is possibly mined. Intend attacking at dawn high water.

At that particular time probably most operational ships in the Royal Navy were at sea, many of them without knowing exactly what was happening. The above signal will be remembered as a heartening tonic to all who read it.

The Admiralty replied:

0136/10 *From Admiralty*

> Norwegian coast defence ships *Eidsvold* and *Norge* may be in German hands. You alone can judge whether in these circumstances attack should be made. We shall support whatever decision you take.

Captain Warburton-Lee drew up his plan of attack and passed it by signal through the snowstorms to his flotilla, as follows:

> Following orders for operation T.N. Final approach to Narvik *Hardy* will close Pilot Station which is close to

Steinhos Light. *Hunter* will follow in support. *Hotspur* and *Havock* are to provide anti-submarine protection to the northward. Ships are to be at Action Stations from 0030. When passing Skredneset Light *Hardy* will pass close to shore and order a line of bearing. Thereafter ships are to maintain narrow quarterline to starboard so that fire from all ships is effective ahead. On closing Narvik *Hardy* will steer for inner harbour with *Hunter* astern in support. . . . Germans may have several destroyers and a submarine in vicinity. Some probably on patrol. Ships are to engage all targets immediately and keep a particular lookout for enemy who may be berthed in inlets. On approaching Narvik *Hardy, Hunter, Havock* engage enemy ships inside harbour with guns and torpedoes. *Hotspur* engage ships to North West. *Hostile* assist on either target. Prepare to lay smoke for cover and to tow disabled ships. If opposition is silenced landing parties (less *Hotspur*) when ordered to land make for Ore Quay unless otherwise ordered. *Hardy's* first lieutenant in charge. Additional visual signal to withdraw will be one Red and one Green Very light from *Hardy*. Half outfit of torpedoes is to be fired unless target warrants more. In order to relieve congestion of movements all ships when turning to fire or opening are to keep turning to port if possible. Watch adjacent ships. Keep moderate speed.

At 0415 *Hardy, Hunter* and *Havock* entered Narvik harbour. The attack was a complete surprise. At 0515 the attack was repeated. By this time visibility was clearing and opposition from shore batteries and ships was increasing. At 0551 three enemy destroyers were seen approaching from the north-east. Captain Warburton-Lee, having done all the damage he could, ordered his ships to withdraw. No sooner had the flotilla formed on a westerley course than they ran into two more German destroyers approaching from ahead.

Hardy, burning, beached herself to the southward. Her Captain was killed. *Hunter* was sunk. The last signal from *Hardy* was:

KEEP ON ENGAGING THE ENEMY

This signal was made only 21 hours after *Glowworm's* last signal was intercepted. The watery graves of those two destroyers and their gallant Captains are only about 150 miles apart.

Hotspur who had been damaged in collision with *Hunter*,

managed to withdraw to the south-westward, covered by *Hostile* and *Havock*. The enemy losses were as follows: Destroyers *Heidkamp, Schmitt,* sunk; *Arnim, Roeder, Kunnem Thiele,* damaged. Seven or eight merchant ships were sunk. Captain Bernard Warburton-Lee was awarded a posthumous Victoria Cross.

AN INVASION HAS BEEN ARRANGED . . . .

2333/   *From Admiralty to all Flag Officers at Home Ports*
1/7   IMMEDIATE
       If a seaborne attack on the British Isles is to be attemped by the enemy during the month of July 1940 there is reason to believe it will be launched during next ten days.

2215/   *From C.-in-C. Nore to General*
12/9   Aircraft report large convoy in position . . course west.
2357   *From C.-in-C. Nore to General*
       My 2215. This is now believed to be phosphorescence.

Midnight *From Admiralty to All Commanders-in-Chief*
13/9   IMMEDIATE
       Following received from British Ambassador Washington source at present ungraded. President has just heard from a source in Berlin which he considers most reliable that invasion of England is timed for 3 p.m. tomorrow, Sunday. Ends.

Before World War II an enthusiastic R.N. sailing sailor, while racing in the Kiel Regatta, was the guest of his German Naval friend and sailing rival in the Pocket Battleship *Graf Spee.*

Came the War: the R.N. officer became our Naval Attaché in Sweden. The German officer became Chief Staff Officer to Grand Admiral Raeder. As the German invasion loomed:

       From British Naval Attaché, Stockholm To Chief Staff Officer, Admiral Raeder.
       I hope you are still making a careful study of the invasion I recommended in *The Riddle of the Sands.**
       Reply
       Your signal. As man to man, have made careful study of Childer's book but must inform you that things are working out rather differently on this occasion.

---

*In Childers' fictional masterpiece the Frisian Islands off Western Germany were mustering points for the invasion barges.

THE DEATH OF A NAVY

Throughout the long history of our love-hate relationship with France, the most poignant moment of all must have been when that one-word executive signal left the transmitting aerials above Admiralty building in the early hours of the early days of July, 1940. It was addressed to C.-in-C. Mediterranean, Admiral Commanding Force H, C.-in-C. Plymouth and C.-in-C. Portsmouth. The word,

CATAPULT

All that June, France was being overrun by Hitler's army. By the end of the month retreating British footprints had been ironed out of the beaches of Dunkirk by the tides. The French army was disintegrating, Paris had fallen, the last Government of the Third Republic had appealed to Hitler for an Armistice. The only weapon France had left was its Fleet, which had sailed intact from French bases before the Germans reached them, and by then was dispersed between Alexandria, Oran, Mers-el-Kebir, Plymouth and Portsmouth.

This Fleet consisted of five battleships, two battle cruisers *Dunkerque* and *Strasbourg*, (which had been designed to outmatch *Scharnhorst* and *Gneisenau*) some twenty cruisers, also destroyers and submarines including *Surcouf*, the world's largest. Untried in battle maybe, but adding up to a far more powerful force than the German navy at that time. Also — and here was the danger — a force which, if combined with the Axis navies, would jerk the balance of sea power out of our hands.

France, avid for favourable armistice terms: ourselves desperate to prevent the French Fleet ranging against us. What a plight for us and our allies of yesterday!

On 27 June, we cast the die. An ultimatum to France, labelled Operation CATAPULT, was drawn up by our War Cabinet.

Broadly, it gave the French Fleet the choice of joining ours, dismantling, interning, or scuttling their ships. Unless one of these ignoble alternatives was carried out effectively and immediately, we would use whatever force was necessary to prevent all French warships within our reach falling into German or Italian hands. "The life of the State and the salvation of our cause was at stake," said Churchill. At 0221/1 July 1940 out went the warning from Admiralty.

PREPARATIVE CATAPULT 3 JULY.

On receipt of the executive signal on 3rd, the operation went smoothly at Portsmouth and Plymouth except that Commander 'Lofty' Sprague — friend of the author's — and one or two others were shot dead on boarding the submarine *Surcouf.* The Mediterranean was different. At Alexandria, our C.-in-C., Admiral Cunningham who was on excellent terms with the French Admiral René Godfroy, remonstrated to Admiralty by signal. He was convinced, he said, that French ships in Alexandria would never join Germany. For Cunningham to attack them, he added, would be disastrous to Anglo-French relationship in Syria and Africa. Both Admirals refused to turn the waters of Alexandria red. Eventually, Admiral Godfroy settled for de-fuelling and disarming his ships. "Admiral Cunningham", he said, "behaved throughout like a gentleman".

At the French occupied ports of Oran and nearby Mers-el-Kebir up the other end of the Mediterranean, it was even more different. At Gibraltar, the nearest British base, Admiral Somerville commanded Force H, consisting of two battleships, a battle cruiser, two cruisers and eleven destroyers. On receipt of Admiralty's CATAPULT warning he demurred, conferring with his officers who included Captain Holland, recent liaison officer at the French C.-in-C.'s headquarters. Holland was popular with the Frenchmen, and spoke their language. A worried Admiral Somerville signalled Admiralty,

> AFTER TALK WITH HOLLAND AND OTHERS I AM IMPRESSED WITH THEIR VIEW THAT USE OF FORCE SHOULD BE AVOIDED AT ALL COSTS. HOLLAND CONSIDERS OFFENSIVE ACTION ON OUR PART WOULD ALIENATE ALL FRENCH WHEREVER THEY ARE.

Admiralty replied sharply,

> FIRM INTENTION OF HIS MAJESTY'S GOVERNMENT THAT IF FRENCH WILL NOT ACCEPT ANY OF YOUR ALTERNATIVES THEY ARE TO BE DESTROYED.

This was softened a little by our Prime Minister's personal signal to Somerville at 2255/2 July.

> YOU ARE CHARGED WITH ONE OF THE MOST DISAGREEABLE AND DIFFICULT TASKS THAT A BRITISH ADMIRAL HAS EVER BEEN FACED WITH BUT

K

WE HAVE COMPLETE CONFIDENCE IN YOU AND RELY ON YOU TO CARRY IT OUT RELENTLESSLY.

When Force H appeared off Mers-el-Kebir early on the 3rd, the French Admiral Gensoul, who had been ordered by Admiral Darlan not to have any relations with the British, had no intention of capitulating. When Captain Holland arrived alongside the quay in the destroyer *Foxhound*, Gensoul refused to see him and informed the French Admiralty the British had ordered him to sink his ships within six hours, or they would use force to make him. "My response" — he added — "Force will be met by force". So he played for time, hoping vainly for reinforcements from Oran.

An hour and a half before the British ultimatum expired, Gensoul agreed to see Holland, who arrived on board *Dunkerque* the French Flagship, at 1500. These two were friends. They talked on and on in the blistering humidity of the Admiral's cabin, but Holland could get no more than vague promises, which he reported to his Admiral by signal. As he was leaving, Gensoul handed Holland a copy of Admiral Somerville's signal, just received:

IF ONE OF OUR PROPOSITIONS IS NOT ACCEPTED BY 17.30 BST I SHALL HAVE TO SINK YOUR SHIPS.

At 17.45 Force H opened fire and sent in bombers from *Ark Royal*. The French battleship *Bretagne* blew up and sank; another battleship *Provence* and battle cruiser *Dunkerque* were badly damaged and beached. *Strasbourg*, though badly damaged, escaped to Toulon. In a quarter of an hour the massacre was over. The French had lost three capital ships, several smaller ones, some 1500 lives and a force which might well have changed the course of World War II.

2303/7/7/40. *From Admiralty to Commanders-in-Chief, Home Ports.*

In order to ensure that French naval forces at Oran were not surrendered intact force had to be used. The result is that all French naval forces must be regarded as hostile. H.M. Ships should be prepared to attack but should not (repeat) not fire first shot.

A MIDSHIPMAN'S SIGNAL LOG

The following signals, made on 29th and 30th March, 1941, after the Battle of Matapan in the Mediterranean, were extracted from the Journal of a Midshipman serving in the flagship, H.M.S. *Warspite* at the time.

29 March   *From D14 (Captain of 14th Destroyer Flotilla.) to C.-in-C.*
Search to port further on point of *Littorio* with no result. Sank *Zara* and *Pola*. Destroyers have a number of survivors, many left in wake in position 237 degrees 50 miles from me now. Further search will be made.

From Havock to C.—in—C. (Repeated) D2, D14,
Sank one destroyer *Vincenzo Geoberto* class by torpedo and gunfire. The last vestige of a burning ship was passed possibly afterwards and the remaining 4 torpedoes fired at a large cruiser which was already damaged by the battlefleet, results unknown but possibly blew up later on as a large explosion was seen in its approximate position. Another large ship burning furiously when contact was broken at 0045. May have been explosion seen on return. Star shells were fired at a darkened ship which intervened. When illuminated its closing inclination gave the appearance of a battleship. Opened fire range 6,000 yards observed hits on the upper works. Turned away and made smoke but surprised fire was not returned. Subsequently identified as *Pola*.

From C.-in-C. to R.A.1.
What did *Barham* fire at last night and to what effect.
Reply
At leading *Zara* class cruiser. First two broadsides hit causing orange flashes and dense volumes of smoke below bridge structure. Remaining broadsides were difficult to spot owing to smoke. When she turned away there was a fire amidships still burning when last

seen. Judging by number of splashes short, 6 each probably straddled.

From D14 to C.-in-C.
Information from survivors state that Italian C.–in–C. was in *Littorio*. Admiral Cantanio in *Zara* was not recovered. Captain Depisa in *Pola* is on board *Jervis*.

From Defender to C.-in-C.
Have 10 officers and 139 survivors on board from Italian cruisers *Fiume* and *Zara*. There are approximately 300 left on rafts.
(Note. Final total picked up by British and Greek units 1,079.)

From R.A.(Air) to C.-in-C. (Repeated) R.A.1.
Report of dusk attack by 6 albercores and 2 swordfish approaching enemy battleship at 1925. They were met by intense AA barrage from all ships and withdrew. They attacked again individually between 1930 and 1945 over a wide area. All aircraft took the battleship as target. One hit on a cruiser was observed which was probably the one contact pistol carried, the remainder being duplex. It is considered unlikely that hits with duplex would have been observed.

From D14 to C.-in-C.
Destroyers have following survivors on board. Read in 3 columns ships, officers, ratings.

Ship	Officers	Ratings
Jervis	22	237
Janus	2	89
Nubian	13	109
Mohawk	7	107
Greyhound	Nil	16
Ilex	1	13
Hereward	Nil	Nil
Hasty	Nil	1
Havock	Nil	31
Hotspur	4	52
Griffin	Nil	29
Juno	4	89
Defender	8	71.

30 March *From D10 to C.-in-C.*

The one you hit first was exploding severely at each end when I left her and I was very near her end. In addition a ship which engaged *Havock*, I think the cruiser, blew up at *Havock's* third salvo or torpedo and I could see no more of her. I engaged the first cruiser till her fire ceased also. I think the burning wreckage found was probably the *Maestrale*. The first destroyer I sank was definitely *Gioberte* which was confirmed by the prisoners from *Pola* I have on board, who say there was no 6 inch cruiser with them after nightfall, only a destroyer screen and the 3 8 inch cruisers. I am doubtful if there are any survivors from *Gioberte* as it blew up. Prisoners on board *Ilex* state destroyer *Maestrale* was sunk. This would fit in with *Havock's* claim.

From C.-in-C.—General.

Estimate damage to enemy

Littorio. . . Heavily damaged (*Vittorio Venetio*)

Zara, Pola, Fiume. . . Sunk.

Bandinere. . . Probably sunk (Definitely sunk*)

Two Destroyers probably sunk. . . (Two definitely sunk*)

Nine hundred prisoners. . . (1079*)

3 Aircraft shot down.

From C.-in-C.—General.

Indicate damage and casualties

Reply:

Warspite	Nil	*Juno*	Nil
Valiant	Nil	*Mohawk*	Nil
Barham	Nil	*Janus*	Nil
Gloucester	Nil	*Havock*	Nil
Jaguar	Nil	*Jervis*	Nil
Ilex	Nil	*Greyhound*	Nil
Hotspur	Nil		

From R.A.1. to C.-in-C.

Italian communiqué claims as follows.

(*Handwritten confirmation added on signal)

Italian aircraft sank British heavy cruisers. German aircraft severely damaged British aircraft carrier with 3 hits heaviest bombs sank destroyer. No mention of action by surface forces.
Reply from C.-in-C.
I regret these heavy losses to our fleet.

"ONE ENEMY BATTLESHIP"
1941

22nd May
1619   *From Admiralty*
            Photographs show *Bismarck* class battleship in Bergen with cargo type merchant ships in vicinity. *Hipper* Class Cruiser nearby and destroyer with three cargo type merchant ships and six auxiliaries, apparently minesweepers, in the vicinity. Destroyer has oiler alongside. One merchant ship berthing alongside *Hipper* Class cruiser.

1939   *From Hatson Air Station*
            Following received from Hatson reconnaissance aircraft over Bergen. Battleship and cruiser have left.

1942   *From Commander-in-Chief Home Fleet. H.M.S. King George V (hereafter C.-in-C.)*
            Prepare for sea.

2042   *C.-in-C. to Arethusa, Manchester.*
        Arethusa is to proceed to take up patrol line. *Manchester* on arrival in area is to take *Birmingham* and *Arethusa* under his orders and dispose ships to patrol the Iceland-Faroes passage to westward of mine barrier.

2043   *From C.-in-C.*
        Request Air reconnaissance be maintained as follows:—
        (a) Iceland—Faroes channel.
        (b) Denmark Strait.
        (c) Faroes-Shetland channel.
        (d) Norwegian Coast.
        Object to detect enemy battleship and cruiser breaking out to westward. Request all forces and authorities be informed of patrols instituted.

2045   *From C.-in-C.*
        Intend to proceed in *King George V* with *Victorious, Galatea, Hermione, Kenya, Aurora,* and seven destroyers passing through Hoxa boom at 2300 Thursday 22 May (initial route given). Commander-in-Chief Rosyth is requested to arrange anti-submarine air escort from daylight 23 May. Code word REBEL.
        Repulse is to join me by noon 23 May.
        In the absence of other information intend Rear-Admiral Commanding Second Cruiser Squadron (hereafter *Galatea*) in *Galatea* with *Hermoine* to patrol to westward off N. Rona-Faroes minefield.

2101   *From Admiralty*
        Positions of our submarines at 0800/23 and movements the following 24 hours include P.31 from patrol position proceeding to patrol 25 miles west of Stadlandet. May be proceeding on surface.

2210   *From Admiral, Iceland*
        Sailed *Arethusa.*

2212   *From Admiral, Iceland*
        Sailed *Suffolk.*

23rd May
0630   *From Admiral, Rosyth*
        Air reconnaissance postponed owing to weather.

1009   *From Rear-Admiral Commanding First Cruiser Squadron in Norfolk (hereafter Norfolk)*
       Suffolk is to patrol within RDF distance of ice edge on a line running North-East and South-West. When clear inshore *Norfolk* will patrol about 15 miles abeam of you. When thick inshore, *Norfolk* will patrol to cover inshore passage. *Norfolk* will make contact with you at 1300 on 24 May. Investigate ice up to minefield on parting company today Friday.

1017   *From Norfolk to Suffolk*
       Enemy may be expected to separate in low visibility or while heavy ship holds off our forces. Intend that *Norfolk* shall try to keep visual contact and engage cruiser if she leaves *Bismarck*. *Suffolk's* object is to shadow *Bismarck*.

1817   *From Admiral, Iceland*
       Study of recent air reconnaissances shows that a well-built ship could make a passage through Denmark Strait about 50 miles inside ice edge.

1922   *From Norfolk to Suffolk*
       One battleship, one cruiser in sight bearing 020 degrees distant 7 miles. Course 240 degrees, (*Suffolk's* position given.)

1939   *From Vice Admiral Commanding Battle Cruisers in Hood (hereafter Hood)*
       Raise steam for full speed.

2032   *From Norfolk*
       One battleship, one cruiser in sight.

(Note: *Norfolk* and *Suffolk* then continued to shadow *Bismarck* and pass reports continually. *Suffolk* made thirty reports by Signal between 1922/23 and 0538/24.)

2055   *From Hood to escorting Destroyers*
       If you are unable to maintain this speed I will have to go on without you. You should follow at your best speed.

2114   *From C.-in-C. to Galatea*
       I am hoping *Hood* may head them off and force them to turn back or to the Southward. Maintain present bearing 7 miles.

2308   *From C.-in-C. to Victorious*
       Primary tasks which will be required of *Victorious* aircraft are Reconnaissance and Shadowing, bearing in mind that

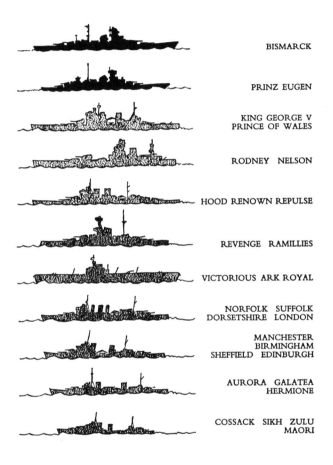

BISMARCK

PRINZ EUGEN

KING GEORGE V
PRINCE OF WALES

RODNEY   NELSON

HOOD RENOWN REPULSE

REVENGE   RAMILLIES

VICTORIOUS ARK ROYAL

NORFOLK   SUFFOLK
DORSETSHIRE   LONDON

MANCHESTER
BIRMINGHAM
SHEFFIELD   EDINBURGH

AURORA   GALATEA
HERMIONE

COSSACK SIKH ZULU
MAORI

the enemy may divide his force. A Secondary task may be provision of torpedo striking force.

If enemy is engaged, *Victorious* with *Aurora* and two rear destroyers from each wing of Screen is to break off to disengaged side.

24th May

0050   *From Admiralty to Force H*

Proceed as soon as ready to join (convoy) after daylight May 26th. Should reconnaissance today indicate one or both German Battle Cruisers have left Brest it will be necessary to alter these instructions.

0120   *From Admiralty*

If still complying with C.in-CHF's instructions and in absence of other orders from him, *Manchester, Birmingham, Arethusa, Galatea, Hermione* should rendezvous 30 miles East of Langanaes to form a patrol line in event of enemy breaking back.

0537   *From Prince of Wales*

One enemy battleship distant 17 miles.

0544   *From Hood*

One enemy battleship distant 14 miles.

0552   *From Bismarck*

Am engaging two heavy units.

0615   *From Norfolk*

Hood blown up in position (given).

0624   *From Prince of Wales to Norfolk*

Hood is sunk. My bridge is out of action. Y turret out of action temporarily. Otherwise damage appears superficial. Will confirm.

0628   *From Norfolk to Prince of Wales.*

I intend to keep in touch with the enemy.

0632   *From Bismarck*

Battlecruiser, probably Hood, sunk. Another battleship King George or Renown damaged and turned off. Two heavy cruisers maintaining contact.

(Note: *Prince of Wales* was mistaken for *King George V* throughout)

0637   *Norfolk to Destroyers in company*

Hood sunk in position (given) proceed to search for survivors.

0705   *From Bismarck*
      Have sunk a battleship in approximate position (given).

0720   *From Prince of Wales*
      A and B turrets in action. Y turret two guns in action. About 400 tons of water in ship mainly abaft armoured bulkhead. Compartment above steering compartment flooded but steering gear in action. Estimated best speed 27 knots.

0731   *Norfolk to Prince of Wales*
      Open out to 10 miles. I may have to fall back on you if the Cruiser tries to drive me off.

0801   *From Bismarck*
      1. *Electrical engine-room No. 4 broken down.*
      2. *Port boiler-room No. 2 is making water but can be held. Water in forecastle.*
      3. *Maximum speed 28 knots.*
      4. *Two enemy radar sets recognised.*
      5. *Intention to put into St. Nazaire. No losses of personnel.*

0839   *From Admiralty to Manchester, Birmingham, Arethusa*
      Proceed with all dispatch.

0903   *From Admiralty to Rodney*
      Proceed with *Britannic* and Screen at best speed, course 290°.

0906   *From Electra*
      Intend landing the three survivors from *Hood* at Reykjavik.

0943   *From Admiral, Iceland to Malcolm*
      Sunderland reports survivors in position (given).

1007   *From Prince of Wales*
      Main armament control undamaged. 9 main armament guns in action. Secondary armament guns in action. Considerable damage bridge. Both forward High Angle Directors out of action. About 600 tons of water in ship, mainly aft, from two or more hits about water line. Estimate maximum speed 26 knots.

1036   *From Admiralty to Rodney*
      If *Britannic* cannot keep up, leave her behind with 1 destroyer.

1110   *From Admiralty to Revenge (Halifax)*
      Revenge is to raise steam with all despatch and proceed to sea.

1126   *From Admiralty to Norfolk*
       Continue shadowing *Bismarck* even if you run out of fuel
       in order that C.-in-C. may catch up in time.

1144   *From Admiralty to Ramillies*
       Proceed so as to make contact with enemy from west-
       wards, subsequently placing enemy between *Ramillies* and
       C.-in-C.

1206   *From Admiralty to Galatea*
       Unless otherwise ordered by C.-in-C., *Galatea* and
       Hermione are to proceed to Faroes and fuel.

1210   *From Norfolk*
       Visibility decreasing.

1235   *From Admiral, Iceland*
       Plot of Sunderland flying boat on return appears to
       indicate *Norfolk's* position accurate. *Bismarck* leaving con-
       siderable wake of oil fuel.

1238   *From Admiralty*
       Situation at 1100.
       Bismarck and *Prinz Eugen* in position (given) course 215°,
       speed 24 knots. *Bismarck* has received some damage.
       (2) C.S.1. in *Norfolk* with *Prince of Wales* and *Suffolk* are
       in touch with enemy. *Prince of Wales* has 2 guns out of
       action. *Hood* blown up by unlucky hit. C.-in-C. in *King
       George V* with *Repulse, Victorious, Kenya, Aurora* may be
       about 230 miles to eastward of enemy's position.
       (3) *Rodney* in position (given) with 3 or 4 destroyers has
       been ordered to steer best closing course.
       (4) *Ramillies* in position (given) has been ordered to place
       herself to westward of enemy.
       (5) *Manchester* is taking *Birmingham* and *Arethusa* under
       his orders and establishing patrol line north of Langanaes,
       North East of Iceland.
       (6) C.S.2 in *Galatea* with *Hermione* is being ordered to fuel
       at Faroes.
       (7) Force H left Gibraltar at 0200/24 and is proceeding
       westwards.
       (8) *Revenge* is about to leave Halifax with orders to close
       enemy.
       (9) *Edinburgh* in approximate position (given) is being
       ordered to close and take over Stand-by Shadower.
       (10) Enemy battle cruisers were in Brest 23/May.

1250 *From Admiralty to Edinburgh*
Close enemy last reported position (given) so as to take over Stand-by Shadower if necessary. Fuel should be conserved reasonably while closing and speed of 25 knots is suggested, but after contact *NO* consideration of fuel must allow you to lose contact.

1314 *From Norfolk*
Have lost touch with enemy in low visibility.

1314 *From C.-in-C. to Repulse*
If this course and speed is continued, report when you must leave to return to Hvalfjord at 20 knots.

1340 *Repulse to C.-in-C.*
At 0500 tomorrow Sunday. This will get me back to Hvalfjord with 8.5% useable fuel remaining.

1349 *Norfolk*
One battleship one cruiser in sight (position given).

1348 *From Bismarck*
1400 approximate position (given) King George with cruiser is maintaining contact. Intention: If no engagement intend to shake off enemy during night.

1350 *From 1st Sea Lord to Chief of Naval Staff, Canada*
Reference Admiralty's appreciation of general situation, I shall be grateful if you would hold long distance aircraft available for reconnaissance from Newfoundland.

1355 *Galatea to C.-in-C.*
I hope they won't get nervous when we don't turn up.

1417 *C.-in-C. to Galatea*
Admiralty is being informed that you are in company.

1420 *From Bismarck to Prinz Eugen*
Intend to shake off enemy as follows. During rain showers Bismarck will move off on westerly course. Prinz Eugen to maintain course and speed until she is forced to alter course or 3 hours after leaving Bismarck. Following this she is to oil from Belchen or Lothringen and afterwards to engage in cruiser warfare independently. Executive on Code word HOOD.

1440 *From C.-in-C. to Galatea*
Take *Victorious* and cruisers to provide a screen for her under your orders and steer for nearest position within 100 miles of *Bismarck* and from there launch torpedo bomber attacks. *Victorious* is not to come under gunfire

from enemy ships. As cruisers run short of fuel they are to be detached to Reykjavik. *Victorious* is to maintain contact as long as torpedo bomber or reconnaissance aircraft are available. *King George V* is altering course more to the Southward.

1442   *From Bismarck to U-boats*
West boats collect in approximate position (given) at dawn. Am approaching from North. Intend to draw heavy units shadowing Bismarck through this area.

1445   *From Admiralty to Norfolk*
Report as follows regarding *Bismarck*:
(1) Percentage of fighting efficiency remaining.
(2) Amunition expended.
(3) Reasons for frequent alteration of course.
Request your intentions as regards *Prince of Wales* re-engaging. Keep a good look-out for U-boats.

1504   *From German Western Naval Headquarters, Paris (Hereafter called Group West) to Bismarck*
English unit made tactical signal at 1223 from approximate position (given). Aircraft reports sighted 12 merchant ships 4 destroyers (position given approximately).

1508   *From Bismarck*
Hood annihilated within 5 minutes by gunfire this morning at 0600. King George turned off after being hit. Bismarck's speed limited. Slightly down by bows owing to hit forward.

1511   *From Group West to Bismarck*
Air reconnaissance of Scapa started. English unit made following to Scapa at 1329. One enemy battleship one cruiser (position given). Renown, Ark Royal and Sheffield left Gibraltar on unknown course during night of 23/24.

1532   *Norfolk to Flying Boat*
Can you report bearing and distance of *Suffolk* on starboard quarter of enemy. Please tell her bearing and distance of enemy.

1535   *From Flying Boat to Norfolk*
Suffolk bears 262 degrees 26 miles, course 140 degrees. She knows enemy position.

1540   *Norfolk to Flying Boat*
Are enemy ships together.

1541   *Flying Boat to Norfolk*
Ships 2 miles apart.

1619 *Norfolk to Admiralty*
Reply to your 1445/24
(1) Uncertain but high.
(2) Engagement 20 minutes also some rounds at cruisers. About 150 expended.
(3) Unaccountable except as effort to shake us off.
Consider *Prince of Wales* should not re-engage until other heavy ships are in contact, unless interception fails. Doubtful if she has speed to force action.

1711 *From Group West to Bismarck*
U-boats will be in approximate postion (given) tomorrow morning.

1715 *Norfolk to Prince of Wales*
As in this visibility we are likely to meet the enemy inside gun range, I am putting you ahead.

1738 *Repulse to C.-in-C.*
If you continue on present course and speed until noon tomorrow I find I can remain with you providing that I then proceed to Conception Bay, Newfoundland at economical speed, arriving with 5% useable fuel.

1747 *C.-in-C. to Repulse*
I am afraid your lack of fuel would not enable you to make contact. Intend detaching you to Reykjavik with destroyers at 2100. Destroyers should have fuel for speed of 20 knots.

1756 *Admiralty to London*
Part company with *Arundel Castle* and destroyers. Order them to proceed in execution of previous orders. *London* proceed at economical speed towards position (given). Your movements should be adjusted to close enemy and you should prepare to take over shadowing duties.

1842 *From Group West to Bismarck*
Hearty congratulations.
Preparations being made at St. Nazaire and Brest concur with intentions of Prinz Eugen. If possible to shake off enemy withdrawal to remote sea area seems advisable for Bismarck. Assume Bismarck's maximum speed 28 knots. Report when draught is above normal.

1914 *From Bismarck*
Short engagement with King George without result. Detached Prinz Eugen to oil. Enemy maintains contact.

1916 *Admiralty to Norfolk, Suffolk*
Shadowing by *Norfolk* has been admirable. Keep it up and good luck.

1925 *From Group West to Bismarck*
5 U-boats will form patrol line at 0600 between (positions given).
One U-boat in (position given) One U-boat in (position given).
Attacks only against enemy warships.
Air reconnaissance Scapa today shows 3 battleships.
Dummies are possible.

1926 *Norfolk to Prince of Wales*
Do not open fire except in response as I do not want to force the enemy away to the westward.

1934 *Norfolk to C.-in-C.*
Enemy turned away when engaged at long range at 1832. Engagement was broken off to avoid forcing him further away from you. Am shadowing him from 232° distance 18 miles.

2010 *Admiralty*
Unless other orders have been received from C.-in-C., *Manchester*, *Birmingham* and *Arethusa* are *NOT* to establish patrol ordered by Admiralty but are to proceed to Hvalfjord and fuel.

2012 *Admiralty*
U.S.A. patrol squadron No. 52 (Catalinas) from Argentia, Newfoundland, has been directed to search area 500 miles SE of Cape Farewell.

2030 *Admiralty*
Oiler *Cairndale* fitted for oiling at sea and with scuttling charges has been sailed from Gibraltar to patrol (position given). *Severn* (submarine) will escort *Cairndale* who is expected to reach patrol area about 31 May.
Oiler is being sent to St. John's, Newfoundland. Capital ships can be fuelled in emergency from oiler in Conception Bay. There are tankers in convoys HX127 and 128 with fuel oil. Enquiries are being made whether any U.S. oiler facilities can be made available.
Oiler *San Adolfo* has been ordered to patrol in (position given) which she should reach about 28 May.

2056   *From Bismarck*
Impossible to shake off enemy owing to Radar. Proceeding directly to Brest owing to fuel situation.

2102   *From Galatea to Victorious*
If enemy situation remains the same, alter course and fly off air striking force at 2200. After flying off intend to steer 220° maintaining 28 knots.

2106   *From Norfolk*
Enemy speed appears to be 22 knots now. Enemy cruiser is probably to the westward of enemy battleship. *Prince of Wales* close astern of me. *Suffolk* on my starboard beam.

2138   *Admiralty to Force H*
In case your force is required for extended operations, destroyers should be sent back to Gibraltar before it is necessary to give them any fuel.

2144   *Norfolk to Suffolk*
I congratulate you on your very fine shadowing. We may rely on you again tonight.

2156   *C.-in-C.*
Hope to engage from the Eastward about 0900/25.

2205   *From Suffolk to Norfolk*
I can still see *Bismarck* and think I can see cruiser to the westward of her.

2211   *From Group West to Bismarck*
In Scapa not 3 battleships and 3 cruisers as previously reported but only two probably light cruisers and gunnery training ships. In the opinion of the Group the enemy is Prince of Wales.

2217   *Suffolk*
Battleship altering course and firing A.A.

2314   *From Group West to Bismarck*
Assume it is no longer intended to proceed to position (given) but to go direct to St. Nazaire.
Make proposals for deployment of 5 U-boats.
Assume earliest time of arrival is evening of 26th.

2315   *Suffolk to Norfolk*
Aircraft approaching from 124°

2331   *Admiralty to Force H*
Steer so as to intercept *Bismarck* from Southward. Enemy must be short of fuel and will have to make for an oiler. Her future movements may guide you to this oiler.

L

2338   *From Bismarck*
        Air attack in approximate position (given).
2351   *Victorious aircraft to Norfolk*
        Interrogative O.K.
2352   *Norfolk to Victorious aircraft*
        O.K.

25th May
0001   *Victorious aircraft to Victorious*
        Have attacked enemy with torpedoes. One hit only
        observed.
0010   *From Norfolk to Prince of Wales*
        One enemy battleship in sight bearing 211°. Open fire.
0020   *Prince of Wales to Norfolk*
        I am not certain that was *Bismarck*.
0028   *From Bismarck*
        Attack by carrier borne aircraft. Torpedo hit starboard.
0037   *From Bismarck*
        Further attacks expected.
0106   *From Suffolk*
        Consider enemy speed under 20 knots.
0129   *From Group West to Bismarck*
        *Unit, probably Admiral in King George class battleship
        repeatedly made three figure tactical Signals. Last
        shadowing report was received at 2234.*
        *Discovery of enemy Radar frequency will be useful for
        fitting jamming gear later.*
0153   *From Bismarck*
        Torpedo hit of no importance.
0252   *From Group West to Bismarck*
        *Afternoon 25th intend to carry out air reconnaissance
        with FW.200 in area North Spanish coast, Brest, Southern
        tip of Ireland and as far as possible to the west.*
        6 U-boats will form a patrol line between (position given).
0401   *From Bismarck*
        *Enemy radar gear with a range of at least 35,000 metres
        interferes with operations in Atlantic to considerable
        extent. In Denmark Strait ships were located and enemy
        maintained contact. Not possible to shake off enemy
        despite most favourable weather conditions. Will be unable
        to oil unless succeed in shaking off enemy by superior*

speed. Running engagement at range of 28,000 metres to 18,00 metres. Hood concentrated fire on Bismarck. Hood destroyed through explosion after 5 minutes. After that target shifted to King George which turned off making black smoke after she received some hits and remained out of sight for several hours. Own expenditure of ammunition 93 rounds. After this King George continued action at maximum range. Bismarck received 2 hits from King George which reduced the speed and put oil bunkers out of action. Prinz Eugen succeeded in escaping because Bismarck engaged cruisers and battleship in fog. Own radar gear liable to break down especially when guns are firing.

0505   *Suffolk to Norfolk*

Lost touch with enemy at 0306 (position 3 on diagram).

0552   *Norolk to C.-in-C.*

Request air search at dawn. Enemy's speed has not exceeded 22 knots for some time.

0605   *Norfolk to C.-in-C.*

Enemy lost at 0306. *Suffolk* is being sent to search to westward. At daylight *Norfolk* follows *Suffolk* and *Prince of Wales* will be sent to join you.

0840   *From Force H*

My position and course (given) speed 22 knots. *Ark Royal* and *Sheffield* in company. Destroyers detached.

0846   *From Group West to Bismarck*

Last enemy contact report 0213. After that 3 figure tactical reports but no more position reports. We have impression that contact has been lost. Operational signals are repeated to Bermuda and Halifax but not to Gibraltar or Force H which is supposed to be in Eastern Atlantic.

0906   *Repulse to C.-in-C.*

Repulse very much regrets having to leave you at this moment and we wish you all success in destroying Bismarck.

0919   *From Admiralty*

Situation at 0600/25 (Positions are shown on diagram.)

(1) 1st Cruiser Squadron lost touch with enemy at 0306 in position (shown).

(2) *Norfolk* and *Suffolk* are searching to the westward. C.S.2 with 4 cruisers and *Victorious* is carrying out an air

and surface search to North-westward of last known enemy position.

(3) C.-in-C. is estimated to be in the vicinity of (position shown). *Prince of Wales* has been detached by C.S.1 to join C.-in-C.

(4) *Rodney's* estimated position (shown).

(5) *Ramillies* estimated position (shown).

(6) *Edinburgh* estimated position (shown).

(7) *London* estimated position (shown) proceeding to search for enemy tanker.

(8) Force H estimated position (shown) proceeding to intercept from the southward.

(9) *Revenge* estimated position (given).

(10) *Manchester, Birmingham, Arethusa* refuelling at Hvalfjord.

0930 *From Dorsetshire*
My position with *Bulolo* and Convoy SL74 at 0930 (given). Intend to leave convoy now and steer 065° at 25 knots to intercept and shadow enemy.

1152 *From Commander-in-Chief Germany Navy to Fleet Commander Bismarck*
Heartiest congratulations on your birthday. May you continue to be equally successful in this coming year.

1313 *From Group West to Bismarck*
7 U-boats will form patrol line between (positions given). 1 U-boat approximately in position (given).

1414 *From Admiralty*
Convoys HX.128 and SC.32 are to reverse courses for 12 hours and then proceed on route ordered.

1424 *From Admiralty*
Ramillies is to join *Britannic* and escort her to Halifax. *Eskimo* now believed with *Britannic* is to report position, course and speed to *Britannic*.

1540 *From Prince of Wales*
Intend to proceed Hvalfjord at 2000. Estimate fuel remaining on arrival will be 6%.

1545 *From Prince of Wales*
Bismarck opened fire, range 23,000 yards just after *Hood*. Fire immediately effective on *Hood*. *Bismarck's* secondary armament opened at 20,000 yards.

1625 *From Adolf Hitler to Fleet Commander Bismarck*
Best wishes on your birthday.

1831   *From Group West*
Reference FW air reconnaissance. No enemy sighting reports.

1932   *From Group West to Bismarck*
Strong air forces available for arrival Bismarck. Battle formation up to 14° west. Patrol line in accordance with my 1313 with 5 U-boats. 3 destroyers for escort. Outer channels of Brest and St. Nazaire under control. If necessary possible to put into La Pallice as well. Report when passing 10° west.

2344   *From Group West to Bismarck*
Assume you will continue directly to French west coast harbour even if no contact with enemy.

26 May

011   *From Admiralty*
Unless otherwise ordered by C.-in-C., one cruiser is to proceed to watch Denmark Straits and remaining two the Iceland-Faroes passage.

0036   *Admiralty to Admiral, South Africa*
Nelson is to proceed as soon as possible to Gibraltar at best speed.

0046   *From Admiral, South Africa*
Nelson expects to arrive Gibraltar 1600 Saturday 31 May.
(Note: During this period many signals were made organising re-fuelling of capital ships, cruisers and destroyers.)

1015   *Admiralty to Suffolk*
Proceed to search area (given) for enemy supply ships subsequently fuelling Newfoundland on relief by *Repulse*.

1025   *Group West to Bismarck*
Reconnaissance started according to plan. Weather situation in Biscay makes extended escort impossible. Therefore only close air cover possible for time being.

1030   *From Catalina aircraft*
One battleship in sight (position 4).

1052   *Force H to Ark Royal*
Do *NOT* break W/T silence.   1052

1052 *Admiralty to Force H*
Renown is not to become engaged with *Bismarck* unless *Bismarck* is already heavily engaged by either *King George* or *Rodney*.

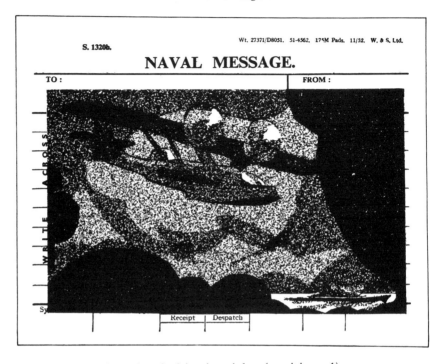

NAVAL MESSAGE.

One battleship in sight (position 4)

1101 *Force H to Ark Royal*
Propose you fly off one or two long range shadowers now. Catalina's report may be somewhat incaccurate.

1103 *Force H to Ark Royal*
Consider we maintain present course until reconnaissance has returned when full scale striking force should be prepared.

1115 *From Ark Royal's aircraft*
One battleship in sight (position given).

(From 1115/26 until 2320/26 Ark Royal's aircraft continuously passed signals reporting the enemy and spotting for gunnery. Destroyers of 4th flotilla shadowed and reported enemy throughout the night, and Ark Royal's aircraft were at it again from first light until 1152/27.)

1154 *From Bismarck*
Enemy aircraft shadowing. Land plane.

1156 *From Group West*
English aircraft reports to 15th reconnaissance group at 1030: One battleship in sight (position 4).

1220   *Admiralty to submarine Severn*
Turn to Gibraltar at maximum speed to establish offensive patrol in Straits of Gibraltar in case *Bismarck* or *Prinz Eugen* endeavours to pass into Mediterranean. *Cairndale* and *City of Dieppe* are to continue in accordance with previous orders.

1228   *Admiralty to Admiral, Gibraltar*
Bismarck reported by Catalina aircraft in (position 4). Establish air and submarine patrols to prevent possible passage into Mediterranean. Patrols are to take preference over convoy duty. Spanish territorial waters need *NOT* be respected for this operation.

1315   *Force H to Sheffield*
Close and shadow enemy battleship to supplement aircraft reports.

1345   *Force H to C.-in-C.*
Enemy position course and speed (given). My position course and speed (given). *Sheffield* detached to shadow.

1424   *From Admiralty*
Repulse is to fuel as rapidly as possible and is then to reinforce *Suffolk* in operation ordered. *Prinz Eugen* may be fuelling in this area. Report probable time of leaving Newfoundland.

1520   *Force H to C.-in-C.*
Air striking force left at 1500.

1553   *From Group West*
Enemy aircraft reports to Plymouth: *Have lost contact with battleship.*

1559   *Force H to Victorious*
Immediately after completion of attack ask aircraft by W/T i enemy is cruiser or battleship.

1722   *Force H to Ark Royal*
Was any attack delivered.

1746   *Ark Royal to Force H*
Yes. 11 torpedoes fired at *Sheffield*. No hits. Afraid instructions to shadow not received in *Ark Royal*. Aircraft left without this knowledge. Your 1345 not decoded and shown to me until striking force had taken its departure.

1800   *Force H to C.-in-C.*
Striking force scored no hits and leaves again at 1830.

1813   *From Group West*
       English Aircraft regained contact at 1600.

1821   *C.-in-C. to Force H*
       King George V had to reduce to 22 knots at 1705 to
       economise fuel. Unless enemy speed is reduced intend to
       return to fuel at midnight. *Rodney* can continue pursuit
       but without destroyer escort. Recommend you remain
       with carrier.

1823   *Ark Royal to Sheffield*
       Striking force leaving 1850 has orders to contact you
       before attacking. Direct them.

1903   *From Bismarck*
       Fuel situation urgent. When can I expect fuel.

1910   *Renown* sighted and challenged destroyers. They identified
       themselves as 4th flotilla (*Cossack, Zulu, Maori, Sikh*).

1935   *Force H to Ark Royal*
       Do you think you could manage a third attack.

1940   *Ark Royal to Force H*
       Intend to make an effort with 6 aircraft. All depends on
       time of return.

1954   *From Bismarck*
       Am being attacked by carrier borne aircraft.

2015   *From Bismarck*
       Ship no longer manoeuvrable.

2054   *C.-in-C. to Force H*
       Request aircraft may give D4 (*Cossack*) visual link with
       enemy.

2056   *Admiralty to C.-in-C.*
       Assume you are organising destroyer night attacks if
       possible. No answer required.

2105   *From Bismarck*
       Aproximate position (given). Torpedo hit aft.

2115   *From Bismarck*
       Torpedo hit amidships.

2117   *Group West*
       *U-boat report at 2000 One battleship one aircraft carrier in
       approximate position (given) course 115° high speed.*

2140   *From Bismarck*
       *Ship no longer manoeuvrable. We fight to the last shell.
       Long live the Fuehrer.*

2225 *Force H to C.-in-C.*
      Torpedo bomber attack scored *one* hit amidships.
2230 *Norfolk*
      My position course and speed (given). Fuel remaining 30%.
      Can operate with *Rodney* or Force H.
2246 *From Captain of 4th destroyer flotilla in Cossack (here-
      after Cossack)*
      Destroyers shadow the enemy.
2307 *Force H to Ark Royal*
      Are you sending off another striking force.
2312 *Ark Royal to Force H*
      No. May have 12 torpedo bombers ready for dawn attack.
      Suggest dawn search. A probable second hit obtained on
      starboard quarter in last attack.
2325 *From Bismarck*
      Am surrounded by Renown and light forces.
2345 *Force H to C.-in-C.*
      3rd torpedo bomber attack not possible tonight. Dawn
      attack tomorrow 12 aircraft. Am turning west for short
      distance to clear you.
2358 *From Bismarck*
      *fight to the last in our belief in you my Fuehrer and in the
      firm faith in Germany's victory.*
2359 *From Bismarck*
      *Armament and engines still intact. Ship however cannot be
      steered with engines.*

27th May
0001 *Admiralty*
      Further examination of photographs of Brest taken on
      May 25th show *Scharnhorst* has moved along the wall 1
      length eastward.
0002 *From Sikh*
      Enemy's speed is 12 knots.
0009 *From C.-in-C.*
      Enemy appears badly damaged. Intend engaging from
      westward at dawn.
0037 *From Admiralty*
      Admiralty appreciation is that *Bismarck* intends to make
      for Brest.

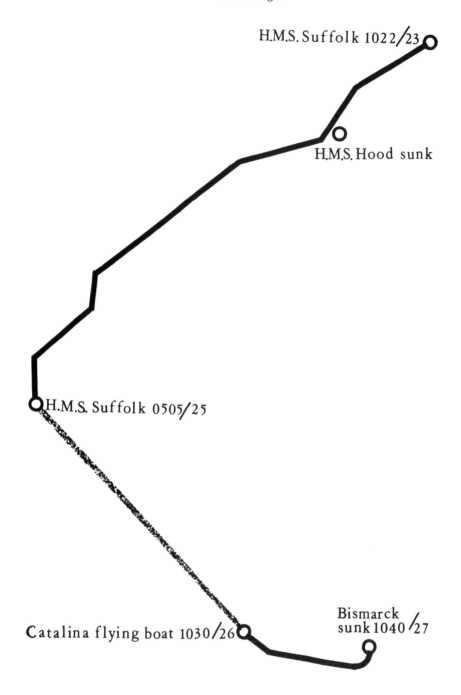

H.M.S. Suffolk 1022/23

H.M.S. Hood sunk

H.M.S. Suffolk 0505/25

Catalina flying boat 1030/26

Bismarck sunk 1040/27

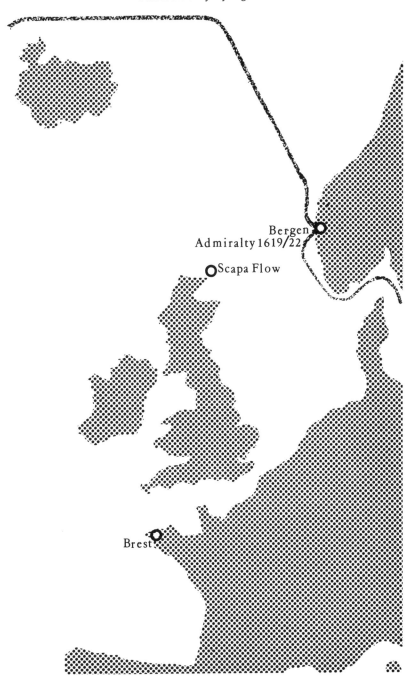

0046   *From Force H to C.-in-C.*
        After being torpedoed *Bismarck* made two complete circles and speed reduced.

0122   *Zulu*
        Have delivered torpedo attack.

0138   *Maori*
        Have delivered attack. Enemy making smoke.

0145   *Maori*
        1 hit confirmed. Extensive fire on forecastle.

0146   *From Cossack*
        Cossack attack completed. Claimed one hit.

0153   *From Adolf Hitler to the Fleet Commander Bismarck*
        I thank you in the name of the German people.
        From Adolf Hitler to the crew of the battleship Bismarck
        The whole of Germany is with you. What can still be done will be done. The performance of your duty will strengthen our people in the struggle for their existence.

0221   *From Fleet Commander Bismarck to C.-in-C. German Navy Propose Lieutenant Commander Schneider, Gunnery Officer, be awarded Knights Cross for sinking Hood.*

0234   *From Sikh*
        Enemy appears to be stopped.

0305   *Force H to Ark Royal*
        At what time will striking force take off. With any luck we may finish her off before Home Fleet arrives.

0320   *Ark Royal to Force H*
        Aircraft ready now but consider attack should not be launched until they can differentiate between friend and foe, shortly after 0600.

0351   *Commander-in-Chief German Navy to Lieutenant Commander Schneider*
        The Fuehrer has awarded you the Knights Cross for sinking the battlecruiser Hood. Heartiest congratulations.

0355   *From Cossack*
        Enemy made good 8 miles 310° between 0240 and 0340 and is still capable of heavy and accurate fire.

0633   *From Force H*
        Air attack postponed. Low visibility.

0637   *Ark Royal to Force H*
        In this weather our torpedo bombers may be a menace to our ships. May I strike down aircraft please.

0707   *Force H to Ark Royal*
      Yes.
0710   *From Bismarck*
      Send U-boat to save War diary.
         (This was the last signal made by *Bismarck.*)
0716   *Admiralty*
      Bomber command is sending a striking force to position
      (given) by 1000 to meet possibility of a second enemy ship
      endeavouring to make French coast.
0940   *From Norfolk*
      Vessel with suspicious marking approaching from South-
      ward.
0942   *From Norfolk*
      Renown approaching from Southward.
1025   *Force H to C.-in-C.*
      Have you disposed of enemy.
1028   *C.-in-C. to Force H*
      Have had to discontinue action for fuel.
1042   *C.-in-C. to Force H*
      She is still afloat.
1044   *From C.-in-C.*
      Any ships with torpedoes are to use them on *Bismarck.*
1045   *C.-in-C. to Force H*
      Cannot sink her with guns.
      Sequence of Signals from Dorsetshire
      German Battleship *Bismarck* is sinking.
      Enemy is sunk.
      Am trying to pick up survivors.
      Am picking up survivors. To rough to lower boat.
      Hundreds of men in water
1107   *From Dorsetshire*
      I torpedoed *Bismarck* both sides before she sank. She had
      ceased firing but her colours were still flying.
1119   *From C.-in-C.*
      I should like to pay the highest tribute for the most gallant
      fight *Bismarck* put up against impossible odds.
1322   *From Group West to Bismarck*
      Reuter reports Bismarck sunk. Report situation im-
      mediately.
1514   *From Admiralty*
      Their Lordships congratulate Commander-in-Chief Home

Fleet and Flag Officer Commanding Force H, and all concerned on the unrelenting pursuit and successful destruction of the enemy's most powerful warship. The loss of *Hood* and her company which is so deeply regretted has thus been avenged, and the Atlantic made more secure for our trade and that of our Allies.

From information at present available to their Lordships there can be no doubt that had it not been for the gallant skill and devotion to duty of the Fleet Air Arm in both *Victorious* and *Ark Royal* our object might not have been achieved.

1610 *From Admiralty to C.-in-C.*

For political reasons it is essential that nothing of the nature of sentiments expressed in your 1119/27 should be given publicly however much we admire a gallant fight.

7th June

1139 *From Admiralty*

Their Lordships desire to be conveyed to the wireless personnel of H.M. ships and shore W/T stations concerned an expression of their appreciation of the good work performed during the operation against the *Bismarck*, the success of which depended so much on efficient wireless communication.

FORCE K
1941

One of the complications of war is that ships hardly ever manage to operate together for any length of time. On the rare occasions that they do their united efficiency soon becomes manifest. One of the ways it shows is by silence. Strange ships have to talk to one another, instructing, reporting, arguing. In a seasoned squadron, everyone knows the form, which eases the load on the signalmen.

Force K consisted of the cruisers *Aurora* and *Penelope,* and the destroyers *Lance* and *Lively.* They worked well and they worked frequently together, molesting the convoys carrying supplies across the Mediterranean to Rommel. No collector of signals would need to leave much space for Force K.

On 8th November, 1941, Force K sailed from Malta to intercept a convoy reported by aircraft. At 40 minutes past midnight the convoy was spotted seven miles away in the moonlight. It was escorted by four destroyers. The Force K rules were to keep in line ahead, and to engage escorts first. As they swept up and down the lines of the convoy *Aurora* alone engaged seventeen targets in 45 minutes. At 0206 Force K withdrew, having estimated their bag as two destroyers, ten merchant ships sunk, two destroyers damaged. Their own casualties amounted to five canaries which died of fright in *Penelope*. During the whole of this neat clear-cut operation only three signals were made.

GENERAL ALARM AND THE BEARING OF THE ENEMY.

REDUCE SPEED TO 20 KNOTS.

DO NOT WASTE AMMUNITION

After the operation *Penelope* signalled to *Aurora*:

CONGRATULATIONS TO AURORA ON HER MAGNIFICENT BOREALIS

The Italian air force attacked Force K on its return to Malta and inflicted "wishful" damage. After this had been reported in the Italian Press, Force K received the following signal from Vice Admiral, Malta:

It is with great regret that I learn from the Italian Press that one of the cruisers received 2 hits and a destroyer 1 hit during torpedo bombing. I can only think in view of the lack of damage I saw today that the Dockyard is more efficient than I thought or your camouflage is excellent.

Force K composed the following reply to Vice Admiral, Malta:

There was an air wap from Taranto

Who set out for exploits gallanto

He sunka da cruise

And get in da nooze

To make up for da kick in da panto.

SIGNAL IK
1941

The Hamburg-Amerika cargo/passenger line *Steiermark* (9,400 tons) was fitted out as a commerce raider and rechristened *Kormoran*. On 19th November, 1941, off the coast of Western Australia, she sighted a cruiser. *Kormoran* turned away immediately, increased to full speed and reported "a disguised raider" in sight. She made the signal as if it had come from the Dutch ship, *Straat Malakka,* whom she closely resembled.

The cruiser, H.M.A.S. *Sydney,* approached eventually to a range of one mile. At this distance *Kormoran's* Captain saw *Sydney* hoist a two-flag signal which he did not understand. He answered it with the order, "Down screens, open fire." A fierce battle followed and both ships were badly damaged. Towards evening *Sydney* steamed away under a dense cloud of smoke and was never seen again. Just before midnight *Kormoran* was abandoned and scuttled. The signal which *Sydney* hoisted was:

IK

(You should prepare for a hurricane or typhoon)

RUSSIAN CONVOY 1942

The finding, fixing and sinking of the *Bismarck* was largely due to the close cooperation between the Admiralty and the Commander-in-Chief, Home Fleet. All available forces were fitted into the picture; nothing was left to chance. Hints were dropped, suggestions made, but the Admiralty did not interfere with the C.-in-C. The kill was left to him. All this is readily revealed in the chain of signals relating to the operation recorded elsewhere in this book.

The following year the pendulum swung the other way. An incident occurred in which cooperation between the Admiralty and the man on the spot failed. Sir Winston Churchill labels it "one of the most melancholy naval episodes in the whole of the war". It led to him being asked by President Stalin if the British Navy had any sense of glory.

By 1942 Russia was in a critical state for war material; the only practical way the Allies could help was for U.S.A. to provide material and freightage and the R.N. to escort it in convoy to North Russian ports. This presented a long gauntlet run for the convoys through enemy-held water and Arctic weather. Our heavy losses were concerning our Commander-in-Chief Home Fleet increasingly, but Roosevelt and Churchill backed Stalin's urgent plea for more, and a larger convoy was planned for midsummer 1942.

German Naval Command sensed this and promptly planned to demolish it. This plan, in signal form, is at long last revealed by our Naval Attaché in Stockholm at that time. His story forms a colourful piece of the fabric on which spy-fiction is woven.

Sweden, with Stockholm its capital, was then the ham in an all-powerful German sandwich. German secret operational information which flowed to and from Norway had to be channelled through Stockholm. Germany, suspecting sympathy between Sweden and Britain, naturally placed our Naval Attaché under rigid German surveillance. Our Attaché and his particular Swedish sympathiser played it off a risky, dangerous cuff. Social contact of any sort between them• was 'out'. The two 'strangers' met and muttered, where and when, at their peril. Nothing was written, everything had to be memorised. Our sympathy goes to our gallant Swedish sympathiser, who was eventually caught.

1218/18/ *From Naval Attache Stockholm to Admiralty*

6/42   Following is plan of attack on next Arctic Convoy begins. It is hoped to obtain early reconnaissance reports when eastbound convoy reaches the vicinity of Jan Mayen Island. Bombing attacks from aircraft will then commence.

Naval movements may then take place as follows. (a) Pocket battleships with six destroyers proceed to Alta fiord. They may also use the anchorage in Sorö Sound. (b) *Tirpitz* with *Hipper*, two destroyers and three T.B's proceed to Narvik area probably Bogen fiord. Naval forces may be expected to operate from these anchorages once the convoy has reached the meridian of 5° East. It is the intention for two groups of surface forces to make rendezvous on Bear Island meridian and then to make simultaneous attacks on convoy supported by U-boats and air units.

Convoy PQ 17 was duly assembled in Iceland and those concerned with escorting it to Russia received this lengthy policy signal from Admiralty before the convoy sailed.

0157/27/ *From Admiralty*

6/42   HUSH

(a) As Admiralty may be in possession of fuller and earlier information of movements of enemy surface forces than our forces will be and as you may not wish to break W/T silence it appears necessary for Admiralty to control movements of convoy as far as this may be influenced by movements of enemy surface forces.

(b) Paragraph (a) will not prevent the C.-in-C. H.F., C.S. One, Senior Officer of escort, or Commodore of convoy

M

giving such orders regarding movements of convoy as local conditions may necessitate.

(c) Should Admiralty consider it necessary to reverse course of convoy the time on which reverse course is to be held will be specified and it is to be understood that it is a temporary measure unless Admiralty give the order for convoy to return to Iceland.

(d) Admiralty may be unaware of weather conditions in the vicinity of the convoy and even though Admiralty may give the order for course of convoy to be reversed it is at the discretion of senior officer present with convoy to ignore the Admiralty order should the weather be thick.

(e) As Admiralty will be exercising control it is essential that they should be kept informed not only of positions and movements of forces but also of any damage incurred. It is not intended above should be carried out when ships, by breaking W/T silence would give away their positions, but only when positions of forces must be known to the enemy.

(f) Generally speaking the safety of the convoy from attacking ships must be met by our covering forces to westwards of meridian of Bear Island and be dependent on our submarine dispositions to eastward of that meridian.

(g) The Admiralty will keep all forces as fully informed as possible of enemy movements.

(h) The movements of the battle fleet covering force will be at the discretion of the C.-in-C. H.F. but it is not expected that this covering force will be placed in the position where it will be subject to heavy air attack unless there is a good chance of bringing Admiral Von Tirpitz to action.

(j) The movements of cruiser covering force will be at the discretion of C.S.One subject to instructions from Admiralty or C.-in-C. H.F. It is not intended that cruiser covering force should proceed to eastward of Bear Island unless convoy is threatened by the presence of surface forces which cruiser covering force can fight. In any case it is not intended that cruiser covering force should proceed eastwards of meridian 25° east.

(k) Our primary objective is to get as much of the

convoy through as possible and the best way to do this is to keep it moving to the eastwards, even though it is suffering damage.

(l) Should the passage of the convoy be barred by a force including Admiral Von Tirpitz in weather of good visibility and to eastwards of meridian of Bear Island, there will be no alternative but to reverse course of convoy. This action may be taken by Admiralty but if necessary C.-in-C. H.F. or Senior Officer of Cruiser Force or Senior Officer with convoy may give this order.

(m) Once convoy is to eastwards of meridian of Bear Island circumstances may arise in which best thing would be for convoy to be dispersed with orders to proceed to Russian ports. It is at the discretion of either C.-in-C., Senior Officer of Cruiser Force or Senior Officer of escort or convoy to give this order.

(n) C.S. One to pass to *Keppel* and destroyers of escort and Commodore of convoy.

On the 27th June 1942 Convoy PQ 17 consisting of 34 merchant ships sailed from Iceland to Russia. By the 4th July only four ships had been sunk after heavy air attack and the convoy was trundling happily along in the calm weather between Bear Island and pack ice with two thirds of its distance run. In close attendance were six destroyers, two anti-aircraft ships, four corvettes and two submarines. Three cruisers and their three escorting destroyers covered the convoy nearby. As day melted into endless twilight there was a lull. Even the enemy shadowing aircraft withdrew for a spell. Suddenly the Arctic's peace was shattered. Not by the enemy, but by three signals which arrived from Admiralty in quick succession:

2111/4   *From Admiralty MOST IMMEDIATE*
        CRUISER FORCE WITHDRAW TO THE WESTWARDS AT HIGH SPEED.

2123/4   *From Admiralty IMMEDIATE*
        OWING TO THREAT FROM SURFACE SHIPS CONVOY IS TO DISPERSE AND PROCEED TO RUSSIAN PORTS.

2136/4   *From Admiralty MOST IMMEDIATE*
        CONVOY IS TO SCATTER.

Those who read these three signals noted the crescendo of priority of the last two, indicating a growing sense of alarm at the transmitting end. They were based on information completely unknown to those with PQ 17, but even so, scattering a convoy from two thousand miles away was unique and had never been done before in our naval history. A convoy is ordered to scatter when it would become an easier target to a superior enemy surface force by remaining concentrated. It is an 'each man for himself' order. The correct way to scatter a convoy is explained in the signal book, but it does not explain there or anywhere else how to round up a convoy with all the ships keeping strict radio silence, once it has been scattered. It is the final and most desperate word in convoy protection. It is the prerogative of the man on the spot when and only when overwhelming enemy forces have arrived on the scene. On this occasion there was no enemy present. The signals gave the ridiculous impression that the Admiralty was watching the enemy coming over PQ 17's horizon.

The second and third of these three signals were sent because the First Sea Lord made up his mind that Tirpitz, Hipper and Scheer were on the point of leaving their base in northern Norway to attack the convoy. The German ships did not in fact sail until 1430 on the following afternoon. When they got to sea they received reports that Convoy PQ 17 had scattered. Satisfied that those merchant ships had been delivered into the hands of their U-boats and bombers, they turned back. Only eleven ships out of the original 34 eventually struggled into Archangel.

It has been said that the ships guarding PQ 17 were never intended to engage heavy enemy forces. This also seems to be implied in the Admiralty's long policy signal. In that case, why were they there? Other convoy escorts had proved what can be done in this respect against fantastic odds. It seems that wireless telegraphy came forty years too soon for PQ 17. Without those three signals whatever else might have happened it would not have become a melancholy naval episode.

NOCTURNE FOR DESTROYERS
1945

Narrative

The above title was appropriately given to an encounter between our "V" Class destroyers and a Japanese cruiser on the night of the 15/16th May, 1945.

The 26th Destroyer Flotilla, consisting of *Venus, Vigilant, Virago,* and *Verulam,* led by Captain M. L. Power in *Saumarez,* were at sea with the Fleet. On the previous night the Admiral got news that some Japanese merchant ships were at large. The 26th Flotilla were ordered to search for them.

At 10 o'clock on the morning of the 15th 'planes from the carriers spotted the enemy convoy about 150 miles to the Eastward. Operations like this in which various forces combine have to have their own label. This one was called MITRE.

The destroyers were off on the scent of the convoy when, at 1150 came the startling news that a Japanese heavy Cruiser, *Haguro,* and a destroyer had been sighted in the same area. The Merchant ships were forgotten. Operation MITRE was cancelled. Captain Power had an unpleasant moment thinking this meant that he was being recalled. The Rear Admiral commanding the 55th Cruiser Squadron soon made it clear that there was no such intention. On went the destroyers, spreading out on to a line of search as they settled down to a speed of 27 knots. They had the whole day in front of them.

Fresh information confirmed the types of enemy ships, and indicated that, having been spotted, they had deserted their convoy and turned Southward towards the protected water of the Malacca Straits. If the Flotilla intercepted this escorted cruiser before dark the odds would be on her side, for she was heavily armed with 8-in. guns with double the range of the destroyers' armament. If they did not make their best speed the enemy would escape. For the moment there was nothing to do but remember the old motto of the Rugger field, "go for the corner flag."

Further reports during the afternoon gave Captain Power no reason to alter his plans. Towards evening, without fuss or bother, he spread his ships on a new line across the approaching course of the enemy.

As the sun went down astern of the destroyers in a blaze of colour, the sea appeared deserted except for the distant coast of Sumatra away to starboard. The destroyers raced eagerly into the approaching darkness. By 7 p.m. the Cruiser was estimated to be about 75 miles to the North-eastward and, as far as they knew, unaware of their presence.

Steaming at that speed, however, very soon introduces a fuel problem. By nightfall Captain Power realised he could do little more than sweep down to the Malayan Coast south of Penang. If he made no contact he would have to turn round and sweep back. He had no intention of being caught close to enemy airfields at dawn.

The night was dark with heavy storm clouds and rain squalls. The destroyers were pinning all their hopes on radar search. But these were the very conditions when radar played tricks. By 10p.m. the crews had been at action stations for 12 hours and were feeling the strain a bit. By 10.30 the thought began to occur that they might be drawing a blank. Then, at 10.45 *Venus,* the most northerly ship, reported a radar contact. At first it was treated with caution; but *Venus* was persistent. Now that it was dark Captain Power had no fear of the result if only he could find the foe. He had a well trained team who knew each other's form well. There was no fear of confusion or lack of understanding. The reported contact certainly fitted in with the plot. He turned his ships towards it. At three minutes past midnight the contact was confirmed by *Saumarez.*

Radar showed a second smaller contact astern of the first—that would be the destroyer. The Flotilla turned to a parallel course and reduced speed to get into their shadowing sectors. When the range had closed to 10 miles the enemy started manoeuvring freely, giving the impression that he was aware of the destroyers. Perhaps he thought they were friendly, coming as they were from the direction of Singapore. That would be the last quarter from which he would expect attack.

Captain Power decided to attack at 1 a.m. At ten minutes to, the situation shaped exactly according to plan. The net was spread and the quarry was steaming into it at a relative speed of 50 m.p.h.

Then events moved fast. The Cruiser turned away to the North-west, spoiling the attack. The Flotilla chased after her, *Venus* bearing down from the Northward. *Saumarez* went "hard over" to avoid colliding with the Japanese destroyer, and opened fire.

The Cruiser replied with everything she had. Near misses drenched everyone on *Saumarez's* bridge. One shell tore its way through her funnel. Then, a direct hit amidships. A blow, a list, escaping steam, and the lights went out. But before this she had got all her torpedoes off at the massive shape as it slid by less than a mile away. On came the lights and away limped *Saumarez* to sort things out behind a smoke screen. Meanwhile other attacks were being pressed home on the Cruiser. Three white plumes of exploding torpedoes were seen. Then a violent explosion from another direction. *Saumarez* thought it was one of the Flotilla. The rest of the Flotilla thought it was *Saumarez*. As Captain Power observed afterwards, "The rest of the Flotilla saw it and apparently eagerly assumed that this marked the end of yet another dictator. Happily, such was not the case." A burst of star shell over *Saumarez* was followed by a report from one destroyer,

AM ILLUMINATING THE ENEMY

The rather cold, though welcome voice of Captain Power replied,

THINK THAT IS ME

Events slowed down a little. *Saumarez* had taken nothing worse than a knock in No. 1 boiler room. The mysterious explosion had almost certainly been the Jap destroyer, stopping someone's torpedo. At 1.30 *Virago* reported the Cruiser's upper deck awash. By then her guns were almost silenced. *Saumarez* lay in the deep field, quite restored and doubtless anxious to join in the final sacrifical rites, but wisely clear of the stray torpedoes which were speeding about in the cruiser's vicinity. Captain Power stayed where he was until he received the report:

CRUISER SUNK

After which he formed up his Flotilla and led them home.

The last paragraph of his report on this brilliant encounter reads as follows:

"The attack was a success; but it was by no means a perfect and polished performance. There is much to be learnt from it, and plenty of room for improvement. The errors and omissions, mostly on my part in the control, were made up for by team work and enthusiasm. The result left me proud of the entire command."

Signals

Throughout these signals

> D 26 addresses Captain Power, commanding the 26th Destroyer Flotilla
>
> C-in-CEI „ Commander-in-Chief East Indies.
>
> B. S. 3 „ Admiral commanding the 3rd Battle Squadron.
>
> C. S. 5 „ Rear Admiral commanding 5th Cruiser Squadron.
>
> (R) means the signal is repeated to the addressees shown.

15th May

0217 *From BS3 to D26*
ATTACKING FORCE DESTROYERS RAISE STEAM FOR FULL SPEED FORTHWITH

0237 *From BS3 to D26*
PROCEED FORTHWITH WITH 26TH D.F. AT 27 KNOTS TO SEARCH FOR ENEMY AUXILIARY VESSEL. RETURN BY SAME ROUTE. AIR SEARCH AND STRIKE FROM CARRIERS WILL BE ARRANGED

0311 *From BS3 to D26*
IF CANCEL MITRE RECEIVED FROM C—IN—CEI OR BS3 REJOIN ME

1000 AIRCRAFT B REPORTS ATTACKING 2 ENEMY MERCHANT VESSELS IN POSITION (given)

1041 *From C.—in—CEI. to D26*
CANCEL MITRE REPEAT CANCEL MITRE

1056 *From D26 to CS5*
REFERENCE C—IN—CEI'S 1041 REQUEST CONFIRMATION OF CANCELLATION IN VIEW OF AIRCRAFT B REPORT

1101 *From D26 to Destroyers*
HAVE BEEN RECALLED. CAN AFFORD TO EASE
DOWN A BIT PENDING REPLY TO MY APPLICATION
TO CONTINUE

1150 *From Aircraft G*
ONE CRUISER ONE DESTROYER IN POSITION
(given)

1155 *From CS5 to D26 (R) BS3, C.—in—CEI*
REFERENCE C—IN—CEI'S 1041 YOU SHOULD SINK
ENEMY SHIPS BEFORE RETURNING

1221 *From D26 to BS3*
MY POSITION IS (GIVEN) AM CLOSING ENEMY
WARSHIPS AT 27 KNOTS

1228 *From Aircraft G*
COURSE AND SPEED OF ONE ENEMY CRUISER
AND ONE DESTROYER ARE (given) TYPE OF ENEMY
REPORTED ARE ONE NACHI CRUISER ONE MINNE-
KAZE DESTROYER

1252 *From CS5 to C—in—CEI (R) D26*
AM PROCEEDING TO SUPPORT D26

1254 *From D26 to Destroyers*
IF REPORTS OF ENEMY CONTINUE GOOD I
SHALL PROBABLY CONCENTRATE BEFORE CON-
TACT. ON SIGHTING AIM IS TO SHADOW AND
CONCENTRATE TO SOUTHWARD

1330 *From D26 to CS5 (R) BS3*
MY POSITION COURSE AND SPEED ARE (given)
INTEND TO INTERCEPT AND ATTACK BY NIGHT

1513 *From D26 to Destroyers*
IF CONTACT IS MADE IN DAYLIGHT KEEP OUT
OF GUN RANGE. TRY TO DRAW ENEMY WEST-
WARD, KEEPING AS FAR SOUTH AS POSSIBLE.
ATTACK BY NIGHT WILL PROBABLY BE SIMUL-
TANEOUSLY FROM DIVERGENT BEARINGS OWING
TO ENEMY'S LARGE TORPEDO ARMAMENT

1551 *From Aircraft*
ONE ENEMY CRUISER AND DESTROYER IN
POSITION(given)

1640 *From Aircraft*
HAVE ATTACKED ENEMY CRUISER WITH BOMBS
RESULT OF ATTACK PROBABLE HITS

1647   *From D26 to Verulam and Vigilant*
        DONT BUST YOURSELVES
1648   *From D26 to Verulam and Vigilant*
        I AM AIMING TO SPREAD BY DARK AND THEN
        CARRY OUT CROSS SEARCH. VIRAGO AND VENUS
        WILL PROLONG THE LINE OTHER THE SIDE OF ME
1651   *From D26 to Virago and Venus*
        FORM ON A LINE OF BEARING (given) FROM ME
        IN SEQUENCE VIRAGO VENUS DISTANCE BETWEEN
        SHIPS 4 MILES
1811   *From D26 to Destroyers*
        FAILING FURTHER REPORT INTEND TO REMAIN
        ON PRESENT COURSE AND SPEED UNTIL MID-
        NIGHT. AT THAT TIME INTEND TO REVERSE
        COURSE AND REDUCE TO 20 KNOTS WITHOUT
        FURTHER SIGNAL
2345   *From D26*
        VESSEL SIZE UNKNOWN DETECTED BY R.D.F.

16th May
0125   *From D26*
        AM ENGAGING ENEMY
0140   *From D26 to C.—in—CEI.*
        CRUISER SINKING
0210   *From D26 to Destroyers*
        V'S FOR VICTORY PICK UP PRISONERS STAY NO
        LONGER THAN 10 MINUTES
0212   *From D26 to Destroyers*
        ON LIGHTS. JOIN ME AT FULL SPEED
        From D26 to C.—in—CEI (R) CS5
        MY POSITION COURSE AND SPEED (given). ENEMY
        CRUISER SUNK. DESTROYER NOT ACCOUNTED
        FOR. ONE BOILER ROOM OUT OF ACTION IN
        SAUMAREZ. REMAINDER OF FLOTILLA NOT
        DAMAGED.

SEND A FRIGATE—1949

Some say China looked upon World War II more as an interruption of its own internal struggle than anything else. As soon as Japan laid down her arms the Chinese Communists up north grabbed all the Japanese military know-how and Japanese weapons they could lay their minds and hands on, and bared their teeth to the southward. The Republicans, with a preference for American weapons, bared theirs back. At Chunking, the Nationalist Chinese Government emerged from its moth balls and floated down the Yangtze—that mighty bisector of China—past Wanshien, and on for another 800 miles to Nanking, their old Capital, to be joined once more by the cortège of Diplomatic Embassies, with their attendant warships. Before long Communists and Nationalists had nothing more to keep them apart than the Yangtze Kiang, which the former determined to cross on 21 April, 1949. Up to this point the civil war was proceeding as Chinese wars usually proceeded; foreigners were unmolested, provided they did not interfere.

Amethyst was a 1,500 ton frigate belonging to our Far Eastern Fleet. About 100 yards long, she carried a few four inch guns and a crew of 160 officers, men and Chinese ratings. An unpleasant sight through the periscope of a U-boat (which she was designed and equipped to destroy) but otherwise a trim, compact, general-purpose little warship, on this occasion proceeding to relieve the destroyer *Consort* at Nanking. Well briefed on the dicey Chinese tension prevailing along the river banks, she sailed from Shanghai on 19th and, according to the River rule-book, anchored over-night. Early next morning, soon after passing where the Delta had decided to become a river, she was fired on intermittently and inaccurately from the north shore. Reassured at such gunnery incompetence she passed quietly on, flaunting a large Union Jack on either side, when suddenly a shell screeched over her starboard side quickly followed by four more which were direct hits; two tearing into her bridge, killing, maiming, spattering blood. Out of control and still under fire, what was left of her limped away to port and grounded on an island. All inside two minutes. The Captain's multiple wounds were to allow him the dregs of two more day's life. The less wounded First Lieutenant took over at the crawl, and mananged to get off a FLASH signal:

From Amethyst to all ships

Under heavy Fire. Am Aground in Approx position
(guessed*) Large Number of Casualties.

Enemy fire soon silenced the after gun, the only one which
would bear. Darkness brought relief and appraisement. The one
remaining telegraphist patched up the radio the (acting) Skipper
signalled to his Admiral at Shanghai,

From Amethyst to Flag Officer 2

Amethyst still aground on Rose Island. Am attempting
to make good vital damage to refloat and proceed to
Nanking. 60 Approx of ship's company including 4
wounded are making way to nearest town. Casualties are
about 17 dead including doctor and sick berth attendant. 20 Seriously wounded including captain.

Followed later by

Please make all signals in plain language as confidential
books destroyed.

Hereafter, all signal communication—upon which so much
depended—was limited by the durability of *Amethyst's* one and
only telegraphist. Another missing necessity was medical knowledge in handling drugs and tending the wounded. A signal from
F.O.2 saying a Sunderland flying boat was bringing an R.A.F.
Doctor was therefore very welcome. The ship was refloated after
dark, ventured a little then anchored, completely exhausted.

The destroyer *Consort* and the 10,000 ton cruiser *London* had
also ventured to *Amethyst's* aid, but were turned back by
overpowering Communist gunfire, with damage and casualties.
F.O.2 signalled:

Am sorry we cannot help you today. We shall keep on trying.
Stay where you are at present unless forced to move. In this
case go upstream. Further instructions will follow.

In the meantime Lieutenant-Commander Kerans, Assistant
Naval Attaché at Nanking was on trek, struggling to find his new
command. With the First Lieutenant almost at the end of his
wound-racked tether, the R.A.F. doctor and the new Captain
eventually arrived on board.

In spite of helpfully-intended suggestions from his Admiral,
Kerans soon realised that the situation was completely in the
hands of the Communists and that *Amethyst* was the jam in the

*Chart was torn to shreds.

sandwich, the bread being the Communist batteries on either side of him. The Nationalists, though friendly, were in no position to help except by lending another doctor. So four days after leaving Shanghai *Amethyst* lay stricken, wedged and alone, still fifty miles short of Nanking. On 22 April F.O.2 surprised Kerans with:

> The safety of your ship's company being now the first consideration you are to prepare to evacuate from the ship and sink her. Report when you will be ready.

Next day, which was St. George's Day, F.O. followed with:

> If I judge the prospect of making a down-stream passage reasonably promising would you feel it practical navigationally at night.

Kerans replied at once in the affirmative. Was the seed of an idea planted here? During the lonely silence of St. George's Day, *Amethyst* intercepted BBC's hint of a probable safe conduct for the ship. Kerans signalled F.O.2:

> Have just heard rough gist of BBC News. Is there any hope of safe conduct which I can pass on to ship's company who are behaving splendidly but nearing breaking point. Have not been fired on again. If I come under fire before dark intend to beach sink destroy and reach Shanghai. Am ready to do this now.

F.O.2 replied:

> You have my approval to act as you think best if fired on again I am trying to arrange safe conduct for you to Nanking but doubtful if this will operate quickly. Try to let me know if you have to abandon. I am full of admiration for all in Amethyst.

But at top level the Communists were unapproachable and now, at ship level their senior bullies started summoning Kerans to periodical conferences ashore and making his release conditional to a full confession from him that the Royal Navy was responsible for, and that they started the whole affair. Each conference was summarised by signals which reached the Commander-in-Chief, Far East. To confirm that the bullies were not getting him down, Kerans signalled in June:

> Rest assured Sir that all on board are determined to hold out come what may.

The C.-in-C. replied:

> I entirely agree your conduct of negotiations and am proud of the spirit and determination of all in Amethyst.

All this was taking place against a background in *Amethyst* of shorter and shorter food and fuel rations, no amenities, great discomfort, humidity and tension. To cap it all, a typhoon in July passed near enough to keep *Amethyst* steaming to her anchors.

All this time Kerans was weighing secretly to himself the chances of escape. There were many aspects but they gradually merged and hardened his lonely reasoning into one resounding challenge—'now or never'. It must be *now*, that very night.

For some time Kerans and his Admiral's Flag Lieutenant had between them been designing a signal cypher. Security was essential. The new cypher was now put into practice:

> *From Kerans to C.-in-C. (repeated) Concord*
> I am going to break out at 10 p.m. tonight 30 July.
> Concord set watch 8290 Kcs.

Without the superb leadership, planning and execution set out in detail, the rest of the story loses much of its lustre. Undetected, *Amethyst* slipped her cable before moon-rise. They struck lucky in finding a merchantman to follow over the section of the river for which her charts had been destroyed, but her guide unintentionally led her into dead trouble with Communist batteries from which luck alone prevented disaster. Thereafter luck held tight and sent her scorching past unexpected hazards at an undreamt of speed, till she screwed up all her courage to face the two big, dreaded Chinese forts at the river's mouth, past which—for reasons only luck will ever know—she romped unnoticed as dawn broke and so on to the freedom of the open sea. On this 150 mile gauntlet-run, only these three signals were exchanged:

> *From Amethyst to C.-in-C.*
> HALF WAY
> *(later)*
> HUNDRED UP
> *Reply from C.-in-C.*
> A MAGNIFICENT CENTURY
> *From Concord (On sighting Amethyst)*
> FANCY MEETING YOU AGAIN
> *Reply from Amethyst*
> NEVER NEVER HAS A SHIP BEEN MORE WEL-
> COME

Kerans' final signal to C.-in-C., put a classic seal on the episode.

> HAVE REJOINED FLEET SOUTH OF WOO SUNG.
> NO DAMAGE OR CASUALTIES. GOD SAVE THE
> KING.

Scrap Log

From now on the reader is faced with a scrapbook—Scrap Log would describe it better—of individual signals.

In the day's work a great deal is said which is not worth recording. So with signals. Most of them are either technical, routine, or just plain dull. Out of the two-hundred odd tons of signals sent during World War II, a mere truckload would cover exciting or interesting episodes of which a handful would be outstanding. Yet, both in war and peace, occasionally there flashes from a lamp or crackles from an aerial a gem which is worth preserving. Some of these may have taken time to compose, others came straight off the cuff. Some are serious; some are humourous and, of those, a few are only funny at the receiving end.

There can't have been much humour, for example, at the transmitting end of:

SOS SOS SOS MAID OF CORK SINKING.

The signals which follow could appear under such headings as: Inspiring, Sarcastic, Witty. But they do not seem to take kindly to grouping; therefore they have been thoroughly mixed up. Without mercy, the reader is jerked from situation to situation. At one moment he is in a sea battle; the next he may be on a peacetime picnic. The point to remember is that the situations are real; they all really happened.

The colour pages of signal flags of the Royal and International (Merchant) navies which follow at intervals show a fair sample of those in use at the outbreak of World War II. Some date right back to Admiral Howe's signal book, and were used by Nelson. Thirteen of the International flags were introduced by the great sailor, Captain Frederick Marryat in 1817. Some flags shown are duplicated in these codes, but the occasion of their use precludes confusion.

The parts some of these flags have played, and their relationship to past visual signals are noted on the pages opposite.

Signalling at sea with distinctive symbols began when ships separated beyond shouting distance from one another. Gradually the symbols evolved into banners, then flags with their codes. How much longer will these colourful bunting designs flutter? Where will they flutter from?

From the decks of modern warships, where masts once grew sprouts electronic cactus, in-and-ex-haling information in clarity, bulk, and speed completely outdating the capability of these pretty flags. Die-hards may cling to signal flags '. . .in case of emergency' Today's top emergency is electric power failure; when power, auxiliary power, and auxiliary-auxiliary power fail, signalling at sea is back in square one.

Flag *A* (Navy) was probably flying from the aircraft carrier *Formidable* when she was attacked by Japanese aircraft in the Pacific.

From *Formidable*, after being attacked by *Kamikaze*, to *Indomitable* (flying flag of Admiral Vian):
LITTLE YELLOW BASTARD.
Reply from *Indomitable:*
ARE YOU REFERRING TO ME.

The Naval *Red Affirmative* may well be the veteran flag of them all, With a slight change of meaning to *Assent,* its colour and design go right back to Admiral Howe's Signal Book, introduced in 1790.

Flag *D* (Navy) was once half of a two-flag signal *DG,* always acceptable to any ship, meaning MANOEUVRE WELL EXECUTED (Damn Good). With the NEGATIVE flag above it, it meant the opposite. In either case, when it appeared at the flagship's halyards it was repeated by all ships present, together with the pendants of the ship addressed. The whole fleet knew whether that ship had done well or badly.

International	1940 — 1945	Royal Navy

A — I am undergoing a speed trial	Aeroplane flag	A — Aircraft — presumed hostile in sight

B — I am taking in or discharging explosives	Ahead flag: Relative position ahead	B — Fire umbrella barrage
	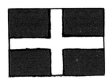	
C — Yes (affirmative)	Affirmative flag: Approved	C — Distinguishing signal for coastguard stations

D — Keep clear of me — I am manoeuvring with difficulty	Aircraft carrier flag: Five minutes notice for air attack	D — Gas alarm

E — I am directing my course to starboard	Battle cruiser flag	E — A semaphore message will be made

International	1940 — 1945	Royal Navy

F — I am disabled. Communicate with me	Battle ship flag	F — Column (or part of column addressed) is to stand by to turn together to port

G — I require a pilot	Black flag	G — Speed flag
	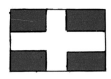	
H — I have a pilot on board	Blue Affirmative flag:	H — 'W' boats in sight

I — I am directing my course to port	Blue flag: Carry out previous manoeuvre	I — Distinguishing signal for leading ships
		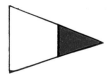
J — I am going to send a message by semaphore	Fleet is to be at immediate notice for air attack	J — Surtace craft detected by RD./F.

Flag *G* (Navy) had, like most of these flags, more than one meaning, but its primary association has always been with that important ingredient of naval warfare — SPEED. Speed is, as the following visual signals suggest, purely a relative term.

*

The Flagship was refitting. The remainder of the Battle Cruiser Squadron were being led up to the anchorage by the mext Senior Captain who had not had much experience in handling the Squadron. The signal to stop engines was hoisted. When it was hauled down the leading ship did not stop her own engines, and soon began to draw away from the others.
From next astern to Leading ship:
    WHAT SPEED ARE YOU STOPPED AT PLEASE.

*

Or, as one Canadian Destroyer put it to another,
    PARDON ME BUT YOUR SHIP IS SLOWING

*

From Terror (very old) to Protector off Sidi Barrani, 1941:
    AM PROCEEDING AT FULL SPEED TO YOUR ASSIST-
    ANCE. MY SPEED 4 KNOTS.

*

On one occasion, through tactless use of its phonetic pseudonym Flag *G* might have ended up on the scaffold.
Scene: Admiral's bridge of H.M.S. *Nelson* with King George VI on board. The fleet was approaching the anchorage in Weymouth Bay. The speed of the fleet was being reduced to 6 knots before anchoring. The following was heard:
Signal Officer to Flag Deck "George 6 Hoist."
Signal Officer to Flag Deck "George 6—execute."
His Majesty is said to have flinched, but he made no comment.

N

Perhaps the most exciting moment in a warship is on sighting the enemy and signalling the sighting report. However much it may have been anticipated, the actual moment when it happens has a thrill of its own.

On 31st May 1916, *Southampton,* flagship of the 2nd Light Cruiser Squadron, was stationed ahead of our Battle Cruisers. It was a fine afternoon; the sea calm, the sun shining through patches of haze. Though the advanced forces had brushed against one another, *Southampton* had taken no part and touch with the enemy had now been lost. The guns' crews were relaxed, the men chatting and smoking; everything seemed quiet and peaceful.

Suddenly, from the foretop, a ship was reported ahead. In a few minutes the German High Seas Fleet could be distinguished. The shutter on the signalling searchlight began clacking. *Southampton* signalled to *Lion,* Admiral Beatty's flagship:

> SIGHTED ENEMYS BATTLE FLEET ON BEARING SOUTH-EAST COURSE OF ENEMY NORTH

*

From Fleetwood to C.-in-C. Portsmouth
> HAVE ONE COLORADO BEETLE ON BOARD. REQUEST DISPOSAL.

*

Two submarines were returning to harbour after the annual inspection by their Admiral, Rear Admiral Dent. He was embarked in one of the submarines and had just retired from the bridge. During the inspection the submarines had to carry out an attack on a battleship, firing a torpedo with a crushable head. After attacking, each submarine recovered its own torpedo and lashed it to the casing. The submarine carrying the Admiral had obviously scored a hit for the head of their torpedo was well crushed. There was no visible damage to the 2nd submarine's torpedo. The following signals were exchanged.

From 1st submarine (with Admiral) to 2nd submarine:
> DID YOU GET A HIT.

From 2nd submarine:
> YES, DENT IS IN THE HEAD BELOW.

From 1st submarine:
> HOW DID YOU GUESS.

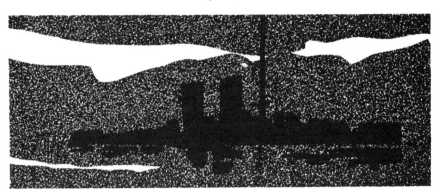

Our light forces were on a sweep in the Skaggerak in World War I in hazy weather. Shortly after dawn the most northerly cruiser signalled:

ENEMY BATTLESHIP BEARING NNE DISTANCE 2 MILES. AM PREPARING TO RAM.

Later came:

CANCEL MY LAST SIGNAL. BATTLESHIP TURNS OUT TO BE A LIGHTHOUSE.

(The lighthouses on the northern shores of the Skaggerak often have twin towers which look like superstructure and turrets.)

*

This contribution from an ex-Signal Bos'n is typical of the keenness of the signal branch between the wars.

"We were lying at Argostoli with all the Mediterranean Fleet. I was in the *Royal Oak* at the time and there was quite a bit of friendly sniping going on. I had caught Barham twice in half an hour before 0930. I then received the following from Fleet Signal Officer:

I HOPE THAT YOUR ADMIRAL IS WELL.

"On investigation I found to my horror that the Admiral's flag was at half mast. I think that is the best one that I was ever caught on."

*

From Gracie Fields (trawler):

GRACIE FIELDS MAKING WATER AND SINKING FAST.

Destroyer flotilla at sea, time 2100. No. 2 destroyer seems to be keeping much too close to the stern of her leader.

From Flotilla leader to No. 2:

WOULD YOU CARE TO JOIN ME IN A GLASS OF PORT.

*

From Ship to Ship:

PLEASE SEND YOUR TECHNICAL EXPERT TO SEE OUR FOREMOST GUN.

Reply:

OUR TECHNICAL EXPERT CAN SEE YOUR FOREMOST GUN FROM HERE.

*

From C.-in-C. Mediterranean, to Cardiff:

YOUR CONFIDENTIAL BOOK OFFICER IS TO REPORT AT MY OFFICE FOR DESTRUCTION.

*

During the operations off Crete in World War II, when cruisers and destroyers which were not sunk were battered and worn out, a flotilla limped into Alexandria. No sooner had they fuelled than they were ordered out again back to Crete. The Rear Admiral commanding Destroyers pointed out to the Commander-in-Chief by signal that his ships were scarcely seaworthy. One of them was leaking badly with one engine out of action and steering defective. Probably one of the toughest signals made during the war was the Commander-in-Chief Mediterranean's reply:

THIS IS NO TIME FOR DESTROYERS TO BE BREAKING DOWN.

*

Two Canadian destroyers approached a semi-frozen anchorage. The first barged her way in through ice and anchored.

From 1st ship to 2nd ship:

ABIE, ABIE, ABIE MY BOY, WHAT ARE YOU WAITING FOR NOW.

Reply from 2nd ship:

ICEHOLES.

When the American Battle Squadron joined the Grand Fleet in World War I, the Americans had great difficulty in mastering our signals. One day when the whole fleet was at sea a signal to turn was hoisted. When it came down the British ships turned one way, the Americans the other. The U.S.N. Admiral Rodman turned to rend his aide, who forestalled him with "Sorry Admiral, I guess I told you wrong." This has since been quoted as an example of the perfect relationship between Admiral and Flag Lieutenant.

From Flag Officer Greenock to Flag Officer Glasgow:
REGRET QUEEN CHARLOTTE CANNOT WAIT FOR DUCHESS OF PORTSMOUTH.

*

A cruiser was trying to secure to head and stern buoys near her flagship in a congested harbour. The Admiral watched the proceedings from his quarterdeck. The cruiser made a good approach and appeared to be judging the manoeuvre well. The Admiral signalled:
GOOD.
Then things started to go wrong for the cruiser. She missed the buoys and got more and more tangled up. After watching for some time the Admiral again signalled:
ADD TO MY PREVIOUS SIGNAL GOD.

*

On a calm summer's evening a destroyer was steaming down the Minches returning to Londonderry after a convoy conference at Greenock. Suddenly, all chances of a final night in harbour were shattered by this signal from the Admiralty, at top priority:

ENEMY AGENT KNOWN TO HAVE BEEN IN ALDER-SHOT RECENTLY SEEN YESTERDAY AT GREENOCK MINGLING WITH TROOPS ABOUT TO EMBARK IN OVERSEAS CONVOY. MOTOR BOAT BELONGING

LIGHTHOUSE KEEPER MULL OF KINTYRE REPORTED MISSING AT 0900 TODAY WEDNESDAY. CONSIDER POSSIBLY AGENT HAS STOLEN BOAT AND IS MAKING FOR IRISH FREE STATE WITH IMPORTANT INFORMATION ABOUT CONVOY SAILING TOMORROW. MOTOR SKIFF HULL GREEN, RUBBING STRAKE ORANGE, TANK FULL. MAN 6 FOOT FAIR FRESH COMPLEXION AND LAST SEEN WEARING KHAKI BATTLEDRESS. NO OTHER SHIP AND NO AIRCRAFT AVAILABLE. SEARCH FOR THIS BOAT. REPORT WHEN YOU HAVE FOUND IT.

With less than an hour's daylight left all the destroyer could do was to guess a likely position and steam for it. As she approached the position a speck was sighted. It became a boat, with a man in it. Man and boat answered the description. The boat was hoisted and searched. It contained a copy of *Mein Kampf,* in German. In that vast area and in fading light it was like a winner coming home at very long odds. In little more than an hour after the arrival of Admiralty's signal:
From Destroyer to Admiralty:
BOAT RECOVERED, MAN ARRESTED.

*

During Russian convoy PQ 16 in May, 1942.
From Ashanti (with convoy) to Admiralty:
NO FURTHER AIR ATTACK TOUCH WOOD. ... THE SHADOWERS LIKE THE POOR ARE ALWAYS WITH US.

*

During World War I an Admiral had invited a friend—Lady A— to lunch the following day. In the morning his Squadron went to sea and he made the following signal to the captain of another ship which was remaining in harbour:
I HAD INVITED LADY A TO LUNCH TODAY BUT AS WE ARE SAILING UNEXPECTEDLY I WOULD BE GLAD IF YOU WOULD GIVE HER LUNCHEON INSTEAD. I AM LEAVING MY BARGE BEHIND WITH ORDERS TO REPORT TO YOU. THIS MAY MAKE IT EASIER FOR YOU TO LOOK AFTER LADY A. PLEASE MAKE WHATEVER USE OF HER YOU LIKE.

Farewell message to departing cruiser commanded by a Captain Wright:
  PROVERBS 6 v.8.[1]

*

Bombardment of Genoa. H.M.S. *Malaya,* in accordance with tradition flying the Malayan Jack at her Port Yard arm. After the second 15-in. salvo enveloped her in smoke and flame *Malaya* received the following signal from Admiral Somerville in *Renown*:
  YOU LOOK LIKE AN ENRAGED P AND O.
(The Malayan Jack and the P. and O. House flag are very similar.)

*

In reply to a complaint by the master of a Merchant Ship that the route he had been ordered to take was dangerous.
From C.-in-C. Med. to Naval Officer in charge, Haifa:
  INFORM THE MASTER OF S.S. . . . . THAT EVERYWHERE IN THE MEDITERRANEAN IS DANGEROUS THESE DAYS.

*

A battlecruiser arrived in harbour after a long patrol at sea to receive a signal from her flagship saying that she—the flagship—was unable to take her turn on patrol, so the returning ship would have to refuel and put to sea again.
  On setting out for the second time the battlecruiser's Marine band were on the quarterdeck, playing a tune which had very rude words. As she passed as close as possible to the flagship:
From Flagship:
  ON LEAVING HARBOUR WHO SELECTS THE BAND TUNES.
The Seagoing ship replied:
  NORMALLY THE BANDMASTER BUT ON SPECIAL OCCASIONS THE CAPTAIN.

---

[1] "Better is a little with righteousness than great revenues without right."

From submarine (returning from Patrol) to Base:
　　EXPECT TO ARRIVE 1800 IF FRIENDLY AIRCRAFT
　　WILL STOP BOMBING ME.

*

C.-in-C. Eastern Fleet after Fleet Air Arm raid on Sabang:
　　WE CAUGHT THE NIPS WITH THEIR HEADS DOWN AND
　　THEIR KIMONOS UP.

*

A submarine had broken down on surface. Another submarine had ordered to close her and take her in tow, thereby delaying the latter's return to harbour considerably. On making contact, the broken down submarine received:
　　TAKE MUMMIES HAND.

*

From Senior officer to submarine, apparently in diffulties:
　　WHAT ARE YOU DOING.
From Submarine:
　　LEARNING A LOT.

*

Dover Patrol 1918. French destroyers were operating with ours. One afternoon enemy destroyers were sighted by a British and French destroyer who immediately gave chase. The Frenchman kept up for a bit then suddenly dropped astern rapidly in a cloud of smoke and steam.
From French destroyer to British ally:
　　CAN GO NO MORE. BOILER GO BANG.

*

*From Canadian Training Establishment to Canadian Flag Officer
　　Atlantic:*
　　RENEWAL OF STOCKINGS REQUIRED WHITE WOMANS
　　AND SHOES BLACK WOMANS.

From both ships simultaneously:
YOO HOO.

*

From Rear Admiral Alexandria—General:
PREPARE TO REPEL SEA BORNE ATTACK.
The situation at Alexandria was tense. *Warspite* and *Valiant* had been put out of action in harbour. As dawn broke the local fishing fleet appeared with their sails billowing, making for the harbour entrance after a good night's catch. The signal was soon cancelled but it showed an intelligent appreciation of what the Italians could have done, had they thought of it.

*

October, 1940. Coastal Command aircraft was laboriously flashing to Cruiser *Dunedin* off Rockall. The ship was returning from Norway.
From Aircraft:
WHAT SHIP.
From Dunedin:
GRAF SPEE.
From Aircraft:
ARE YOU NAVAL TYPES STILL SO FAST ASLEEP THAT YOU HAVEN'T HEARD OF THE END OF THE GRAF SPEE.
From Dunedin:
WHICH END.

From Coastguard Station:
A SMALL BOAT APPEARS TO BE STATIONARY OFF
BROADSTAIRS ABOUT ¾ MILE. THE MILITARY HAVE
BEEN FIRING AT IT BUT GET NO REPLY.

*

One gunboat was being followed up a Chinese river by a second.
The first ship rounded a bend and slowed down to wait for the
other. As her consort did not appear she called her up by radio.
WHAT IS THE DELAY.
The second gunboat had run aground, and replied:
REGRET HAVE BECOME A SEMI-PERMANENT
FEATURE OF THE CHINESE LANDSCAPE.

In 1916 a young naval officer was married on board the Flagship H.M.S. *Queen,* at Taranto. Much to his embarrassment and annoyance an Italian officer approached him after the ceremony and kissed him on both cheeks.

In 1941, this naval officer,, by then a Rear Admiral, commanding the Mediterranean aircraft carrier Squadron, met his erstwhile best man, another Admiral. The best man reminded the bridegroom that the culprit was now Commander-in-Chief of the Italian Battlefleet.

After the carrier's raid on Taranto the following signals were exchanged:

From ex Best Man:
CONGRATULATIONS ON PAYING OFF SO WELL A 25 YEAR OLD DEBT.

From ex Bridegroom:
THANK YOU YERY MUCH, BUT SO FAR ONLY ON ONE CHEEK.

*

From Captain D, Plymouth to C.-in-C., Nore:
INTEND PUTTING FISHER GIRL OUT OF ACTION FOR 7 DAYS FOR SCRAPING OF BOTTOM.

*

From Submarine returned from war patrol to flotilla Captain:
PSALM 17 v.4.[1]

*

From Admiralty to Admiral Commanding Orkneys and Shetlands:
PYROTECHNICS SIMULATING FLASH OF TRAMWAY TROLLEY BUSES NOW AVAILABLE FOR CAMOUFLAGE PURPOSES. REPORT NUMBER REQUIRED.
Reply from Admiral commanding Orkneys and Shetlands:
YOUR . . . NIL. NO TRAMS.

---

[1] Concerning the works of men by the word of thy lips I have kept me from the paths of the destroyers.

Admiral Lord Charles Beresford, as C.-in-C. Mediterranean, was flying his flag in H.M.S. *Bulwark,* anchored off Corfu. Some midshipmen from the flagship were picnicking on a neighbouring island on which there stood a German convent. As no boat arrived to collect the midshipmen some of them, who were due back on board, stripped and swam off to the ship. Some nuns from the convent were horrified and reported the matter to the Kaiser who was in residence at his Palace at Corfu:

From His Imperial Majesty to Commander in Chief:
    I AM SORRY TO INFORM YOU THAT THE NUNS ON THE ISLAND OF ... HAVE BEEN SHOCKED BY THE ATTIRE OF SOME OF YOUR YOUNG OFFICERS THIS AFTERNOON.

From C.-in-C. to His Imperial Majesty:
    THE INCIDENT IS GREATLY REGRETTED BUT YOUR MAJESTY IS MISINFORMED ON ONE POINT. THE YOUNG GENTLEMEN IN QUESTION HAD NO ATTIRE.

*

In World War I H.M.S. *Essex,* patrolling off New York, intercepted on radio a foreign vessel endeavouring to relay a weather forecast. The result was recognisable but unintelligible. When she had finished an American Shore Station cut in with:
    NOW TRY THE OTHER FOOT.

*

H.M. Submarine *Truant,* operating in the Far East at the beginning of the war, experienced distresssing conditions of humidity. She included in her subsequent report readings of wet and dry thermometers while diving. This produced the following observation from Flag Officer, Submarines:

From Flag Officer Submarines, to Truant:
    THE FIGURES YOU REPORT WILL NOT SUPPORT LIFE.

*

From Admiralty to W.R.N.S. Training Establishment:
    REFERENCE ADMIRALTY LETTER DATED ... FOR SEXEY QUALITY READ SEX EQUALITY.

Scene: Foul Atlantic weather, one destroyer comes across another which has been dismasted.

1st destroyer:
HOW COME.

2nd destroyer:
SCRAPING UNDER VERY LOW CLOUD.

*

Convoy ONS5 marked the turning point of affairs between U-boats and escorts in the Battle of the Atlantic. For days the convoy was reported and shadowed. Then in came the U-boats in wolf pack formation to attack. Each time they ran into the tough ring of escorts and were either sunk or fought off. This was virtually the last appearance of the wolf-packs. On arrival at St. John's, Newfoundland, the signal message was received.

From Prime Minister to Escorts of Convoy ONS5:
MY COMPLIMENTS TO YOU ON YOUR UNCEASING FIGHT WITH THE U-BOATS. PLEASE PASS TO COM-MODORE OF THE CONVOY MY ADMIRATION FOR THE STEADINESS OF HIS SHIPS.

A Russian convoy, was being steadily shadowed day and night by relays of Blom and Voss flying boats. The aircraft flew round and round the convoy keeping low on the horizon and well out of range of the escorts' guns. An irritated escort leader told his signalman to make by lamp to the German:

YOU ARE MAKING ME DIZZY, FOR GOD'S SAKE GO ROUND THE OTHER WAY.

The signal was read and acknowledged and the flying boat complied immediately.

*

H.M.S. *Duke of York* was lying alongside Parlatorio wharf, Grand Harbour, Malta, repairing damage resulting from an electrical fire. The work took longer than expected, much to the consternation of all on board who wanted to press on to the Far East and get at the Japs. Finally, on leaving, this signal was made:

1738 25 May/45 From Duke of York to Admiral Superintendent Malta:

IN ENTERPRISE OF MARTIAL KIND
WHEN THERE IS ANY FIGHTING
WE'D RATHER NOT BE LEFT BEHIND
IT ISN'T SO EXCITING.
BUT WHEN THE FLAMES BEGAN TO LICK
AROUND OUR MULTICORIO
WE VERY NEARLY ENDED UP
THE DUKE OF PARLATORIO.

*

From Senior Officer after inspecting small ship:

STANDING ORDERS PROVIDE FOR OVERALLS BEING WORN FOR DIRTY WORK ON BOARD IN WHICH CATE-GORY I DO NOT INCLUDE AN INSPECTION BY ME.

*

From Escort Leader to Corvette:

THE DUCHESS OF RUTLAND IS SHOWING A DIM LIGHT LOW DOWN AMIDSHIPS.

During exercises in peacetime.
From Warspite to destroyer Volunteer:
> THANK YOU FOR RECOVERING OUR TORPEDO. ONE
> VOLUNTEER IS BETTER THAN 10 PRESSED MEN.

*

Admiral Sir John Fisher signalled to a Captain who was making a mess of a manoeuvre:
> WHAT THE DEVIL ARE YOU DOING.

The Captain, on his dignity, asked for a repetition of the third word, whereupon the Admiral hoisted:
> DEVIL, DEVIL, DEVIL, DEVIL,

on all the yard arm halyards.

*

From Corvette (returning to base) to Motor Torpedo Boat (setting out on patrol):
> GOOD LUCK.

Reply from M.T.B.:
> THANKS. ACTUALLY WE RELY ON SKILL.

*

From Mid. East to Bombarding Force
> ... PRISONERS EXCEED 25,000 INCLUDING 2 CORPS
> COMMANDERS, 4 DIVISIONAL COMMANDERS, 1
> BISHOP ACCOMPANIED BY 3 NUNS (REPEAT) NUNS.

*

A signal made as H.M.S. *Phoebe* parted company from one command to join another:
> ROMANS CHAPTER 16 VERSES 1 and 2.[1]

---

[1] "I commend unto you Phebe our sister ... that ye receive her in the Lord, as becometh Saints, and thatt ye assist herin whatsoever business she hath need of you; for she hath been a succourer of many, and of myself also."

H.M.S. *Belton,* on Fishery Protection Duty, has trouble with a trepassing trawler, and signals Senior Officer Fishery Protection:
>AT DOVER WITH JESUS OF NAZARETH IN CUSTODY
>*(later)*
>JESUS OF NAZARETH PLEADED GUILTY TO CHARGES OF USING AN ILLEGAL SIZED NET.

*

If Flag *N* (Int) — also Flag *Z* (Navy) — are no longer required at sea, they will always be a very relieving sight to the racing motorist.

An admiral entertained his officers to dinner, but owing to a stomach upset he had to retire early in the evening. When the squadron weighed anchor and proceeded to sea the next morning the admiral led his ships out of harbour flying the general signal
>*NEGATIVE* DUFF GEORGE

(Signal D G then meant:
>FOLLOW THE ADMIRAL'S MOTIONS MOST CARE-FULLY AS HE MAY ALTER COURSE OR SPEED WITHOUT SIGNAL.)

International

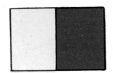

K — You should stop your vessel instantly

L — You should stop. I have something important to communicate

M — I have a doctor on board

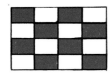

N — No (negative)

O — Man overboard

1940 – 1945

Destroyer flag

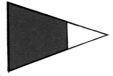

Division flag: Am undergoing D.G. test

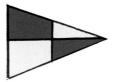

Fishery flag: Fishery protection duty

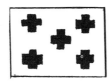

Negative:

Optional flag: It is optional to follow the Admirals motions

Royal Navy

K — Stand by to turn together to port

L — Suspicious vessel in sight

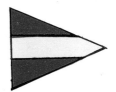

M — Mine in sight

N — Enemy in sight

O — 'E' boats in sight

International	**1940 — 1945**	**Royal Navy**
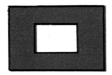		
P — In harbour: All persons are to repair on board as the vessel is about to proceed to sea.	Port flag: Relative position port	P — Submarine in sight on my port side
		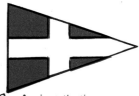
Q — My vessel is healthy and I request free pratique	Preparative flag	Q — Am investigating a contact
		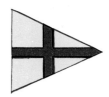
R — The way is off my ship; you may feel your way past me	Red flag: Harbour. National air raid warning Red	R — Resume previous course together after flight operations

S — My engines are going full speed astern	Screen flag	S — Submarine in sight my starboard side
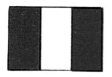		
T — Do not pass ahead of me	Squadron or flotilla flag: Gas spray alarm.	T — Torpedoes approaching

Flag *P* (International) — also Flag *Cruising Disposition* (Navy) belongs for ever to the Merchant Navy as "Blue Peter", probably the best known signal flag of them all. Who amongst us has not, at some time or another, reacted to its appearance either by swallowing our drink, saying goodbye, and scuttling down a liner's gangway, or scuttling up a liner's gangway, saying hallo, and swallowing our drink.

*

Flag *Q* (Navy) — and Black Pendant later — were hard worked by convoy escorts during the Battle of the Atlantic, when many pairs of ears spent many hours considering whether the contact their Asdic held was a shoal of fish or a U-boat, (and hoping to use either Flag *P* or *S* after their next depthcharge attack.) A United States patrol aircraft wasted no time deliberating. His signal:

SIGHTED SUB SANK SAME.

*

Long before air raids were invented the Red Flag shown here was symbolic of mutiny afloat. In 1797 it flew from the mastheads of H.M. Ships at Spithead, and the Nore. Ships' companies were firm in their protests but they didn't shed blood, in fact the Red Flag was struck on 4th June, in honour of the King's birthday, and rehoisted the next day. At the Invergordon Mutiny in 1931 the Red Flag was sung, but not hoisted.

*

Flag *T* is a gentle reminder of more rigid etiquette, when it was about as much as a junior Captain's life, let alone his chances of promotion were worth to cross his Admiral's bows at sea without asking permission, irrespective of the Rules of the Road.

*

From dissatisfied Admiral during manoeuvres to private ship
        WOULD IT NOT HAVE BEEN BETTER TO HAVE
        TURNED TO STARBOARD.
Reply
        YES

o

On 30th June 1928, the 4th Destroyer Flotilla left the Mediterranean Fleet, then at Navarro, to return to the United Kingdom to Pay Off. The Flotilla steamed between the lines of anchored ships with each ship flying a hoist comprising one line of *Auld Lang Syne*.

*

An Admiral, leading a line of carriers, watched one of the destroyer screen trying to cut through the line between his ship and the next astern. The destroyer Captain, anxious not to make the obvious mistake of getting across No. 2's bows, cut too close to the flagship's stern. Sure enough an unlucky roll brought his sea boats' davits in contact with the carrier's stern. The Admiral growled "Make that young blighter a signal." Everyone waited to hear the great man's anger put to words.
From Flag Officer to Destroyer:
    IF YOU TOUCH ME THERE AGAIN I SHALL SCREAM.

*

After the Battle of Matapan.
From Captain of Destroyer Flotilla to C.-in-C. Mediterranean:
    HAVE   ITALIAN   SURVIVORS   INCLUDING   THE
    ADMIRAL. HE HAS PILES.
Reply from C.-in-C. Mediterranean:
    I AM NOT SURPRISED.

*

Mediterranean cruisers were practising taking up their escorting positions on the Royal Yacht. A Frigate was acting as Royal Yacht. Several senior N.A.T.O. officers were watching the incident including a French Admiral in the Frigate. The C.-in-C. intended the occasion to be spectacular. The cruisers turned inwards at 25 knots into line abreast and turned again, passing about 50 feet either side of the Frigate, who received the full benefit of their bow-waves.
From Cruiser to Frigate:
    WHAT DOES IT FEEL LIKE TO BE THE MEAT IN THE
    SANDWICH.
From Frigate to Cruiser:
    NOT GOOD. NO ROOM FOR THE FRENCH MUSTARD.

From C.-in-C. Portsmouth to Admiralty, repeated to C.-in-C.
Plymouth, C.-in-C. Nore, C.-in-C. Rosyth:
REFERENCE ADMIRALTY MESSAGE . . . A CHAOTIC
SITUATION HAS ARISEN. WRENS ARE NOT ALLOWED
CLOTHING COUPONS ON THE ASSUMPTION THEY
RECEIVE UNIFORMS, BUT THERE IS NO UNIFORM
AND OVER 1,000 WRENS IN THE PORTSMOUTH COM-
MAND ARE STILL IN PLAIN CLOTHES. AT SOME
ESTABLISHMENTS NEW ENTRY WRENS ARE NOW
WORKING IN BARE LEGS TO SAVE THEIR PAIR OF
STOCKINGS FOR WALKING OUT. IN DUE COURSE A
LARGE NUMBER OF WRENS WILL BE WORKING IN A
STATE OF NATURE WHICH ON MANY GROUNDS
WOULD BE UNDESIRABLE. . . .
From C.-in-C. Plymouth to C.-in-C. Portsmouth:
SUGGEST YOU APPLY FOR FIGHTER COVER.

*

From extremely fussy destroyer flotilla captain to destroyer
about to go to sea for exercises:
HOW LONG DO YOU EXPECT TO BE AFTER LEAVING
HARBOUR.
From Destroyer:
310 FEET AS USUAL.

From Coastguard Station:
A MINE HAS BEEN WASHED INTO . . . BAY. THERE IS A
SMALL BLACK BAND ROUND THE MINE.

From Flag Lieutenant to Senior Officer, Port:
WHO DO YOU RECOMMEND FOR ADMIRAL'S WOMAN.
The Senior officer ashore was most perturbed, and asked for a repetition of the signal. In due course he received this amendment.
From Flag Lieutenant to Senior Officer, Port:
REFERENCE MY SIGNAL PLEASE INSERT WASHER BETWEEN ADMIRAL AND WOMAN.

*

From Flotilla leader to U.S. destroyer who has sunk six Japanese submarines in twelve days:
DAMMIT. HOW DO YOU DO IT.
From destroyer escort:
PERSONNEL AND EQUIPMENT WORKED WITH THE SMOOTHNESS OF WELL OILED CLOCKWORK. AS A RESULT OF OUR EFFORTS RECORDING ANGEL IS WORKING OVERTIME CHECKING IN NIP SUB-MARINERS JOINING HONOURABLE ANCESTORS.

*

At a Spithead Review it was decided that all ships would cheer together. A time table was made out to synchronise the cheering allowing for the distances between ships. At the last moment another ship joined the Fleet and was anchored furthest away from the track of the Royal Yacht. She received the following signal:
From C.-in-C.:
CHEER SHIP 5 SECONDS BEFORE SIGNAL TO CHEER SHIP IS HAULED DOWN.

*

Destroyer *Diamond* had just collided with Cruiser *Swiftsure* during manoeuvres at sea. The destroyer was technically in the wrong. When they had sorted themselves out:
From Swiftsure to Diamond:
WHAT DO YOU INTEND TO DO NOW.
From Diamond to Swiftsure:
BUY A FARM.

Admiral conducting bombardment to remainder of Battle Squadron:

WHO KNOCKED THAT LIGHTHOUSE DOWN AND WHY.

*

From Flagship to private ship:

WHAT ARE YOUR WASH CLOTHES HANGING UP FOR.

Reply from private ship:

SUBMIT TO DRY.

*

The following signal indicates weather conditions in which Minesweepers worked in North Russia:

2054/26 January. From Captain of 1st Minesweeping Flotilla to Senior Base Naval Officer, North Russia:

REGRET TO REPORT THAT AT 1000/26TH JANUARY HARRIER PASSED THROUGH IOKANKA ENTRANCE BROADSIDE ON WITH BOTH ANCHORS DOWN THERE-BY DISREGARDING KOLA INLET GENERAL MEMOR-ANDA NOS. 36 AND 37. THIS PROCEDURE WAS ADOPTED AS THE ONLY ALTERNATIVE TO GROUND-ING ON MEDYEJI ISLAND. WHEN SHORTENING IN CABLE IN WIND SOUTH WEST FORCE 10 THE SHIP DRAGGED FASTER THAN THE WINCH COULD HEAVE IN . . . SEAGULL LEFT HARBOUR IN A SIMILAR MAN-NER. OXLIP LEFT WITHOUT INCIDENT. HYDERABAD WAS REPORTED UNABLE TO PROCEED AND WAS ORDERED TO RETURN TO KOLA INDEPENDENTLY.

From Fleet Air Arm Commander in Carrier to airborne Squadron who are not obeying instructions:

THIS IS MASTER QUOTING HEBREWS CHAPTER 12 VERSE 8. I QUOTE: BUT IF YE BE WITHOUT CHASTISEMENT WHEREOF ALL ARE PARTAKERS THEN ARE YE BASTARDS. UNQUOTE. I SAY AGAIN BASTARDS. OUT.

*

When the New Zealand Cruiser *Bellona* was preparing to sail for U.K. for the Coronation in 1953, it was decided that as many young ratings as possible should go in her. New Zealand Navy Board made the following signal:

RATINGS DRAFTED TO BELLONA FOR PASSAGE TO UK SHOULD BE VICE TRAINED MEN.

*

Operation COAT was the codeword given to the passage of a reinforcement from Force H, at one end of the Mediterranean to the Mediterranean Fleet at the other end. The force was late, and only arrived one day before the already planned attack on Taranto.

From C.-in-C. Mediterranean to Flag Officer Force H:

THANK YOU FOR MY COAT. I NEARLY CAUGHT A COLD WAITING FOR IT. I STILL HAVE NO TROUSERS BUT INTEND TAKING THOSE OFF MUSSOLINI SHORTLY.

*

H.M.S. *Queen Elizabeth* and Cunard liner *Queen Elizabeth* met for the first time in mid-Atlantic.

Queen Elizabeth to Queen Elizabeth:

SNAP.

*

From Royal Yacht off Cowes to H.M.S. *Bittern,* one of the first small ships fitted with stabilisers:

WILL YOU PLEASE ROLL YOUR SHIP FOR HER MAJESTY.

Two frigates approaching Portland Harbour in Channel gale, visibility nil.

From 1st Frigate:

WHEN DO YOU EXPECT TO SIGHT PORTLAND BREAK-WATER.

Reply:

FIFTEEN MINUTES AGO. ESTIMATE MY POSITION 4TH FAIRWAY, CAME GOLF COURSE.

*

From personal friend of Imperious Admiral who had recently fallen from his barge into the sea.

I AM SURPRISED THAT A MAN OF YOUR EXPERIENCE SHOULD ATTEMPT TO DO WHAT ONLY ONE MAN HAS DONE BEFORE—WALK ASHORE.

*

From Captain of 2nd Destroyer Flotilla in 1940 when his flotilla, while trying to draw the enemy, were being chased by two Italian cruisers.

Hyperion to Destroyers in company:

DON'T LOOK ROUND NOW BUT I THINK WE ARE BEING FOLLOWED.

*

Early in May, 1943, enemy resistance in Tunisia was collapsing. British naval forces were disposed to prevent any large scale withdrawal of the enemy by sea from the Cape Bon area. He was to be given no chance of staging a Dunkirk evacuation.

1251 8th May. ,From C.-in-C. Mediterranean to Destroyers on patrol—Laforey, Bicester, Aldenham, Jervis:

SINK, BURN AND DESTROY. LET NOTHING PASS.

*

From Local Naval Base to destroyer which has grounded in vicinity:

REQUEST YOU WILL CONSIDER YOURSELVES HON-ORARY MEMBERS DURING YOUR STAY.

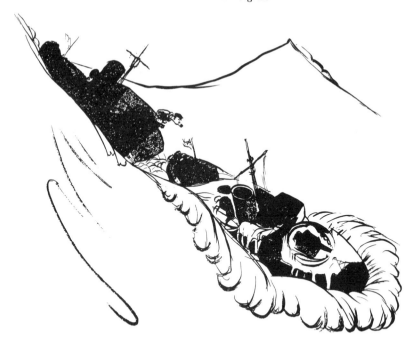

From one corvette to another in full Atlantic gale:
HAVE JUST SEEN DOWN YOUR FUNNEL. FIRE IS
BURNING BRIGHTLY.

*

Before World War I, the combined Mediterranean and Channel
Fleets were lying at Lagos. The following general signal was sent
by the flagship:
HIS MAJESTY THE KING OF PORTUGAL HAS KINDLY
PRESENTED SEVEN TINS OF TUNNY FISH TO EACH
SHIP. BOATS ARE TO BE SENT TO COLLECT AT 1600.
Only one ship sent a launch capable of carrying seven tons.

*

Signal made on conclusion of a Mediterranean operation.
From Flag Officer Force H to C.-in-C. Mediterranean:
... ABSENCE OF AIR OPPOSITION LEADS ME TO
SUSPECT THAT NEIGHBOURING TENANT IS FEEDING
MY BIRDS.

Two ships wishing to exchange movie films:
   WILL BE GLAD TO EXCHANGE FANNY BY GASLIGHT
   FOR TWIN BEDS.

*

Between two Atlantic convoy escorts:
1st ship:
   COMMENCE HOSTILITIES WITH JAPAN.
2nd ship:
   REQUEST PERMISSION TO FINISH BREAKFAST FIRST.

*

There was no particular signal to initiate the Normandy Landing. The huge operation ran to a time table, with each Assault
Force operating independently, once D day had been established.
The initiation was metaphorically a nod from the meteorologists.
   On the other hand, once the operation started there must have
been many signals, of which the following is typical. The first
groups of landing craft from the Portsmouth area sailed at 0900,
5th June. As the first convoy left Spithead the signal:
   GOOD LUCK. DRIVE ON.
was hoisted in *Largs* (Admiral Talbot's flagship) anchored at the
Eastern end of the lines of landing craft. It remained flying until
Largs got under way at 2145.

*

One night a corvette chased a U-boat away from a convoy and
attacked it. The attack was successful, the U-boat surfaced and her
crew started to abandon ship. For a few moments the Scottish
captain observed the scene lost in admiration of his achievement.
The he "came to" and realised the gap between him and the
convoy was widening rapidly. He also remembered that picking up
U-boat survivors was secondary to guarding the convoy. Shining
his Aldis Signal lamp in an Easterly direction therefore he steamed
past the U-boat, and to ease his conscience he said through the
loud hailer:
   MY LIGHT IS SHINING ROUGHLY IN THE DIRECTION
   OF GERMANY—GOOD NIGHT.

Extract from a signal from Senior Naval Officer Archangel to Senior Naval Officer North Russia:

> ... HE IS A TALKATIVE MAN AND IS ALLEGED TO HAVE TOLD RADIO OFFICER MOFFAT OF EMPIRE BARD THAT HE RETURNED LAST NIGHT TO FIND TWO DANES IN BED WITH HIS WIFE AND THAT HE SHOT THEM BOTH. CONSEQUENTLY HE WOULD DO ANYTHING TO BE ALLOWED TO RETURN TO U.K.

*

H.M.S. *Southampton,* cruiser flagship, had the ship's name designed in an unusually dazzling plaque. In harbour one evening when this plaque was illuminated she received the following signal from a senior admiral:

> AS A SHAREHOLDER IN THE SOUTHERN RAILWAY I MUST PROTEST ON WHAT CAN ONLY BE CALLED PILFERING ON THE PART OF YOUR FLAGSHIP OF ONE OF THE PLATFORM SIGNS OF THE STATION WHOSE NAME YOU BEAR.

*

> REQUEST THE PLEASURE OF THE COMPANY OF ADMIRAL AND MRS ... AT DINNER TONIGHT 1930.

Reply:

> VERY MANY THANKS. ADMIRAL AND MRS ... HAVE A DAUGHTER.

Reply:

> QUITE UNDERSTAND. HEARTIEST CONGRATULA-TIONS.

*

From Commander-in-Chief, Western Approaches to the Senior Officer of a special flotilla formed for training our Escort Groups in the Atlantic:

> THE TRYING CONDITIONS OF A FULL GALE ON SATURDAY NIGHT AND EASTER SUNDAY MORNING MIGHT WELL HAVE PERSUADED A LESS RESOLUTE TEAM THAN YOURS TO HAVE ABANDONED THE EXERCISES FOR SHELTER.

From Admiralty:
    IT HAS BEEN DECIDED TO DISCONTINUE USE OF BALLOONS IN ALL THEATRES WITH POSSIBLE EXCEPTION OF FAR EAST.

*

From Flag Officer Eastern Fleet—General:
    0831/24/12/1943. EVERYBODY WISHES EVERYBODY ELSE A VERY HAPPY CHRISTMAS AND NEW YEAR. NO FURTHER SIGNALS ARE TO BE MADE. THINK OF THE SIGNALMEN AND THE PAPER SHORTAGE.

*

In winter, 1940, when Wrens were buying up all available serge to make trousers, a Commander-in-Chief made the following signal:
    WRENS CLOTHING IS TO BE HELD UP UNTIL THE NEEDS OF SEAGOING PERSONNEL HAVE BEEN SATISFIED.

*

27th April, 1941. From Athens wireless station (as Germans entered Athens):
    CLOSING DOWN FOR THE LAST TIME HOPING FOR HAPPIER DAYS. GOD BE WITH YOU AND FOR YOU
    Then . . . silence.

Eastern Fleet, returned from sea, "hove to" outside Trinco-
malee waiting to proceed one by one up the swept channel to the
anchorage. Apart from ships being vulnerable to torpedo attack
everyone was short of sleep and touchy. Suddenly an American
Merchant ship appeared and, ploughing through the waiting ships,
shaped up for the swept channel. The tricky situation was relieved
by Admiral Sir James Somerville's ability to sum anyone up
quickly:

C.-in-C. to U.S. Merchant ship:
    AS MAE WEST SAYS, ONE AT A TIME BOYS.

*

The Bombardment of Genoa on 9th February, 1941, by Force
H was followed by 48 hours' wireless silence. Then from Flag
Officer Force H to Admiralty:
    BOMBARDMENT   COMPLETED.   (Pause.)   FROM   ALL
    ACCOUNTS GENOA IS IN A BLOODY FINE MESS.
This was followed by a further silence of 48 hours.

*

From small South Korean craft to British Patrol vessel:
    WE PUT TO PATROL AT 2000. THE SEA IS BAD. MY
    SHIP SHE IS LIKE RAGS AND I HAVE NO CONFIDENCE
    IN HIM THIS WEATHER. I BEG WITH PARDON YOU
    MUST TELL ME PUT ASHORE.

*

In 1940 submarine *Sealion,* after attacking a convoy in the
Skaggerak was rammed and heavily depth-charged. When she
eventually surfaced she was a shambles. No periscopes, no wireless,
but still alive. As she was surrounded by enemy D/F stations any
signal she sent would have to be short. Eventually the wireless was
repaired and the following signal transmitted:
From Sealion to Flag Officer Submarines:
    SEALION RAMMED AND RETURNING TO BASE. BLIND
    BUT BLYTH.
The last word signalled was *Sealion's* intended destination, and
was understood as such.

From Bairoko (American ship) to H.M.S. Cossack:
> SHIPS BEING ACCEPTED BY HELO WILL KEEP CLEAR
> OF FANTAIL CRANE AFTER MOUNT FORWARD AND
> DEPRESS AND SEND CREW INDEPENDENTLY TO
> PLACE WIND 30 DEGREES ON STARBOARD BOW.

or, in other words
> WHEN HELICOPTER ARRIVES, QUARTERDECK IS TO
> BE CLEARED AND Y TURRET TRAINED FORWARD
> AND GUNS DEPRESSED. SHIP IS TO ACT INDEPEND-
> ENTLY TO PLACE WIND 30 DEGREES ON STARBOARD
> BOW.

*

On her maiden voyage to Malta the paint peeled in a distressing manner from the sides of H.M. Yacht *Britannia*. The captain reported the matter in detail to the Commander-in-Chief, Mediterranean, on 20th April, 1954, concluding his signal as follows:
> ... PEELING HAS EVEN OCCURRED RIGHT UP MY
> STERN.

From Commander-in-Chief, Mediterranean:
> I AM MUCH RELIEVED TO FIND THAT IT IS YOUR SHIP
> AND NOT YOU WHO WILL BE UNFIT FOR POLO.

*

The famous brothers, Admirals Howard and Joe Kelly, rarely demonstrated their affection for one another. These signals followed the grounding of Admiral Howard Kelly's yacht, when he was Commander-in-Chief, China Station between the wars.

From J. to H.:
> GLAD YOU'RE SAVED.

From H. to J.:
> GLAD YOU'RE GLAD.

*

From Base to ship:
> HAVE (BLANK) WOMEN FOR YOU

Correction:
> HAVE TWO MEN FOR YOU

During the Munich crisis a destroyer and a submarine were carrying out exercises together off Gibraltar. On return to harbour a large and heavy-laden German freighter passed nearby.
From Submarine to Destroyer:
 REQUEST PERMISSION TO START THE WAR.

From Vice Admiral Dover to C.-in-C. Nore:
 THE SERVICES OF LADY BRASSEY LAST NIGHT IN WHAT MIGHT HAVE BEEN A DIFFICULT PREDICA-MENT WERE MUCH APPRECIATED, PARTICULARLY BY WAR NIZAM.

*

A carrier was flying on aircraft which necessitated her steaming head to wind. By the Rules of the Road she should have given way to an approaching cruiser flagship but she remained on her course. The cruiser passed very close indeed astern of the carrier.
Cruiser Flagship to Carrier:
 LUCKY THE TAIL OF YOUR SHIRT WAS NOT HANGING OUT.

*

Reply to signal received by an officer, congratulating him on his promotion:
 VMT. PSALM 140, 2ND HALF OF VERSE 5.[1]

---

[1] "They have set gins for me."

Sailors have their own views about the pronunciation of ships' names. *Penelope,* for example, they usually call Pennyloap. When she met destroyer *Antelope* at sea, the following signal was made:
From Penelope to Antelope:
AT LONG LAST ANTELLYPEE MEETS PENNYLOAP.

*

Ex-Corvette *Coreopsis,* hired by Ealing Studios for making the film "The Cruel Sea," entered Portland Harbour after a day's "shooting." She was meant to look as if she had been battered about in Atlantic weather, and she did. Her white ensign was being exchanged for a red one as she passed U.S.S. *Missouri,* "the Mighty Mo," berthed in Portland Harbour:
From U.S.S. Missouri to Coreopsis:
WHAT SHIP.
From M.V. Coreopsis:
H.M.S. COMPASS ROSE SAILING THE CRUEL SEA (pause) WHAT SHIP.
No reply.

*

A ship was carrying out low level A.A. practice at a drogue target supposed to be at 2,000 feet. The pilot of the plane obviously had not read the orders for the exercise, and for an hour he flew up and down over the ship at 5,000 feet. Finally the pilot signalled to the ship:
I AM AT 5000 FEET. SHALL I COME DOWN.
The ship replied:
I THINK IT WOULD BE QUICKER IF I CAME UP TO YOU.

*

From Captain Walker to his famous Atlantic Escort Group, when he had come to the conclusion that the particular underwater Asdic contact they were investigating was not a U-boat:
I AM AFRAID WE MUST LEAVE AND PUT IT DOWN TO AN ICHTHYOLOGICAL GEFUFFLE.

Flag *W* (Int) Frequently hoisted by merchant ships in convoy in wartime, and accompanied by such visual signals as:

> PLEASE CAN YOU LET ME HAVE SOME SORT OF MEDICINE FOR SOME SORT OF RASH.

or

From Salvage tug to C.-in-C. Plymouth

> HAVE ONE HAND WITH SEPTIC FOOT.

*

UNION FLAG. First mentioned in the Admiralty Book of Signal Instructions dated 1673. It is worn afloat in place of an Admiral's flag by an Admiral of the Fleet.

A smaller version is worn at the jack staff for'd by HM Ships in harbour, or at sea when ships are dressed.

From Senior Ship to Junior Ship

> YOUR JACK IS UPSIDE DOWN.

From Junior Ship

> THIS IS HOW IT WAS RECEIVED FROM NAVAL STORE OFFICER PORTSMOUTH.

From Senior Ship

> SOME PEOPLE WOULD DRINK SULPHURIC ACID IF IT CAME IN A GIN BOTTLE.

*

1059/10/12/44. From Senior Naval Officer afloat—General

> SHIPS ARE TO DRESS WITH MASTHEAD FLAGS IN HONOUR OF HIS MAJESTY'S ASCENSION TOMORROW MONDAY.

(Shark infested waters only). Correct use of the I'm-all-right-JACK.

Pendant 1
Evolution completed

Pendant 2
Repeat last flag signal made
by you

Pendant 3
Exercise completed

Pendant 4
Guide of fleet

Pendant 5

Answering Pendant

Pendant 6
Military Pendant

Pendant 7: Horary Pendant

Pendant 8: Am about
to fire torpedo for
exercise

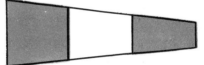

Pendant 9: Stand by to
turn together to
starboard.

In port:
Gin Pennant.

Pendant 0: Signal exercise
is suspended

Bearing Pendant:
International code meaning

1940 — 1945   Royal Navy

Black Pendant: By convoy
escort. Am investigating
a contact

Blue Pendant: The column
addressed is to standby to
turn together to starboard

Church Pendant: At the
dip man overboard

Course Pendant:

Deployment Pendant: In
harbour. Clear the upper
deck of men not on duty

Disposition Pendant:
Resume previous
disposition

Formation Pendant:
Reform

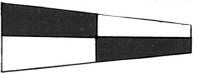

Interrogative Pendant

Numeral Pendant

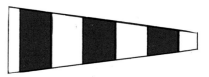

Order Pendant: Resume
previous order

Red Pendant: In harbour.
Have service telegram for
ship indicated

White Pendant: Fifteen
minutes notice for air
attack

Flag *Z* (Int). When dressing ship a destroyer had this flag upside
down. The phonetic alphabet used in the Navy frequently changes;
at the time of this incident *Z* was Zulu.

1st Destroyer:
> I BET YOUR FLAG ZULU IS UPSIDE DOWN

2nd Destroyer:
> IT IS A TOSS UP WITH SOME OF THESE FLAGS

1st Destroyer:
> IN THIS PARTICULAR CASE HEADS I WIN TAILS
> ULUZ

*

The late Captain F. J. Walker, C.B., D.S.O. and three bars,
showed a quality of skill and leadership which became a legend in
the Atlantic battle against U-boats. His enthusiasm is reflected in a
signal after a fifteen-and-half hour hunt which ended in sinking of
U-473, on 5th May, 1944. Shortly after midnight the U-boat
surfaced in a desperate effort to escape on her diesel engines.
Starling, Wren and *Wild Goose* pursued her and a running gun
battle followed. Finally the U-boat, out of control, circled, and
after receiving several direct hits up went her bows and she sank.
As she disappeared Captain Walker made his first signal of the
action from *Starling*:
> CEASE FIRING. GOSH WHAT A LOVELY BATTLE.

An example in cooperation between Royal Naval and Merchant
Naval flag signalling at a Spithead Review: A yacht sailed by a
particularly beautiful girl is closely observed by Admiral and Flag
Lieutenant from quarter deck of cruiser flagship. Admiral instructs
Flag Lieutenant to make a suitable flag signal to the yacht in
international code. Flag Lieutenant thumbs through vocabulary
and instructs flag deck to hoist three flag signal: D-I-N, which
means:
> I WILL KEEP CLOSE TO YOU DURING THE NIGHT.

Signal is acknowledged by yacht. Through powerful glasses girl's
shoulders observed heaving but whether from laughter or suppressed indignation will never be known by Admiral.

P

Time 0700. Squadron at sea, having sailed the previous midnight from port at which the entertainment had been lavish:

From ship to Flagship:
SUBMIT, GOOD MORNING.

From Flagship:
NOT APPROVED. THE MATTER WILL BE RECONSIDERED AFTER BREAKFAST.

*

Concluding remarks by Flag Officer Force H to signal report of Malta convoy operation on 25th July, 1941:
I HAVE RESTORED GOOD CONDUCT BADGE TO FORCE H GUARDIAN ANGEL, DEPRIVED FOR OFFENCES COMMITTED ON DAY 1 AND DAY 3.

*

Extract from a signalled report on operation STYLE, 4th August, 1941.
... FAILURE OF ENEMY TO DEAL WITH FORCES ENGAGED ATTRIBUTED TO PREVIOUS ROUGH HANDLING OF SURFACE FORCES BY MEDITERRANEAN FLEET AND SUCCESSFUL OPERATIONS OF OUR SUBMARINES. ENEMY IN FACT APPEARED TO HAVE BEEN COMPLETELY BOTCHED, BEGGARED AND BEWILDERED.

*

From American destroyer to Flag Officer Queenstown:
HAVE ATTACKED AND SUNK ENEMY SUBMARINE. WHERE AM I.

From Flag Officer Queenstown:
TOP OF THE CLASS.

*

From C.-in-C. Mediterranean to Vice Admiral, Malta:
DRIVE A LONG HAT PIN INTO THE STERN OF THE OFFICER RESPONSIBLE FOR REPORTING MERCHANT SHIPPING MOVEMENTS.

Two destroyers home from abroad securing alongside dockyard jetty. Both ships have been friendly rivals throughout commission on foreign station.

From 1st Destroyer to 2nd Destroyer:

> IF THE BEARDED CAPTAIN WILL GET IN TOUCH WITH THE LADY ON THE JETTY PUSHING THE PRAM HE WILL LEARN SOMETHING WHICH WILL TAKE THAT GRIN OFF HIS FACE.

*

From Vice Admiral (Air) to Glorious:

> I PROPOSE INCORPORATING THE FOLLOWING IN MY LETTER OF PROCEEDINGS, HEARD ON R/T FROM GLADIATORS PATROL THIS AFTERNOON—TALLY HO TALLY HO I SEE THE BASTARDS. THIS ALLEGATION ON THE PARENTAGE OF THE CREW OF THE JUNKERS 87 ATTACKED WAS PROVED TO BE UNFOUNDED WHEN THEY WERE SUBSEQUENTLY RESCUED.

*

Narvik, the railhead of the Norwegian iron ore industry, was in German hands.

To the north of the town the railway follows the coast and enters a tunnel about ¼ mile long.

Two destroyers were patrolling in the vicinity one sunny morning in May 1940. Destroyer B received the following signal from A:

> ORDERS FOR OPERATION LETS PLAY TRAINS. THE 11.30 FROM NARVIK IS ALMOST DUE. DESTROYER A WILL TAKE STATION TO SOUTHWARD AND HASTEN TRAIN INTO TUNNEL WITH H.E. AFTER 2ND SALVO DESTROYER B IS TO COMMENCE GREETING TRAIN IN SIMILAR MANNER AT NORTHERN END OF TUNNEL.

*

In July, 1943, a minesweeper entered Syracuse harbour towing a captured Italian submarine. She looked very pleased with herself. Another minesweeper leaving harbour signalled:

> IS THAT YOUR FIRST TODAY.

On an occasion when Fleets were being mobilised some Royal Marine Bandsmen got all mixed up due to an error in drafting. One ship made a general signal.

I CAN OFFER 2 PICCOLOS AND A BASSOON IN EXCHANGE FOR 3 TROMBONES AND A BIG DRUM.

*

Two Mediterranean destroyers being attacked periodically by enemy aircraft.

From 1st Destroyer:

TODAY IS CORONATION DAY.

Reply from 2nd Destroyer:

HOPE YOU DON'T GET CROWNED.

*

A classic understatement when *Illustrious* rejoined the Mediterranean Fleet the morning after the brilliant Fleet Air Arm raid on Taranto.

From Commander-in-Chief to Illustrious:

MANOEUVRE WELL EXECUTED.

*

The Senior Officer of a Motor Torpedo Boat Flotilla, operating from a temporary base, had quarters in the local hotel. He returned one night late from London to find his room was occupied. Next day he sent the following signal to the flotilla:

OFFICERS ARE REMINDED THAT THE S.O.'S CABIN IS NOT REPEAT NOT TO BE USED FOR PURPOSES OTHER THAN THOSE LAID DOWN IN THE BOY SCOUT MANUAL.

*

To add to the strain of the operations off Crete, there was an abundance of signalling. Everyone from Admirals downwards signalled their day and night intentions. At dusk one destroyer, fed up with reading all these signals, grumbled to another ship:

THE ROAD TO CRETE IS PAVED WITH NIGHT INTENTIONS.

Destroyer reporting having to leave refugees without any food:
... THEY REMAIN SANS BEURRE ET SANS BRIOCHES.

*

From C.-in-C. Mediterranean to Sunderland aircraft which has
just announced proudly by signal that she has shot down a small
Italian shadower.
YOU GREAT BIG BULLY.

*

When the Australian Cruiser *Brisbane* was visiting Hongkong the
flagship of the China Fleet, H.M.S. *Hawkins,* gave an "At home"
to enable the officers of the *Brisbane* to meet the local ladies.
Whilst this At home was in progress a swarm of bees settled on the
quarterdeck awning of the *Brisbane.* The Officer of the watch in
the *Hawkins,* observing this phenomenon through his telescope
immediately made a signal to the *Brisbane:*
HOW MANY BEES IN BRISBANE.
Back came the reply from the Australian Officer of the watch:
HOW MANY HAWS IN HAWKINS.

*

From Corvette to Base:
AM TIED UP TO NO. 5 BERTH.
From Base:
SHOE LACES ARE TIED UP. H.M. SHIPS ARE SECURED.

*

In a Mediterranean convoy operation *Nelson,* flying the flag of
Flag Officer Force H, was torpedoed.
From C.-in-C. Mediterranean to Flag Officer Force H:
I HOPE THAT THESE MY CONGRATULATIONS WILL
COMPENSATE FOR A SLAP IN THE BELLY WITH A WET
FISH.

From Flag Officer Force H to C.-in-C. Mediterranean:
THANK YOU. AT MY AGE KICKS BELOW THE BELT
HAVE LITTLE SIGNIFICANCE.

On a Russian convoy in May, 1942, U.S.S.R. gunboat collided with H.M.S. *Harrier.* Later the following signal was sent:
From Rubin to Harrier:
> I AM VERY SORRY WHAT INJURED YOUR SHIP BY APPROACH TO BOARD FOR WHAT I MUST TO BEG PARDON. WE ARE PROUD OF STAUNCHNESS AND COURAGE ENGLISH SEAMENS OUR ALLIES.

*

H.M. Minesweeepers *Prompt* and *Jason* were built, launched, commisssioned and operated together. They were chummy ships and much friendly rivalry existed between them. One day *Prompt* struck an acoustic mine. While she was settling down in the water with upper deck awash:
From Prompt to Jason:
> FIRST AGAIN.

*

From Senior Base Naval Officer, North Russia to Senior Officer, Force R (visiting):
> THE RUSSIAN ADMIRAL HAS SENT TO MY OFFICE A PRESENT TO BE FORWARDED TO YOU BUT I REGRET VERY MUCH THAT THE CUSTOMS FORMALITIES IMPOSED ON ME BY OUR BRAVE ALLIES PREVENTS ME FROM SENDING IT TO YOU UNTIL PASSED FOR EXPORT. IT IS ALSO MOST UNFORTUNATE THAT I HAVE FELT COMPELLED TO WITHHOLD FROM HIM THE PRESENT THAT C.-IN-C. HOME FLEET SENT HIM UNTIL OUR GLORIOUS ALLIES ALLOW ME TO RECEIVE OUR OWN PRIVATE MAIL WHICH YOU BROUGHT OUT. THE ADMIRAL HAS BEEN INFORMED IN EACH CASE. PLEASE EXPLAIN TO COMMANDER IN CHIEF.

*

From Admiral to Ship:
> WHILST AFLOAT WITH MY FLAG FLYING I PASSED YOUR SHIP AT 1250. IT REMINDED ME OF AN AVIARY WITH THE SHIP'S COMPANY SITTING ON THE RAILS WITH TAILS TOWARDS ME LIKE BIRDS ON A TWIG.

In the Mediterranean a submarine was ordered to try out a new route through a supposed enemy minefield, which entailed an all day dive in thickly mined waters. It was a grim form of trial and error, but it was the only way of finding a channel through which our submarines could pass. The result of the experiment, as received by the Captain of the submarine flotilla at Malta after hours of suspense was:
From Submarine Urchin:
    NEXT PLEASE

*

The Flag of the Zeebrugge Association is derived from the following signals.
From Warwick (destroyer flying the flag of Rear Admiral Roger Keyes leading force to attack Zeebrugge on eve of St. George's Day 1918):
    ST. GEORGE FOR ENGLAND.
From Vindictive (Captain Carpenter, shortly to win V.C.): MAY WI TWIST.

*

A Corvette was passing the Bar light vessel off Liverpool when she touched a magnetic mine somewhere in the shallows. It did not do much damage beyond bending the main shaft. A signal was sent by the Corvette to the Port War Signal Station reporting the incident.
    From Commander-in-Chief Western Approaches came the somewhat heartless reply:
    DO NOT SINK IN THE SWEPT CHANNEL.

*

22nd December 1854, Crimean War. Vice Admiral James Dundas was turning over to Rear Admiral Sir Edmund Lyons. The relationship of these two officers is revealed in the parting signals:
From Britannia (Admiral Dundas) to Agamemnon (Admiral Lyons):
    MAY SUCCESS ATTEND YOU.
Reply from Agamemnon:
    MAY HANGING AWAIT YOU.

From Cruiser to Admiral:
MY SEAPLANE IS OUT OF ACTION DUE TO SEAGULLS STROPPING THEIR BEAKS ON FABRIC.

*

From 1st Cruiser to 2nd Cruiser (in harbour at anchor):
YOUR MOTORBOAT HAS JUST DESTROYED MY STARBOARD GANGWAY. IT SEEMS THAT YOUR COXSWAIN COMPLETELY LOST HIS HEAD.
Reply:
PLEASE SEND BACK MY COXSWAIN'S HEAD.

*

From Renown:
AM BEING ATTACKED BY ELEVEN DIVE-BOMBERS.
Later:
SEVEN DIVE-BOMBERS WILL NOT BAT IN SECOND INNINGS.

*

Signal being received:
... THE FLEET WILL ACT AS A HOLE IN A BAYONET (pause).
Correction:
THE FLEET WILL ACT AS A WHOLE IN OBEYING IT.

*

Winter afternoon, 1940. Four destroyers approaching Scottish coast from the Atlantic. Filthy weather. Low cloud, low visibility. No means of knowing their exact position.
From Kipling to Kelly:
ATTENTION IS INVITED TO THE TEMPEST ACT I SCENE I LAST 4 LINES.[1]

---

[1] "Now would I give a thousand furlongs of sea for an acre of barren ground—long heath, broom, furze, anything. The walls above be done! but I would fain die a dry death."

1914-18 War. *Cyclamen to V.A. Malta* (after sinking Allied Italian Submarine mistaken for U-boat):

> HAVE RAMMED AND SUNK ENEMY SUBMARINE. SUR-VIVORS APPEAR TO SPEAK ITALIAN

*

From Cruiser entering harbour to Base:

> HAVE YOU ANY NEWS OF LADY BLANCHE.

From Base:

> HAS LADY IN QUESTION LEGS OR PROPELLORS

*

Destroyer *Virago* was in collision with *Emperor* while transferring stores at sea.

From Captain of Flotilla:

> IN SPITE OF YOUR NAME YOU MUST GET OUT OF THE HABIT OF SNAPPING AT THESE GREAT BIG MEN.

*

A severe air raid at Algiers coincided with a Fourth of June Etonian Dinner. Subsequently a question was asked in the House of Commons as to whether service fireworks had been used at public expense for an Old Etonian celebration. The following is an extract of Commander-in-Chief Mediterranean's signal on the matter.

> ... THE ONLY INCIDENT BEARING ON THIS SUBJECT IS THAT DURING A 4TH JUNE OLD ETONIAN DINNER AT ALGIERS AN AIR RAID TOOK PLACE ON THE PORT. DURING THIS RAID THOSE DINING WERE TREATED TO A SPECTACULAR ROCKET DISPLAY WHEN THE PROJECTORS WERE FIRED, AN OFFICER BEING HEARD TO REMARK IN APPRECIATIVE TONES ON THE FIREWORK DISPLAY SO KINDLY ARRANGED FOR THEIR FESTIVAL BY THE NAVY. IT IS REGRET-TED THAT THE EXIGENCIES OF WAR SHOULD HAVE GIVEN COLOUR TO THE IDEA THAT GOVERNMENT SUPPORT WAS BEING GIVEN TO THE ACTIVITIES OF THIS NEFARIOUS SECT. SHOULD IT BE CONSIDERED

OF SUFFICIENT IMPORTANCE TO JUSTIFY THE WASTE OF TIME AND EFFORT I CAN OF COURSE CONTINUE MY ENQUIRIES THROUGH ALL THE PORTS IN NORTH AFRICA, IN WHICH CASE PERHAPS THE HON. MEMBER WILL FURNISH MORE DETAILS. I AM HOWEVER OF THE OPINION THAT THIS IS THE BASIS OF THE STORY, AND THAT THE HON. MEMBER'S INFORMANT MUST ALSO HAVE BEEN CELEBRATING.

*

Ships assembled to greet Her Majesty who is about to pass in Royal Yacht. One ship is in doubt as to how many "hips" should precede "Hooray" when giving three cheers.
1st Ship to 2nd Ship:
INTERROGATIVE 2 HIPS OR 3.
Reply:
2 AS IN MARILYN MONROE.

*

From Commander-in-Chief—General:
DRESS FOR COMMANDER-IN-CHIEF'S PICNIC TOMORROW SUNDAY, PLAIN CLOTHES. THIS DOES NOT INCLUDE MIDSHIPMAN . . .'S YELLOW PLUS FOURS.

*

Gibraltar Signal Station to passing ship:
WHAT SHIP?
Reply:
WHAT ROCK?

*

Flotilla of Canadian Motor Launches in line ahead. Fog descends, fog buoys are streamed. Fog lifts completely, all fog buoys are recovered except one, whose owner has apparently forgotten its existence.
From M.L. following to owner of fog buoy:
TELL THE CAPTAIN THERE'S NO BEER LEFT IN THIS KEG.

From Cruiser relieving Malta:
WE ARE DELIVERING THE MILK. ANY EMPTIES TO COLLECT.
Reply:
YES, 26 GERMAN AND ITALIAN PRISONERS OF WAR.

*

Two submarines were accompanying a Russian convoy. One submarine Captain thought it would be a good idea to show himself if the convoy was attacked. He therefore made a signal to the Senior Officer of the escort.
IN THE EVENT OF ATTACK BY HEAVY SURFACE FORCES, INTEND TO REMAIN ON THE SURFACE.
The destroyer Escort Commander replied immediately:
SO DO I.

*

From Commander-in-Chief Mediterranean, Admiral Cunningham to Admiral Commanding Force H, Admiral Somerville, already K.B.E., on the occasion of his receiving the K.C.B.
FANCY, TWICE A KNIGHT AND AT YOUR AGE. CONGRATULATIONS.

*

From St. Helena to Bermuda:
ASCENSION ADVISES THREE DENTURES FOUND IN CAR AFTER CRICKET SUNDAY, 7 DECEMBER. DO THEY BELONG TO YOU PLEASE, IF SO INDICATE DISPOSAL.
From Bermuda to St. Helena:
ARE TEETH MARKED WITH BROAD ARROWS.

*

From Cruiser to destroyer who is acting as a Merchant ship in a trade defence exercise, and has been captured.
HAVE YOU ANY WOMEN ON BOARD.
From Destroyer:
NO, THEY HAVE ALL BEEN SHOT. THEY PREFERRED DEATH TO DISHONOUR.

H.M.S. *Shah,* escort carrier, built in Vancouver, was entering San Francisco on her maiden voyage down the West Coast.
From San Francisco Port War Signal Station to Shah:
WHAT SHIP.
From Shah:
HMS SHAH.
Port War Signal Station:
REPEAT.
After several repeats:
NEVER MIND WE WILL FIND OUT WHEN YOU GET IN.

*

Manoeuvres were being carried out by destroyers conducted by a Cruiser flagship. They finished up with the somewhat hair-raising V.I.P. escort manoeuvre, in which two divisions of destroyers approached the V.I.P. (Cruiser) on opposite courses, turning inwards to form a close escort. One destroyer misjudged the distance and finished by passing much too close to the V.I.P.
From Admiral to Destroyer:
THE EMPEROR WAS MUCH IMPRESSED BY THAT MANOEUVRE BUT NOT SO THE BRITISH NAVAL ATTACHE WHO HAS GONE BELOW TO CHANGE HIS TROUSERS.

*

Admiral Sir James Somerville on first sighting his Eastern Fleet off Ceylon, observed a mixed party with hardly any two ships of the same class present:
C.-in-C. Eastern Fleet to Eastern Fleet:
SO THIS IS THE EASTERN FLEET. WELL NEVER MIND. THERE'S MANY A GOOD TUNE PLAYED ON AN OLD FIDDLE.

*

Dark night, North Sea.
From Destroyer A to Admiralty:
HAVE BEEN HIT RIGHT AFT BY MINE.
From Destroyer B to Admiralty:
REFERENCE DESTROYER A'S SIGNAL. NOT MINE BUT ME.

From Cotswold
    BELGIA BOMBED BY SUNK LIGHT VESSEL.

*

When H.M.S. *Valiant,* newly refitted battleship, was exchanged from the Western Mediterranean for H.M.S. *Malaya,* the latter suffered from condenser and other troubles. C.-in-C. Med. made a polite "thank you" signal to Flag Officer H, hoping *Malaya* would serve him well. The reply from Flag Officer Force H was carefully coded up as follows:

    THOUGH NOT WISHING TO LOOK A GIFT HORSE IN THE MOUTH, I UNDERSTAND THAT THIS (THREE CORRUPT GROUPS) HAS TROUBLE WITH HER TUBES.

*

From 1st Destroyer to 2nd Destroyer:
    MY PORT SHAFT IS RUNNING HOT.
From 2nd Destroyer to 1st Destroyer:
    AS THE SEWING MACHINE SAID IN THE NUDIST CAMP, SO WHAT.

A convoy escort developed a defect which necessitated her limping home from her mid-Atlantic charges. There was a thick fog as she lay close to the senior officer's ship receiving her instructions.

From S.O. to Escort:

'... HOPE YOU FIND NECESSARY FACILITIES IN BELFAST.

From Escort to S.O.:

HOPE I FIND BELFAST.

*

After the Battle of Jutland:

JOIN ME. WHERE AM I.

*

From Flag Officer, Gibraltar:

SMALL ROUND OBJECT SIGHTED 180 DEGREES 5 MILES FROM EUROPA POINT. PROBABLY MINE.

From Flag Officer Force H:

CERTAINLY NOT MINE.

*

A cruiser was leading some destroyers on an operation against enemy coastal shipping. After much bad weather and no navigational fixes they found themselves not where they expected to be and almost certainly in a minefield.

From Cruiser to Flotilla Leader:

WHAT DO YOU CONSIDER IS OUR POSITION OTHER THAN PRECARIOUS.

*

Returning to Malta, after the bombardment of Catania, Sicily, on 17th July, 1943, H.M.S. *Warspite,* with paravanes streamed, made good 23½ knots in her thirtieth year.

From C.-in-C. Mediterranean to Flag Officer Force H:

OPERATION WELL CARRIED OUT. THERE IS NO QUESTION WHEN THE OLD LADY LIFTS HER SKIRTS SHE CAN RUN.

From Boom Defence Officer to C.-in-C., Portsmouth:
WRECKS OF SIX SISTERS AND OUR LADDIE HAVE
BEEN REMOVED.

*

H.M.S. *Ark Royal* on first emerging for sea trials *circa* 1938,
passed another of H.M. ships.
From Ark Royal to passing ship:
HOW DO I LOOK.
Reply
GO BACK TO LOCH NESS.

*

The British Pacific Fleet included a very small Rescue tug which
tried hard but which could not keep up with the other ships
during the assault on Japan. Commander-in-Chief's signal to
Admiralty concerning this tug ended:
. . . AM ORDERING HER TO RETURN TO BASE. I
RECOMMEND STRONGLY SHE SHOULD SEEK
FURTHER EMPLOYMENT ON THE THAMES BUT NOT
BELOW TEDDINGTON LOCKS.

*

From Liverpool W/T Station to Admiralty:
FOLLOWING RECEIVED FROM UNKNOWN SHIP. AM
BEING INTERFERED WITH.

*

After *Kelly* was torpedoed in the North Sea on 8th May, 1940,
and again after *Javelin* was torpedoed in the Channel on 29th
November, 1940, Captain Lord Louis Mountbatten, who was on
board both these ships, made the same reply to the same signal
from the next Senior Captain on each occasion.
Signal:
IS CAPTAIN (D) ALIVE
Reply:
YES. YOU ARE NOT IN COMMAND OF THE FLOTILLA
YET.

Pendant 2. (Navy. There are no International pendants)
From Destroyer to unknown Trawler
> WHAT IS THE SIGNIFICANCE OF THAT SIGNAL
> YOU ARE FLYING.

From Trawler
> REGRET I DO NOT KNOW. FLAGS SMELT OF FISH.

*

Pendant 3. In the combined RN and Merchant Navy signal book provided for operating convoys in World War II, this pendant acquired the sinister meaning: CONVOY IS TO SCATTER. It spelt tragedy to a particular Russian-bound convoy in the Arctic on 4 July 1942, by delivering it on a plate to hungry German U-boats and bombers.

But like all tragedies, this one had its lighter side. After a heavy air attack before the convoy scattered, the Admiral and officers on the bridge of H.M.S. *London,* flagship of the convoy's cruiser covering force, felt hungry; the Admiral approved the suggestion of hoisting Pendant 7 which still has an additional meaning that 'Flag and Commanding Officers have time for the next meal.' No sooner had the champagne and caviar — or whatever — arrived on the flagship's bridge than the Arctic peace was shattered by the Admiralty's MOST IMMEDIATE signal ordering the convoy to scatter. Away went the meal; down came Pendant 7 to be rammed ignominiously back into its locker with strict orders from the Admiral it was never to be used thus in his Squadron again.

International	1940 — 1945	Royal Navy
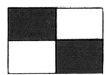		
U — You are standing into danger	Starboard flag: Relative position starboard	U — Use proper amount of rudder

V — I require assistance	Stationing flag: Disregard my motions	V — Relative position, the van

W — I require medical assistance	Subdivision flag:	W — Relative position, the centre
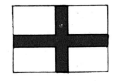		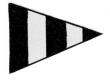
X — Stop carrying out your intentions and watch for my signals	Submarine flag	X — Relative position, the rear

Y — I am carrying mails	Union flag A Court Martial is sitting onboard	Y — In contact with a submarine on my port side

International	1940 – 1945	Royal Navy

Z — To be used to address or call shore stations

R.N. Numeral flags

O — Take up cruising disposition against air attack.

Z — In contact with a submarine on my starboard side

1 — Take individual avoiding action

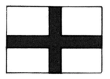

2 — Clear the line of fire against torpedo aircraft attack

3 — Stand by for attack by Torpedo Bombers

4 —

5 — Open fire

6 — Cease fire

7 — Take up close screen against torpedo aircraft attack

8 — Stagger the line

9 — Take up cruising disposition against air attack.

Church Pendant. Easily distinguishable, and, depending on where it appears, proclaiming that either the ship's company is at Divine Service, the ship is working anchors and cables, or someone has fallen overboard.

An American destroyer new to our signal methods was seen in the Atlantic flying two flags: Church Pendant and Interrogative Flag. On being asked what the signal was intended to mean she replied:
GOD, WHERE AM I.

*

Deployment Pendant. A lot of signals have been made by a lot of senior officers complaining about untidiness or behaviour of men on the upper decks of HM Ships in harbour. One rebounded.

From permanently irritated Admiral, to Cruiser Flagship lying alongside (whose Admiral he took to be ashore):
I OBSERVE MEN ON YOUR UPPER DECK WHO ARE NOT IN THE CORRECT RIG OF THE DAY.
From Senior Cruiser Admiral, who was in fact on board:
I OBSERVE THAT YOU OBSERVE TOO MUCH.

*

Course Pendant. Cruiser flagship *Trinidad* was attacked repeatedly returning from a Russian convoy. In a further attack by dive bombers she was set on fire and put out of action. Having regained control the Admiral, for the benefit of the escorting destroyers, hoisted a signal:
I AM PROCEEDING TO THE WESTWARD.
Half an hour later it was decided to abandon ship. Destroyer *Matchless* was ordered to sink her with torpedoes. This signal was still flying when *Trinidad* eventually sank.

*

Interrogative Pendant.
From Flagship to Cruiser which is out of station
WHAT ARE YOU DOING.
From Cruiser
20 KNOTS.

Q

Following the brilliant Fleet Air Arm raid on Taranto.
From Flag Officer Force H to C.-in-C. Mediterranean:
CONGRATULATIONS ON SUCCESSFUL DE-BAGGING.
IF THIS GOES ON UNCLE BENITO WILL SOON BE
SINGING ALTO IN THE CHOIR.

*

Senior Officer Atlantic convoy escort to rejoining corvette in
very bad weather:
WHY HAVE YOU TAKEN SO LONG TO REJOIN
CONVOY.
Reply:
IT WAS UPHILL ALL THE WAY.

*

The troubles reported by Naval Officer in charge, Mersa Matruh,
when the port was first re-opened were as follows:
From Naval Officer i/c Mersa Matruh to Rear Admiral, Alexandria:
SOME GENIUS HAS SENT 1,000 AUSTRALIANS HERE.
THEY ARE SITTING ON THE PIER SHOUTING FOR
FOOD. I HAVE NO FOOD, NO SHIPS, NO STORES, NO
TRANSPORT, NO INSTRUCTIONS, NO REPLIES TO MY
SIGNALS. SITUATION IS IMPOSSIBLE.
Reply from Rear Admiral, Alexandria:
DON'T LET THEM EAT YOU REPEAT YOU. HELP IS ON
THE WAY.

*

From Corvette to C.-in-C. Plymouth:
ROMAN EMPEROR IN TOW BADLY DAMAGED PLEASE
SEND TUGS.
From C.-in-C. Plymouth:
REVELATIONS CHAPTER 3 VERSE 11.[1]

[1] "Behold I come quickly: hold that fast which thou hast, that no man take
thy crown."

In 1937 H.M.S. *Cumberland* was returning from China with a collection of exhibits for the Chinese Ceramics Exhibition. On arrival at Portsmouth she made the customary signal to Commander-in-Chief Portsmouth.

REQUEST PERMISSION TO SALUTE YOUR FLAG.

C.-in-C. replied:

APPROVED, PROVIDED YOU DONT BREAK THE CHINA.

Signal flying from destroyer as she emerges from a near miss.
PHEW.

*

During General Drill:

From Commander-inChief (Admiral Joe Kelly):

SEND BAND TO FLAGSHIP TO PLAY POPULAR TUNE. HAS ANYONE HERE SEEN KELLY IS NOT REPEAT NOT CONSIDERED A POPULAR TUNE.

*

From Tug towing battle practice target to firing cruiser whose shots are falling too close:

WE AIM TO PLEASE. YOU AIM TOO PLEASE.

From 1st Destroyer to 2nd Destroyer:
YOU HAVE A LIGHT SHOWING ON YOUR STOKERS MESSDECK.
Reply:
YOU ARE LOOKING ON TO MY STOKERS MESSDECK. HAVE JUST BEEN IN COLLISION.

*

From Protector to C.-in-C. Mediterranean:
EXPECT TO ARRIVE ALEXANDRIA 1600. HAVE 1,500 ITALIAN PRISONERS ON BOARD, MIXED BUNCH RANGING FROM LIBYAN SOLDIER AGED 10. ALL VERMINOUS.

*

From Base Routing Officer, Norfolk, Virginia to Admiralty:
LOUISE EJECTED FROM CONVOY KS529 FOR EXCESSIVE SMOKING.

*

Carrier joining Fleet after having been painted with new camouflage design receives following greeting from C.-in-C.:
YOU LOOK LIKE A FRIESIAN COW IN CALF.

An aircraft was towing a drogue target down a line of cruisers who were firing at the target with A.A. armament. Suddenly a shell burst in front of the aircraft. The pilot immediately broadcast by Radio telephone:

I AM PULLING THIS BLOODY THING, NOT PUSHING IT.

*

R/T message from Free French pilot in Hurricane.

ENGINE NO GOOD. I JUMP.

*

A U.S. destroyer was ordered alongside a battleship at sea to fuel. She made several attempts to get into position but each time something went wrong and she sheered off and circled around for another try. When the Admiral commanding the Task Force could stand it no longer he signalled to the battleship:

SUGGEST YOU TRY GOING ALONGSIDE THE DESTROYER.

*

From U.S. Admiral Merrill, after leading his task force into action:

BOMBARDMENT FINISHED. TWO CRUISERS SUNK IN ADDITION. WHAT IS BAG LIMIT THIS YEAR ON THOSE BASTARDS.

Admiral Halsey replied:

THOROUGHLY PROUD OF YOUR BAG. IN THESE WATERS IT IS ALWAYS OPEN SEASON AND THE GAME WARDENS ARE ON VACATION. CONGRATULATIONS TO YOU AND YOUR GANG.

*

At Guadalcanal U.S. Intelligence learned that a Jap submarine would land a certain high official one night at Cape Esperance. Admiral Halsey's signal to the Commander of that area ended:

. . . IMPORTANT S.O.B. ABOARD. GET HIM.

Later the area commander replied:

SANK SUBMARINE. S.O.B. STILL ABOARD.

Q2

From Base to Trooping Carrier:
> CAN YOU FREIGHT 12 LIVE SOMALI SHEEP FROM ADEN TO CEYLON.

Reply from Trooping Carrier:
> SHIP WILL ONLY BE STOPPING OFF COLOMBO TO DISEMBARK OFFICERS. CONSIDER IT WOULD BE INAPPROPRIATE TO LAND SHEEP IN SAME BOAT.

*

One winter H.M.S. *Sabre,* a destroyer, was alongside a dockyard wharf under repair. She had no steam and only a few men on board. A gale blew which parted her lines and she charged helplessly across the harbour bouncing off anything in her path.

Eventually dockyard tugs appeared and took her firmly in hand. As they were bringing her back to her berth the only officer on board signalled to the resident Admiral:
> STONE COLD SABRE.

*

When part of a cypher message is either coded or transmitted incorrectly, and therefore can't be read at the receiving end it is known as a Corrupt Group, and a repetition is asked for. In the middle of one night in World War II, Sir Winston Churchill was awakened and handed a bunch of signals, including one which read
> FOR CORRUPT GROUP READ ADMIRALS.

*

Off the Pentland Firth in a fresh easterly gale, a small Landing Craft was prancing and wallowing her way into the wind and performing antics which caused some anxiety to the captain of a passing battleship who signalled:
> ARE YOU ALRIGHT?

Reply from the Sub-Lieutenant in command:
> YES THANKS VERY MUCH

Then, as the landing craft turned to round Duncansby Head her Skipper added
> MY NEXT PERFORMANCE WILL INCLUDE THE INDIAN ROPE TRICK.

When the visit of a cruiser to a hospitable Commonwealth port came to an end, and the cruiser sailed away, she found she had one absentee, his name, Able Seaman Thomas John Clark. In due course the cruiser received the following signal from the Resident Commissioner:

ABLE SEAMAN THOMAS JOHN CLARK REPORTED AT THE RESIDENCY AT 1430 TODAY TUESDAY. HE WAS SOBER, WELL DRESSED, AND IN HIS RIGHT MIND. TRANSPOSITION OF HIS CHRISTIAN NAMES WILL INDICATE THE CAUSE OF HIS DELAY. HE IS NOW WORKING ON MAIN ROAD TO DISPEL SURPLUS ENERGY.

*

Signal Books enable ships to exchange quantities of instructions or information by hoisting even a single flag. There are still occasions however, when a ship may have a sudden urge to convey a message to other ships in company simultaneously, and quickly, but there is no help from the Signal Book. Yet, when a green pendant (frequently bearing an appropriate design in white at the head) is seen flying from the starboard yard-arm of one of H.M. Ships in harbour it is universally recognised as the GIN PENDANT, and as long as it is flying, you're welcome.

*

A Signal Officer was very anxious to inform a brother Signal Officer in a passing ship of his first happy family addition, but private signals at sea between junior officers were forbidden.
Signal Officer to Signal Officer:
NEW RECEIVING SET DELIVERED LAST FRIDAY. EXCELLENT CONDITION.

*

A spick and span destroyer was fuelling at sea from a cruiser when suddenly, through mishandling at the destroyer's end, the fuel hose parted, spraying her immaculate superstructure, deck, and side with thick black furnace oil fuel.
Cruiser to Destroyer:
THERE'S NO FUEL LIKE AN OIL FUEL.

After the spectacular Air strike on the Central Phillipines in September, 1944, which accounted for 59 Jap ships and 478 of their planes, Admiral Halsey expressed his enthusiasm thus:

BECAUSE OF THE BRILLIANT PERFORMANCE MY GROUP OF STARS HAS JUST GIVEN I AM BOOKING YOU TO APPEAR BEFORE THE BEST AUDIENCE IN THE ASIATIC THEATRE.

The audience referred to proved to be Manila and when the Japs had been driven out Admiral Halsey said:

THE RECENT EXCEPTIONAL PERFORMANCE YIELDED GRATIFYING GATE RECEIPTS AND ALTHOUGH THE CAPACITY AUDIENCE HISSED VERY LOUDLY LITTLE WAS THROWN AT THE PLAYERS. AS LONG AS THE AUDIENCE HAS A SPOT LEFT TO HISS IN WE WILL STAY ON THE ROAD.

*

A pint-size Captain, who could only just see over the bridge screen of the great battleship he commanded was passed at sea by a destroyer-leader, commanded by probably the largest Captain afloat.

Destroyer to Battleship:

WHAT A SMALL DRIVER FOR SUCH A GIGANTIC CONTRAPTION.

Reply:

WHILE LARGE APES STILL CLING TO SMALL BRANCHES.

*

Two Frigates entering harbour together to refuel and then berth.

1st Frigate:

ARENT YOU HEADING FOR THE WRONG TANKER.

2nd Frigate:

NOT ON YOUR HORATIO NELLY. THIS ONE GIVES TRADING STAMPS.

*

When an Admiral strikes his flag at the end of an assignment, it is a custom for Captains who have been serving under him to man

a ship's boat and row him ashore. Recently, one of the Captains who was about to leave his ship to perform this function to an unpopular officer received from a passing contemporary
MICHAEL ROW THE BRUTE ASHORE ALLELUIA

*

A Sloop was towing a king-size gunnery practice target in a very rough sea when a destroyer inadvertantly passed between the Sloop and the target, fouling the towing hawser. The Sloop signalled
HOW CAN I DANCE WITH YOU STANDING ON MY TOW.

*

On a foreign station. A cruiser squadron at sea. One cruiser is leaving the squadron to return home and pay off. The departing cruiser signals the flagship,
I HOPE I HAVE SERVED YOU WELL
Reply:
ADMIRAL IS CONSULTING SQUADRON VET WHOSE VERDICT WILL BE PROMULGATED IN DUE COURSE.

*

When the Germans produced the magnetic mine in World War II, our answer was to de-magnetise ships' hulls; a process technically known as 'de-gaussing' or more commonly 'wiping'. A warship at sea received the following signal from Commander-in-Chief, Nore,
PROCEED TO CHATHAM FORTHWITH TO HAVE YOUR BOTTOM WIPED.

*

In a recent exercise in the Eastern Fleet, observing officers of all nations over-ran the space available to accommodate them. There just weren't enough ships. The dissatisfaction of two Siamese officers at the accommodation provided reached the Commander-in-Chief's ears, but there was nothing he could do about it, except signal,
BLESSED BE THE THAI THAT BINDS.

A submarine flotilla was going to sea in the early hours of the morning after a farewell dance ashore.

1st Submarine:
I CAN NOT SEE YOUR STARBOARD BOW LIGHT.

2nd Submarine:
TRY THE OTHER EYE. MY STARBOARD BOW LIGHT IS BURNING PASSIONATELY AND DANCING GAILY IN SHIMMERING GREEN.

*

In World War I, before the days of carriers and patrolling aircraft, an American Battle Squadron was at sea, in close formation, towing kite balloons.

U.S.S.sTexas to U.S.S. New York:
PLEASE ASK YOUR BALLOON OBSERVER TO STOP PISSING ON MY NAVIGATOR.

*

A landmark in the Battle of the Atlantic in World War II was this signal made by Commodore Western Isles, the famous 'Monkey' Stephenson, to the Commander-in-Chief, Western Approaches,

H.M.S. CLOVER THE THOUSANDTH VESSEL TO BE WORKED UP AT TOBERMORY SAILED AT NOON TODAY.

From C-in-C:
HEARTY CONGRATULATIONS ON THE THOUSANDTH VESSEL. THE UNIQUE METHODS OF TRAINING EMPLOYED AND THE HIGH STANDARDS YOU HAVE SET HAVE BEEN OF THE UTMOST VALUE IN DEFEAT-ING THE U-BOAT AND PRESERVING THE OLD TRADITIONS. HELEN OF TROY'S HISTORIC ACHIEVE-MENT WAS NO GREATER AND WAS PROBABLY GAINED WITH CONSIDERABLY LESS EFFORT.

From Commodore:
YOUR REFERENCE TO HELEN OF TROY. MAY I SAY THAT YOU ARE THE FIRST OF MY FRIENDS TO APPRECIATE MY FACE VALUE.

An Atlantic convoy emerged for the first time during the voyage from thick fog. When the cacophony of sirens faded, and ships sorted themselves out, the Escort Commander made the following general signal to the convoy,

JOB CHAPTER 42 VERSE 5*

*

A certain Commander-in-Chief, who insisted on everything running smoothly and like clockwork always had his movements reported to Headquarters by radio. On one occasion he was visiting one of H.M. Ships and the radio reports came into H.Q. as follows,

C-in-C ARRIVED ON BOARD.

C-in-C INSPECTING SHIP.

INSPECTION COMPLETED.

C-in-C's BARGE ALONGSIDE.

C-in-C LEAVING SHIP.

(The sea was rough, and as the Admiral was stepping into his barge he slipped and fell in the water.)

C-in-C IN SEA.

*(I have heard of thee by the hearing of the ear now mine eyes seeth thee.)

The *Queen Mary*, gliding gracefully at 25 knots through a rough Atlantic sea noted the obvious discomfort of her escorting destroyers. She signalled one of them,

HOW ARE YOU GETTING ON?

Reply:

SHIP IS OK IT IS MY NEW TEETH THAT ARE TAKING THE IMPACT.

*

From Local Manager New Zealand Shipping Company, Wellington NZ to Commander SS Kororata:

PROCEED AT YOUR UTMOST SPEED IN ORDER TO OBTAIN MAXIMUM GANGS FOR 0800 START MONDAY MORNING.

Reply:

AM UTMOSTING.

*

Before carrying out high speed manoeuvres in close formation, the Navigating Officer of one of the battleships (possibly recalling the tragic occasion in 1893 when H.M.S. *Camperdown* rammed and sank H.M.S. *Victoria*), signalled privately to his opposite number in the flagship

WHO ORGANISES THESE JUGGERNAUTICAL DARE-DEVILMENTS

Reply:

IT IS I BE NOT AFRAID.

*

During Desert operations in World War II, a Corvette was making her way up the Tobruk inlet when she came upon a small coaster which appeared to be making no headway against the strong current. The corvette circled the coaster preparatory to offering her a tow, and in the process she ran aground. She signalled the coaster,

AM AGROUND.

Reply:

SHAKE BUDDY. THIS IS MY FOURTH DAY. WALK ABOARD.

At the Coronation Review at Spithead, Trinity House vessels were conventionally escorting the Royal Yacht round the fleet when the Duke of Gloucester, Master of Trinity House, on board *Surprise,* spotted Sir Winston Churchill, an Honorary Elder Brother of Trinity House, on board *Patricia,* wearing a monkey jacket, while all the other officers wore frock coats. The Master signalled,

WHY IS SIR WINSTON NOT IN THE RIG OF THE DAY?

Reply:

AD and PT.

(Anno Domini and Purchase Tax.)

*

On the same occasion an assembly of distinguished Admirals levelled their telescopes and binoculars provocatively on Field Marshal Alexander of Tunis, wearing his moustache with his Trinity House Elder Brother's uniform. Sensing their concern Alex signalled,

BET I WOULD MAKE A BETTER ADMIRAL THAN YOU LOT WOULD MAKE GENERALS.

*

Some years ago, on a flat calm day a launch arrived at the Eddystone Lighthouse, out of which emerged a young wife carrying a small baby which she placed in the arms of her husband, the lighthouse keeper on duty, saying "I'm fed up with him, its your turn." She then returned to the launch and disappeared back to Plymouth. In due course the local Trinity House H.Q. received the following signal,

REQUEST IMMEDIATE INSTRUCTIONS, FOOD, AND EQUIPMENT FOR MAINTENANCE OF THREE MONTH OLD BABY.

*

H.M.S. *Ark Royal,* signalling details of an absentee,

BORN 27 JUNE 1943 UTTOXETER WEARING BLUE/GREEN LOUNGE SUIT BROWN SHIRT AND TIE NO OVERCOAT.

To H.M. ship at anchor from Senior Naval Officer ashore:
MILITARY AUTHORITIES REQUEST INFORMATION AS
TO STATE OF HEALTH OF SHIP'S MONKEY WHICH
RECENTLY BIT A PRIVATE OF THE BLANKSHIRE
REGIMENT WHILE HE WAS ON BOARD YOUR SHIP.
TWO VETERINARY CERTIFICATES OF ABOUT TEN
DAYS INTERVAL WOULD BE APPRECIATED IN ORDER
TO COMPLY WITH THE LOCAL REGULATIONS.
Reply:
SHIP'S MONKEY REPORTS SLIGHT TOOTHACHE BUT
OTHERWISE SHE IS IN PERFECT HEALTH.

*

From Admiralty to Admiral Commanding Aircraft Carriers:
HAVE ONE DUCK AIRCRAFT AVAILABLE FOR YOU IF
REQUIRED.
(No reply)
MY . . . IS THIS AIRCRAFT REQUIRED.
(No reply)
ANSWER MY . . .
From Admiral commanding Aircraft Carriers:
LORD LOVE A DUCK.

*

Having refuelled from tanker during a NATO exercise in
international waters, a British Frigate captain signals a Russian
trawler, who had been shadowing the manoeuvres closely for
several days,
DO YOU REQUIRE REFUELLING
Trawler:
NOT IF YOUR EXERCISE FINISHES ON TIME.

*

From Senior Officer Port Said to C-in-C Mediterranean
REQUEST APPROVAL TO ENTER ONE WREN CYPHER
OFFICER FORTHWITH
Reply:
YOUR . . . APPROVED PROVIDED NECESSARY FOR-
MALITIES AND PRECAUTIONS ARE TAKEN.

From Lochinvar to H.M.S. Wasperton

SPDC EAGLESCLIFFE PUMP NO LONGER MANUFAC-
TURED ALTERNATIVES OFFERED ARE LEFT HAND
HANDLED PUMP UNIT AND RIGHT HANDED HANDLED
PUMP UNIT. YOUR 232000Z FEB ASKING FOR PUMP
HANDLES NOT UNDERSTOOD. DO YOU REQUIRE 1 IN
NO GREASE PUMP HAND OPERATED LEFT HANDED
HANDLE AND 1 IN NO GREASE PUMP OPERATED
RIGHT HANDED HANDLE OR ONE LEFT HANDED
PUMP HANDLE FOR A LEFT HANDED HANDLED PUMP
TOGETHER WITH ONE RIGHT HANDLED HANDLE FOR
A RIGHT HANDLED HAND OPERATED PUMP.

*

From Admiralty to C-in-C East Indies

BRITISH SAILOR CAPACITY APPROXIMATELY 7500
TONS DUE SAIL SHORTLY DESTINATION TRINCO-
MALEE.

*

From Loch More to Senior Naval Officer Afloat:

0800 EXPECT TO ARRIVE BANGKOK 1600/2 JUNE

Shortly after making this signal H.M.S. *Loch More* was unfor-
tunate enough to run aground.

From Senior Naval Officer aground to Senior Naval Officer afloat:

CANCEL MY 0800/2

*

When Radar (RDF) was first introduced to H.M. Ships a rumour
spread that anyone passing through the beam when the instrument
was transmitting was liable to be rendered impotent. To quash this
alarming rubbish, Captain (D) Liverpool signalled the ships of his
Liverpool Escort Force:

COMMANDING OFFICERS ARE TO REASSURE THEIR
SHIPS' COMPANIES FORTHWITH THAT THE REMARK-
ABLE ACHIEVEMENTS OF RDF WILL NOT REPEAT
NOT INCLUDE THE PRODUCTION OF UNABLE
SEAMEN.

C-in-C to passing Destroyer:
   THERE IS A MAN ON YOUR FO'C'SL WITH FLAP DOWN REGARDING ME
Destroyer to C-in-C:
   THIS IS VERY MUCH REGRETTED. DISCIPLINARY ACTION IS BEING TAKEN.
C-in-C to Destroyer:
   THE EXISTENCE OF MY SIGNAL IS SUFFICIENT DISCIPLINARY ACTION.
(Note: Undoing the flap of bell-bottom trousers relaxes the stomach)

*

While "shadowing" a Soviet warship in the Atlantic,
From Russian warship to H.M.S. Londonderry:
   YOU ARE LAGGING BEHIND. RECOMMEND YOU CONNECT ADDITIONALLY A WASHING MACHINE TO THE SHAFT OF YOUR SHIP.
From H.M.S. Londonderry to Russian Warship:
   I AM ONLY RUNNING ON WASHING MACHINES AT THIS SPEED. MY MAIN ENGINES ARE STILL IN RESERVE.

*

In the early 60's a Captain (D) led his Mediterranean Destroyer Flotilla into the Black Sea, where he soon sighted a squadron of Russian Cruisers closing his flotilla at high speed.
From leading Russian Cruiser (by light)
   WHAT ARE YOU DOING IN THE BLACK SEA.
   Turmoil ensued amongst the Staff on the flotilla-leader's bridge while signal logs were sent for and Diplomatic Clearance discussed. At last Captain (D) raised an elegant hand for silence, and said quietly to the Signalman,
Reply:
   TWENTY-ONE KNOTS.

*

From Penelope (refloated after grounding) to C-in-C, Home Fleet:
   I AM NOW AFLOAT IN TOW OF ESKIMO.

From Admiralty to General:

IN CERTAIN INSTANCES TYPE 252 HAS BEEN REN-
DERED INOPERATIVE BY THE SETTING OF THE BIAS
MORE THAN 3 NOTCHES FROM THE SQUITTER MEN-
TIONED IN OPERATING INSTRUCTIONS. THE TERM
SQUITTER IS USED TO DESCRIBE A CONDITION OF
SELF-OSCILLATION WHICH IS HEARD AS A DISTINCT
SQUEAL. TYPE 252 SHOULD BE CHECKED FOR COR-
RECT SETTING AT HALF HOUR INTERVALS WHEN IN
CONTINUOUS OPERATION OR WHENEVER SWITCHED
ON DURING IRREGULAR OPERATIONS.

*

From Admiralty to General:

GERMAN BROADCAST ON 7 DECEMBER CLAIMS H.M.
SUBMARINE SEAL HAS BEEN COMMISSIONED FOR
SERVICE AS U-BOAT.

*

Section of Commander-in-Chief Mediterranean's situation
report as signalled to Admiralty dated 23/5/1941.

LOSSES AND DAMAGE TO NAVAL UNITS ARE TO BE
EXPECTED IN VIEW OF THE IMPOSSIBILITY OF
FIGHTER PROTECTION AND GENERAL DIMINUTION
OF AMMUNITION. H.M.S. *GLOUCESTER* HIT ABANDON-
ED AND SUNK. H.M.S. *FIJI* HIT AND SUNK LATER.
DESTROYERS *GREYHOUND, KELLY,* and *KASHMIR*
SUNK. *WARSPITE* AND *VALIANT NAIAD AJAX* AND
CARLISLE ALSO RECEIVED DAMAGE.

*

A submarine having made complete mess of a dummy attack
surfaced to receive this rocket by signal from the Skipper of the
target ship:

YOU BLUNDERING BATHYBIUSTIC BUFFOON.

Reply from submarine:

REGRET YOUR SIGNAL NOT UNDERSTOOD. I DO NOT
HOLD FLAG OFFICER CYPHER.

From Wick W/T:
> IMPORTANT.
> FOLLOWING RECEIVED FROM AMERICAN STEAMER SCANPENN.
> FOLLOWING W/T MESSAGE RECEIVED FROM GERMAN SUBMARINE. QUOTE. TRANSMIT TO MR CHURCHILL. UNKNOWN STEAMER SUNK (APPROX. 200 MILES N.W. OF STORNOWAY). SAVE CREW IF YOU PLEASE. SIGNED SUBMARINE COMMANDER. UNQUOTE. AT 1550/11 Sept./1939.

*

A U.S. Submarine in World War II was unexpectedly diverted to an Australian Base which it was customary to enter and leave by night. Being a stranger to R.N. she did not know British Submarines had names. As she approached she received the following signal from base:
> KEEP GOOD LOOKOUT FOR BRITISH SPIRIT PASSING YOU SHORTLY.

Her Reply:
> WHAT MAY BE THE NATIONALITY OF OTHER GHOSTS POLTERGEISTS OR HOBGOBLINS I MAY ENCOUNTER ROUND HERE.

*

from C-in-C American and West Indian Stations, H.M.S. Calcutta to Empress of Australia 27 July 1927
> TO THE RIGHT HONOURABLE STANLEY BALDWIN. IF THERE IS ANY WAY IN WHICH I OR ANY OF MY SHIPS CAN SERVE IT WILL BE A VERY GREAT PLEASURE TO US ALL.

Reply:
> GREATLY APPRECIATE YOUR KIND MESSAGE. I WILL NOT FAIL TO APPEAL TO YOU SHOULD NECESSITY ARISE. STANLEY BALDWIN.

How far backwards can VIP's who pass in the night bend over?

From Commander-in-Chief Mediterranean to First Sea Lord:
> EVERY SUBMARINE THAT CAN BE SPARED IS WORTH
> ITS WEIGHT IN GOLD. THEY ARE DOING EXTREMELY
> WELL. 1933/17/9/1941.

*

Rear Admiral commanding Destroyers, flying his flag in a cruiser, is at sea with his flotillas.

Destroyer to Flagship:
> REQUEST PERMISSION TO SEND ONE RATING TO
> FLAGSHIP FOR MEDICAL EXAMINATION.

Flagship:
> SIGNAL SYMPTOMS.

Destroyer:
> MAN INSISTS HE IS SAINT GEORGE BUT THAT HE
> ONLY HOLDS ACTING RANK OF SAINT AND IS NOT
> PREPARED TO TAKE ON DRAGON UNLESS RATED
> FULL SAINT BY AN ADMIRAL.

Flagship:
> SEND SAINT GEORGE WITH ESCORT. KEEP DRAGON.

*

In Northern Ireland, at the mouth of the river Foyle, a tanker was moored throughout World War II as a compulsory filling station for convoy escort ships. To those based at Liverpool, wasting precious relaxation fuelling at Moville after a tough convoy run in Atlantic weather was not popular.

In the middle of a foul night, two Liverpool-based destroyers cast off from the tanker, set course for Liverpool, and rang down 28 knots.

The Navigator of the second destroyer noticed his leader was cutting off the corner into the Irish Sea by steering south of Rathlin Island, through a tide-race which could be dangerous. He reported to his Captain who immediately signalled his senior officer:
> LEAD US NOT INTO TEMPTATION.

Back whipped the reply:
> BUT DELIVER US FROM MOVILLE.

Family Gram: (From Base to member of crew of polaris submarine on diving patrol)
> WINE IS ON THE CHILL I AM ON THE PILL HAVE ABSTAINED SINCE FEBRUARY IS POLARIS NECESSARY?

*

In World War I, when Air Power joined the Royal Navy, a Sopwith Camel, perched on a raft, set forth in tow of a destroyer of Vice Admiral Sir Reginald Tyrwhitt's Harwich Force. On receipt of a Zeppelin report the Admiral endeavoured to entice it by making a smoke screen; the Zeppelin's Captain, feeling safe at 19,000 feet, responded.

The Camel, piloted by Lieutenant Scully, took off successfully and climbed for an hour until he reached his ceiling. Still 200 feet below Zeppelin L 53, Scully pulled back his stick, stalled, emptied his two Lewis guns, and broke away to reload.

Returning to the attack he saw spurts of flame along the gasbag suddenly sweep into a meteor of flame, plummeting down into the sea leaving behind a pillar of smoke.

With petrol dangerously low Scully searched in vain for the squadron until, breaking out of cloud to land alongside some Dutch fishing trawlers, he spotted our ships.

The Admiral watched the pilot's exhuberant antics of relief as he looped and rolled; then he signalled to his squadron,
> ATTENTION IS CALLED TO HYMN 224, VERSE 7.[1]

---

[1] Oh happy band of pilgrims,
Look upward to the skies,
Where such a light affliction
Shall win so great a prize.

Has communication shrunk the world?

Ask Atlas